UNLATCHED

Praise for *Unlatched*

"*Unlatched* is a deeply engaging, highly personal, well-researched, and thoughtfully balanced account of how modern society has denormalized breastfeeding. Jennifer Grayson does not expect every mother to follow her example and breastfeed babies for three or four years. Instead, she asks us to consider how formula feeding became the norm and how government policies perpetuate it as the norm (see especially the stunning chapter on the Women, Infants, and Children program). She argues compellingly that our challenge as a society is to restore breastfeeding as the default for feeding babies, and to provide the support—political as well as emotional—that mothers need to breastfeed successfully."

—Marion Nestle, professor of nutrition, food studies, and public health at New York University and author of, among other books, *What to Eat*

"*Unlatched* is an intelligent, often funny, deftly written page-turner. Honestly, I'm surprised at how enthusiastically I find myself recommending a book about breastfeeding. Perfect not just for new parents, but for anyone who loves a good read."

—Anne Hathaway

"I'm hearing more and more that the root of much evil in our bad health is formula feeding instead of breastfeeding, and with terrific investigative chops Jennifer Grayson nails the most insidious part of this: the government's role in hocking formula to the most vulnerable among us."

—Michael Moss, Pulitzer Prize–winning investigative reporter and *New York Times* bestselling author of *Salt, Sugar, Fat*

"Grayson's book beautifully explains how we got to the breastfeeding brouhaha that exists in America today. This book is recommended reading for anyone who has breasts or loves them."

—Ricki Lake and Abby Epstein, filmmakers of *The Business of Being Born*

"Why can American women expose their breasts to sell magazines, cars, and beer, but not publicly nurse their children? It is time for an unflinching look at the breastfeeding obstacles women face in our society and in *Unlatched*, we have it. This is a must-read book for every mother and mother-to-be."

—Alyssa Milano

"Grayson's personal journey into the world of breastfeeding is fresh, accessible, and infused with humor—a must read for anyone embarking on the path to parenthood."

—Dana Ben-Ari, filmmaker, *Breastmilk*

"As an ob-gyn I have been guilty of speaking to new mothers about the benefits of breastfeeding instead of warning them of the risks of not breastfeeding. *Unlatched* is an essential book, not only for every parent-to-be, but also for physicians. Jennifer Grayson asks all the right questions, and it is clear that we must stop letting politics, money, and societal expectations trump good science."

—Dr. Lauren Streicher, associate clinical professor of obstetrics and gynecology at Northwestern University's Feinberg School of Medicine and author of *Sex Rx: Hormones, Health, and Your Best Sex Ever*

"*Unlatched* is a fascinating story about the history of breastfeeding and baby formula and how moms have been caught in the middle."

—Robyn O'Brien, bestselling author, food industry analyst, and mother of four

"Connecting the dots between women's health, women's work, and public policy, Grayson sheds new light on the origins of America's breastfeeding controversies and points to a way beyond the mommy wars. Anyone who cares about women's well-being and rights in twenty-first-century America should read *Unlatched*."

—Nancy L. Cohen, historian and author of *Breakthrough: The Making of America's First Woman President*

UNLATCHED

The Evolution of Breastfeeding and the Making of a Controversy

Jennifer Grayson

HARPER

NEW YORK • LONDON • TORONTO • SYDNEY

HARPER

This book is written as a source of information only. The information contained in this book should by no means be considered a substitute for the advice, decisions, or judgment of the reader's physician or other health professionals. All efforts have been made to ensure the accuracy of the information contained in this book as of the date published. The author and publisher expressly disclaim responsibility for any adverse effects arising from the use or application of the information contained herein.

HarperCollins books may be purchased for educational, business, or sales promotional use. For information please e-mail the Special Markets Department at SPsales@harpercollins.com.

FIRST EDITION

Designed by Jamie Lynn Kerner

Library of Congress Cataloging-in-Publication Data has been applied for.

ISBN 978-0-06-242339-9 (pbk.)

16 17 18 19 20 OV/RRD 10 9 8 7 6 5 4 3 2 1

For Izzy and Mika

Contents

INTRODUCTION

It was my younger daughter Mika's second birthday, and my husband Matthew and I decided that the uncharacteristically drizzly and cold day would be the perfect time to take Mika and her older sister, Izzy, to the Los Angeles Zoo for a quiet family celebration.

Normally, the LA Zoo is, well, a zoo. Fighting through the fray of visitors on prior visits, we ordinarily had to hoist our girls up on our shoulders just so they could get a peek at their beloved giraffes and flamingoes. But since no one in our typically sun-blessed city dares to venture out in the rain, on that day as the girls raced down the trail from one exhibit to the next in their bright pink galoshes, they found to their delight that they had the entire park to themselves. Correction: they had a vast swath of *nature* to themselves. I had never noticed it before among the masses, but the LA Zoo is, in fact, plunked in the northeast corner of the 4,000 acres that comprise the city's Griffith Park, the largest stretch of municipally managed urban wilderness in America.

As I've done since I was a little girl anytime I found myself in the middle of nature with few others about, I tried to imagine what the very place in which I stood must have looked like five hundred years ago; ten thousand years ago; one million years ago. Shielded from the rain beneath a densely woven canopy of soaring eucalyptus, mulberry, and palm trees and listening to the howls of monkeys and birds overhead, it wasn't hard to imagine that I was no longer in the second-largest city in the United States but in the midst of a primeval forest. And in the light rain as we made our way toward our favorite exhibit, the zoo's "Chimpanzees of the Mahale Mountains," a dense cloud of mist seemed to form, promising a path to another time. Then I was yanked out of my lovely daydream and thrust back into the twenty-first century.

"Oh my God, look! That mom is breastfeeding!" a woman shouted and then erupted into laughter. A crowd gathered, and I could hear people snickering as smartphones were pulled from pockets and raised before the vast stretch of safety glass that separated humans from primates. I hoisted Mika onto my hip and held tightly to Izzy's hand as we inched closer for a better look. What I saw didn't make me laugh; it momentarily took my breath away.

There, in the crook of what appeared to be a young female chimpanzee's gangly, fuzzy arm, I spied one miniscule wrinkled pink ear. A pair of tiny hand-like feet dangled about a foot below. As if in response to the clamor on our side of the partition, a miniature head popped up, and its uncannily humanoid face stared, bewildered, at the crowd. Then almost as quickly, the infant turned back toward the substantial comfort of its mother, stretched its mouth open wide, and rooted around a bit before rediscovering the protruding brown nipple on its mother's chest. The baby latched on firmly, once more shielded from view by a motherly embrace.

Near me, a young boy of about eight tugged at his father's

iPhone-wielding arm and asked what the creatures were doing. But Mika had glimpsed her baby chimpanzee doppelganger (only slightly furrier and with somewhat sleepier brown eyes), and needed no such explanation.

Mommy milk! she exclaimed, clawing at my chest with the tenacity of an excited puppy. I gave the baby carrier I was wearing around my hips a yank and pulled it up around her snugly, to shield her from the rain. Just as quickly, I inched down the top of my shirt. Like the little ape, Mika latched on hungrily, her eyelids soon drooping drowsily at her first respite from a full day of running around.

I suppose I had half-expected the crowd to then turn from the glass and point their cell-phone cameras at *me* as I nursed my two-year-old birthday girl (not the most common sight even in laid-back LA). So I was relieved when they only turned their attention to a pair of tussling adolescent chimps instead. Matthew held up Izzy to give her a better look at the two chimps and as he did, I noticed that the chimpanzee mother, clearly distressed by the gawking and smartphone-wielding horde, had protectively backed herself and her nursling away from the window and was already some distance off.

With Mika neatly tucked into the carrier, now almost fast asleep as she continued to nurse, I slipped away from the group and followed the mommy chimp and her nursling as I moved down the length of window. The mother climbed to the top of the hill at the edge of the habitat and then, using only one arm while her infant dangled from her chest, she scaled twenty feet of rock wall to the top of a cave. At that point, she must have judged herself safe from the onslaught, and she rested at the top, gently stroking her baby's head with her long fingers. All at once, her eyes met mine and she seemed to acknowledge my gaze—and Mika.

For the next ten minutes, we stayed as we were, eyes locked, nursing our babies silently, and I felt myself slip back in time once more: It was just me, my daughter, and our ancestors from 13 million years ago. Then I broke the spell by wondering, *When had the wall been so firmly wedged between us, just like that glass barrier?*

I looked back to see where Matthew and Izzy had gotten to and saw the crowd of iPhone gawkers dissipating in the distance. When I returned my gaze to my new chimp friend, she had turned her back to me, once more shielding her baby from the view of strangers.

FOR ALL THE MONTHS THAT I HAVE WORKED ON THIS PROJECT, the story above is the one I have always kept in the back of my mind. While the breastfeeding controversy has come to encompass many, many issues (including whether or not it's acceptable to breastfeed in public, how long it is "appropriate" to nurse, the snarky media and message board back-and-forth as to whether the benefits of breastfeeding are all they're cracked up to be), for me the essence of the story is what transpired that day at the zoo: It's all about us, as we peer through a barely discernable barrier at a reflection of 98.8 percent of our own DNA and see an image that we do not recognize. It's all about us, as we hurtle headfirst into the Digital Age without stopping to consider the momentous significance of what we may have impulsively left behind.

Only recently, I learned another part of the story at the

zoo. That summer and again that autumn before our visit with our two girls, there had actually been *two* chimp babies born at the LA Zoo, both to first-time mothers. One was Johari, the inquisitive imp I saw nursing that day. But there was also Oliver who, on that day, was off-exhibit. Oliver's mother had tried to nurse him, but it proved unsuccessful and the zoo staff had made the decision to hand-feed (that is, formula feed) him until he became strong enough to rejoin his mother and the group.

Before completing my research for this book, I had, like so many others, assumed that breastfeeding was an ingrained mammalian instinct that we humans—in our fast-paced modern world—had *made the choice* to subvert, once a convenient alternative became readily available. But the truth is that while the rooting and sucking reflexes are hardwired *in a baby*, a mother's knowledge of how to breastfeed is not. For humans and members of the larger primate order to which we belong, that knowledge is culturally based and it is largely learned. It is unclear why, specifically, Oliver was unable to connect with his mother, but what we do know is that in the absence of literally generations of female know-how (or in an alien environment as in the case of an animal held in captivity), even a chimpanzee mother might not be able to assume the seemingly instinctive task of feeding and nurturing her young.

In America today and to a larger extent in the rest of the rapidly developing, industrializing, and technologizing world, this is the very situation in which we find ourselves. Unlike the time in which I was born when half of all babies were exclusively formula-fed from birth (as I was), nearly

80 percent of US mothers now start off breastfeeding. And yet about half of all new mothers give it up (either entirely or start supplementing with formula) after just a few weeks. A meager 19 percent of American infants receive the six months of exclusive breastfeeding now recommended for optimal health by the American Academy of Pediatrics and the World Health Organization. And, inexplicably, the concept of "optimal health" with regard to breastfeeding remains a murky, ill-defined one for so many new mothers and fathers who sincerely want the best for the precious progeny they are bringing into this world.

For all those new parents and parents-to-be—and for all those of our species who care deeply about the health, well-being, and future of our descendants, and wish to make the most informed choices possible—this book is for you.

one

Formula-Fed Me

When we try to pick out anything by itself, we find it hitched to everything else in the universse.

—JOHN MUIR

The lactation consultant strode briskly into my hospital room. She was a middle-aged Orthodox Jewish woman clad in a long, frumpy skirt that brushed the tops of her sneakers as they squeaked across the Lysoled linoleum. Her traditional wig-instead-of-kerchief, perched on top of her real hair, framed her face in an awkward helmet of matte brown. I was thinking how incongruous it was that such a modestly dressed woman could appear so self-assured in such an intimate situation. I was thinking about that when she arrived at my bedside, grabbed my naked breast, and then matter-of-factly readjusted its position in my newborn's mouth.

A few years prior, I would have been put off by her, well, chutzpah. But now I felt strangely comforted by the woman's confidence. I knew she was likely an experienced mother

(Orthodox Jews view procreation as a religious duty and often have many children) who could help me with a dilemma even more pressing than my optimal nipple position. I glanced over at my husband, Matthew, who was sitting on the edge of his sleeper chair and fidgeting with his iPhone. I was praying that this woman could tell us how to handle our insatiably breast milk–thirsty almost two-and-a-half-year-old daughter, who was no doubt wondering when Mommy and her breasts would return home.

"I don't really need help latching on," I told her. With a nervous chuckle, I explained that I was a veteran breastfeeding mother with a still-nursing *twenty-eight-month-old* back at our apartment. "But what do I do about breastfeeding both of them?" I asked her. Matthew looked up anxiously. "How soon after bringing home the new baby should we wait before weaning our older one?"

The lactation consultant considered me for a moment and then gazed at my new little bundle, cozy and contentedly nuzzling up against my breast. With one calm sigh, the woman drained all the apprehension from the room. She said gently, "You know, it used to be common to breastfeed not just until age two but until age four. It was only a few generations ago that nearly every person on earth could *remember* being breastfed."

And with that, everything crystallized for me.

The endless debate—to breastfeed or not to breastfeed, to do it in public or private, to what age it is socially acceptable to nurse—all of this had taken center stage in the modern world, yet in reality, we had forgotten the basics. Forgotten that for thousands, perhaps millions, of years of human history, breastfeeding was a natural, intuitive experience that all

Homo sapiens and previous human ancestors had shared and knew intimately. It was a biological process that informed not only our personal physical development but also our unique psychological evolution and even our earliest memories here on earth.

I thought then not just about my precious new daughter at my breast but about my first child—the little girl with the golden hair back at the house who drifted off to sleep in my arms each night, her delicate mouth still suckling the air, her arms reaching out for me in dreamland after I unlatched her, laid her in bed, and tiptoed out of the room. I thought about myself as a baby, my own arms reaching out for something that would never be there.

IT WASN'T UNTIL I ENTERED THE FOURTH DECADE OF MY LIFE AND became a mother of two that I had a powerful, if not obvious, realization: the building blocks of my life were manufactured.

Exclusively formula-fed as a baby, I have little memory of seeing a naked breast throughout my entire childhood. Sure, there may have been a flash of flesh as my mother wrapped a towel around herself after a shower, but I have no recollection of ever discussing the question: *What are those things for?*

Breasts were something secret, and they certainly didn't have anything to do with feeding babies. Like many American children raised in the 1980s (and as far back as the 1930s and even still, in fact), my baby dolls were fed with bottles. So was my younger brother. It wasn't as though breastfeeding was held out as an option but rejected. As far as I knew, it didn't exist.

Mine was not a unique experience. My brother and I were children of the Great Formula Age, and at the time of my birth, 1979, only half of all American babies had ever been breastfed. Just one in five were still breastfed at the age of six months. It hadn't been much different for my mother and father as infants, either. It was during the post–World War II baby boom that commercial infant formulas became entrenched in American culture, after a handful of food companies and, later, pharmaceutical companies had supplanted the home-made formula market. Breastfeeding rates, nearly universal less than a century before, halved between 1946 and 1956. (My father was born in 1949; my mother, 1953.)

If either of my parents had been breastfed, it hadn't been for long, and they certainly didn't remember it. So when in the years before I was born, infant-formula maker Nestlé became embroiled in scandal after a report surfaced linking the company's marketing push in third world countries to the deaths and malnutrition of millions of children, it didn't have a lasting impact on my parents' future decision-making process. The controversy also didn't have an immediate effect on infant-feeding practices here at home. There was a landmark boycott of Nestlé products—the then largest nonunion consumer boycott in US history, in fact—and breastfeeding rates did increase slightly as the scandal brought the bottle-versus-breast debate to light. But formula feeding remained the norm in the United States, especially among upper-middle-class, educated white women. With access to clean water, sterilized bottles, routine health care, and vaccines, bottle-feeding didn't seem to pose the urgent health threat that it did for infants living in unsanitary conditions in developing countries. For many, including my parents, the reaction to the Nestlé scandal wasn't *Let's go back to breastfeeding*, but rather *Which formula should we buy instead?*

For my parents, the answer to that question was a trendy "healthier" soy formula, which actually didn't seem all that incompatible with my otherwise wholesome and natural upbringing. My mother had birthed both of us sans medication, even through a thirty-six-hour labor with my nearly nine-pound brother. We shopped at the health food store when Whole Foods was still a start-up. I didn't taste store-bought bread until I was well into elementary school; my mother baked her own bread every week from scratch. I spent my hours after school and on weekends rambling through the woods in our backyard and breathing in the piney Connecticut air.

It wasn't until right before my first daughter was born that I even noticed the formula-feeding anomaly of my childhood. One day, a package arrived addressed to me. Inside was a full-size container of powdered infant formula. Clearly, my pregnancy magazine subscriptions had tipped off the formula marketers and I was now on their radar, along with millions of other mothers to be.

I'm embarrassed today to admit that, even though I am a journalist well acquainted with the advanced marketing tactics of Big Industry, when I held that hefty canister of formula in my hand, my knee-jerk reaction was *Hey, this might come in handy. I should put this aside, just in case.* Just in case? I had planned on breastfeeding. At least, that's what I kept telling myself. And it was what I kept informing various friends, family members, and random mothers in supermarkets who always seemed to enjoy approaching very pregnant women to inquire into their personal birthing and feeding plans: I'll be breastfeeding, thanks for asking.

Because while breastfeeding rates in the United States are still low, the slogan "breast is best" has undeniably inched its way into the (albeit conflicted) public consciousness, and it had made its way into my own consciousness, as well. I had planned on a medication-free birth, so breastfeeding certainly seemed to fit right into that picture along with my most-things-natural lifestyle. I also knew there would be lactation consultants provided at the nonprofit hospital where my first child would be born, and they would be ready to help me with any bumps I encountered along my breastfeeding way.

Still, I didn't know quite what to expect. Intellectually, I knew I wanted to be a mother, but truth be told, I wasn't really "feeling" it. Did I really want to let some little alien child glom onto my nipples for untold hours each day and for months on end? So when that canister of formula arrived, I toted it over to the closet where I was building a small mountain of baby accoutrements in anticipation of D-Day (which meant *delivery* day but which, as time went on, was feeling more like a reference to a large-scale invasion. An Earth Mother to be I was not).

"What's that?" Matthew asked.

"Um, infant formula," I said. "It came in the mail."

He scowled at me. "You realize that's some formula company trying to get you to start buying their product, right? What's in that stuff?"

My eyes quickly scanned the back of the package. *Corn syrup solids, partially hydrolyzed nonfat milk, whey protein con-*

centrate solids, vegetable oil . . . The list of somewhat familiar commercial ingredients was followed by a plethora of unpronounceable lab-created vitamin additives. And then, all of a sudden, I wondered, was *I* fed something like this as a baby? I had spent much of my young adult life battling chronic health issues that were now being linked to potential dietary causes. I remembered being told that as an infant, I had such a severe case of reflux that I had to sleep sitting up at night, strapped into a chair, for the first three months of my life. It was as though my body had been saying, *No thank you.* I wasn't sure that the ingredients on the back of that formula package were directly responsible for my ailments—after all, generations of people had been raised on the same stuff, and they didn't all have hypothyroidism as I did, did they?—but for the very first time in my life, I considered the possibility that there could be a connection.

Both the midwife and the pediatrician I had met with were recommending six months of exclusive breastfeeding (no additional foods or fluids, not even water) per the American Academy of Pediatrics (AAP) and World Health Organization (WHO) recommendations for optimal growth, development, and health. But if my daughter *wasn't* going to be breastfed, my only option was the powder in that container I held in my hands (or some iteration thereof). Those ingredients, manufactured as they were, would be the sole source of nourishment for her developing bones, muscles, and organs; they would inform her earliest sense of taste and be drawn upon to forge the synapses that would wire her brain. They would become the building blocks of *her* life.

I wasn't taking any chances. The container of formula

went in the trash. Yet it seemed somehow wasteful to just toss it out. Shouldn't I donate it to a food bank so that a needy infant wouldn't have to go hungry? But when I contemplated the industrialized ingredients on the back of the package, my mind began to spin. If I didn't think it was OK to feed my own baby whey protein concentrate solids, then why would it be OK to pass on such questionable edibles to someone else's baby? And if a mother and child truly were needy, then why would infant formula be the first choice when it costs money and breastfeeding is free? Expense, in fact, was one of the supporting reasons why I, a work-from-home freelance journalist (with a then-unemployed husband) was considering exclusive breastfeeding for my firstborn. "See, having a kid won't cost us anything!" I had gleefully announced to Mathew when he started expressing anxiety about the added expense of our impending arrival.

"How much does formula cost, anyway?" he wanted to know, and in a flash, the laptop came out. We quickly discovered that formula could easily run up to $200 a month—a sizable expense for most American families, let alone a low-income family. That's when I uncovered an even more surprising statistic: The federal government's Women, Infants, and Children program, also known as WIC (which provides supplemental foods as well as health assistance to low-income pregnant women, new mothers, infants, and children under the age of five), buys and distributes more than *half* of all the infant formula sold in the United States every year, making the US government the formula manufacturers' biggest customer.

For mothers, though, it seemed that the clear economic

winner was exclusive breastfeeding. While our taxpayer dollars were subsidizing an intricate system of formula funding, needy families were still paying out something for additional formula they required, mothers were forfeiting their own self-reliance, and only the corporations were the big winners. Pre-baby, the issue seemed pretty black-and-white to me: I would give my unborn daughter the best start I could possibly give her by breastfeeding, at least for the first six months of her life, and our little family would be more self-sufficient in the bargain.

Of course, I had yet to personally encounter any of the realities or challenges of being a mother.

FOR ALL MY RELUCTANCE IN BECOMING A MOTHER, INCLUDING twenty-six hours of active labor that didn't go as naturally as I had planned (I caved at hour twenty-two and had an epidural), the moment my daughter was brought into the world was as magnificent as any cliché anyone has ever conjured. She was placed on my chest, and when I gazed into her already open eyes, I was utterly lost in their midnight blue. Everything that had led up to that moment simply fell away.

Then when she, mere minutes old, inched up to my breast and planted her rosy little lips upon my nipple, the sucking instinct literally encoded in her DNA by way of millions of years of evolution, I was mesmerized. Yes, I had just given birth in a hospital with advanced medical equipment all around me. Via smartphone, photos of my newborn baby were beaming their way to relatives all over the country. Outside, the night sky was so awash in light pollution that no stars were visible. Yet here I was feeding my child just as women had done since the dawn of humanity. In an instant, I was connected to every human who had ever graced our beautiful blue planet. The bond to my daughter and the all-consuming love I felt for her were both immediate and staggering. When those little lips connected us, I knew there was nothing I would not do to protect her.

A little later on, however, the breastfeeding thing was not quite so easy. Although at first in the hospital, I seemed to be getting the hang of it: Isobel woke up crying every couple of hours; I put her to my breast and comforted her; she fell back asleep. The lactation consultant came in the next morning, readjusted my positioning, uttered a few encouraging words, and gave me a couple of handouts. I felt empowered knowing that when I nursed my baby, she was receiving the magical colostrum that would buffer her immune system in those first days. My real milk wouldn't come in for a few days yet.

Then, back at home, it did. My breasts, always a nice reliable C cup, swelled to porn star–size proportions. The things ballooned to just below my chin, sending my brother (on a surprise visit to meet his first niece) into a full-on snicker fit. Desperate to do anything to relieve the throbbing, I tried heat then cold; I even resorted to an old wives' remedy that involved stuffing cabbage leaves into my bra. But each time my daughter moved her lips hungrily toward my breast, I winced—then later, sobbed—in pain. My mom and other female relatives were sympathetic but could only shrug at my pleas for remedies. If they had nursed, it had been a brief experience and they simply didn't remember the mechanics. Three times I schlepped back to the lactation consultant for help, with my tiny daughter in tow. Each time I felt a bit more heartened, but my patience was wearing thin. If the pain continued another week, I wasn't sure I could last.

Then, as if a spell had lifted, the swelling and the pain subsided, and Izzy and I eased into a lovely sort of reverie. I had always been a go-go-go type, but now I relished the quiet time with my newborn daughter, watching her grow content and full from the nourishment my body was giving her.

It wasn't all a breeze, of course. Matthew went back to work a week after the birth, and his demanding new job meant that I alone was up at night with our teeny but ravenous (and incredibly loud) daughter. Then there was the three-day stretch when Izzy wailed all night, both on and off the breast, until I called my mom at five o'clock in the morning and she gently suggested that I might want to burp the baby. (The lactation consultant had insisted that breastfed babies didn't need to be burped.)

I went back to my freelance writing schedule at almost full tilt when Izzy was eight weeks old, even though I was struggling to string together sentences on a brain diet of three-hour snippets of sleep. By and large, though, the two of us fell into an easy pattern. I nursed my daughter while conducting phone interviews with scientists and CEOs. I strapped her into a baby carrier and went for long hikes in the mountains, popping a boob in her mouth whenever she got fussy. I soon discovered that breastfeeding was not only something I could handle, but actually an insecure new mother's dream: no measuring, no sterilizing, no scheduling, no forgetting. For me, breastfeeding became instinctive and was just not all that mysterious. My daughter cried out in hunger; I fed her. She clamored to my breast for comfort; I gave it to her.

For many of my new-mom friends, however, confusion reigned. We'd meet for lunch, and they'd whip out their iPhones and check their breastfeeding apps to see if it was an accepted time to feed their babies. One of my friends exclusively pumped her milk and fed her baby daughter by bottle, explaining that she had tried breastfeeding once but thought her naked breast in her daughter's mouth looked creepy. Another friend preferred feeding her daughter pumped breast milk by bottle so that she could properly gauge how much her baby was drinking. She didn't quite accept that the invisible milk inside her breasts could adequately nourish her infant, but bottle measurements she could trust. I stared as her eighteen-pound three-month-old sucked back a ten-ounce bottle of breast milk and then reached out for more. Childhood obesity was epidemic in this country. Why wasn't her doctor warning her not to overfeed?

At the same time, though, I definitely felt shy about nursing in public, and the reactions of my friends and family didn't help much. Matthew would rush to drape a baby blanket around me before I even unclasped my nursing bra, whether we were out at a restaurant or at home with friends. My mother would start stammering apologies about invading my privacy any time she realized I was breastfeeding near her and not just cradling the baby. Once, during a casual girls' lunch at a friend's apartment, I began to nurse my yelping daughter and then watched as women scattered from the table like flies fleeing a swatter. (Is it worse table manners to discreetly feed your baby at the dining table or heartlessly let your baby wail while you finish your chopped salad?) Then there was the time I was breastfeeding in an examining room at my LA internist's office, and the doctor—a medical professional supposedly well acquainted with the workings of human anatomy—interrupted our conversation to cloak me with a "nursing cover" she adroitly fashioned from a sheet of exam-table paper, much to the surprise of my startled infant.

Still, I forged on. But even in Los Angeles, which is by and large a breastfeeding-friendly town (despite its preponderance of silicone mammaries and curiously modest internists), contradiction was everywhere. In my postnatal yoga class, it wasn't unheard of for a health-conscious young mother to yank down her tank top and smile endearingly as her scampering toddler playfully latched on. But most of the women I knew personally had given up breastfeeding by the time their babies were six months old, either switching to formula or relying on bagged breast milk they had frantically pumped and stockpiled in their freezers.

And maybe that's too bad, because my friends who had stopped breastfeeding complained that they couldn't travel any real distance or even get out of the house to fill up a cart of groceries without the help of a babysitter or grandparent. Meanwhile, I could go anywhere knowing that I had an infallible pacifier always at the ready. I hopped on a plane with Izzy and flew with her cross-country, listening to other babies scream like banshees while mine cozily snuggled against my breast. When my daughter began eating solid foods at six months, breastfeeding got even easier. No longer needing to nurse around the clock, she latched on for shorter feeds in between meals and started sleeping for longer stretches at night.

I had signed on for the recommended minimum six-month stint. *Why not continue?* I wondered, even though I knew I would be in the minority. While 79 percent of new American mothers now breastfeed at birth, a mere 19 percent of babies receive the AAP- and WHO-endorsed six months of exclusive breastfeeding (around half are breastfed for six months, but only by supplementing with formula and food). One month past that milestone, nearly 60 percent of moms have switched to formula entirely, despite the academy's recommendation that babies continue to be nursed for a year or more. These suboptimal stats persist for a number of complex reasons, to be explored in this book, but one obvious reason is that many women simply have to go back to work, since the United States is one of only a few countries in the entire world (and the only developed country) without paid maternity leave. By law, employers must provide a place other than a bathroom for employees to express breast milk, but as any working-and-pumping mother will tell you, it's more than a challenge to maintain a working-and-pumping schedule that works for both baby and employer. It's no wonder breastfeeding rates drop off sharply once women return to their jobs.

I was fortunate in that I was a freelancer and worked from home. There seemed to be no reason *not* to continue breastfeeding Izzy. Sure, I second-guessed myself whenever a new baby tooth started coming in (which exasperatingly proved to be every two weeks) and she woke during the night with the breast her only comfort. I even began to envy friends whose already-weaned babies had learned to self-soothe. Yet somehow another bleary but blissful six months whizzed by, and I was about to celebrate my little girl's first birthday.

AROUND THIS TIME I CAME ACROSS AN ARTICLE ABOUT "EXtended" breastfeeding, a term that was entirely new to me. The very word, *extended*, implied something outside the realm of normal, and at least in this country, it is. The annual Centers for Disease Control and Prevention (CDC) Breastfeeding Report Card doesn't even bother to publish data for mothers nursing past the twelve-month mark.

I was intrigued. Everything I had already read suggested that there was no harm in continuing to breastfeed. If anything, there was a clear benefit, which is why WHO recommends breastfeeding for two years or longer. Toddlers who nurse continue to receive all the important immune factors that babies do, as well as valuable fats that boost brain growth, plus other vital nutrients. One recent landmark study even revealed higher IQs in children who breastfed past one year.

Mothers have been shown to have a clear advantage, too, with longer durations of breastfeeding linked to lower rates of uterine, ovarian, and breast cancers. One particularly large study showed that for every year a woman breastfed, her risk of breast cancer was reduced by 4.3 percent. For mothers with more than one child, those breastfeeding years can really add up. Thinking of my grandmother who had died from breast cancer twenty years earlier, the breastfeeding–breast cancer link didn't seem one to take lightly.

Yet, more than anything, continuing to breastfeed my daughter was what I knew she needed emotionally. At a year old, Izzy was joyful and active but also high-strung. Her behavior could devolve into mini tantrums at the first taste of frustration. Later, in full toddlerhood, she could become so caught up in emotion that she would bang her head on the floor. Other kids had pacifiers and lovies as their comfort. Why shouldn't nursing be Izzy's solace, her reset button? In fact, those pacifiers and lovies seemed to me man-made substitutes for a more natural instinct that had been prematurely subverted. It didn't seem fair to take "Milky" away from her just because her father and I had arbitrarily decided that it was time.

IN 2012, THE MAY 21 ISSUE OF *TIME* MAGAZINE HIT THE NEWSstands and promptly set off a media firestorm that lasted for weeks and beyond. On its cover, an attractive blonde named Jamie Lynn Grumet breastfed her nearly four-year-old son, who though tall for his age, posed on a stool to latch on. The boy stared back into the camera, breast in mouth, as though he had merely been interrupted helping himself to a glass of chocolate milk from the fridge.

I was nursing an eighteen-month-old at the time (though mostly in private and definitely not on magazine covers). By this juncture, I had come to believe that breastfeeding a child into toddlerhood, while outside the norm, was certainly not abnormal. If anything, it was natural. Anthropological evidence supports a biological weaning age for humans that is anywhere from two and a half to seven years of age. My friends and family, however, didn't give a hoot about anthropological evidence. Matthew begged me to promise that I wouldn't still be breastfeeding our daughter at the age of four. My mother and brother teasingly warned that I would be on the next cover of *Time* with Izzy climbing up for a drink. The consensus among my friends was no better: Breastfeeding for years, not months, is *insane*!

The American media—and, by and large, public opinion—concurred. And it wasn't only the *Time* magazine cover that stirred up controversy. By 2012, everything that had to do with breastfeeding was stirring up controversy. "Breast is best" may have been deposited into our national consciousness, and it may finally have become consensus in the medical establishment, yet still, we all felt pretty conflicted, even queasy, about breastfeeding. Seemingly each day (or was I now simply more aware since I was breastfeeding a toddler?), another breastfeeding blowup found its way into the headlines: "Facebook Removes Photos of Women Breastfeeding, Citing Content as 'Offensive'!" "Michelle Obama and Michele Bachmann Come to Blows on the Politics of Breast Pumps!" "Gisele Bündchen Reveals Breastfeeding Selfie on Instagram!" Even the release of scientific breastfeeding studies sent thousands of commenters running to the message boards, as women proclaimed themselves either "lactivists" or proud bottle feeders, each camp pointing fingers at the other.

I, too, was conflicted. Up to this point, breastfeeding my daughter had felt right, but I also didn't feel completely comfortable with the prospect of one day breastfeeding a four-year-old. Then again, I wasn't ready to wean, even though I was expecting again. Pregnant and exhausted, it was pretty great having an excuse to lie down and get cozy with my otherwise unstoppably active toddler. And given my past health struggles, it certainly didn't seem like a bad idea to give her the two full years of nursing recommended by WHO for her optimal health. My doctor gave me the go-ahead to continue breastfeeding, although she explained that the few children still nursing at this time ordinarily stop by themselves because hormones later in pregnancy can change the taste of the milk. *Perfect*, I thought. *Izzy will wean herself right around the two-year mark.*

But Izzy didn't. Not only was she still nursing as the pregnancy wore on, she seemed to find her Milky more delicious than ever. Her second birthday came and went, and then it didn't seem fair to wean my daughter just a couple of months shy of the birth of her new baby sister. After all, I didn't want her to resent the new addition to our family. Like all parents about to welcome a new sibling, I was determined to do anything to ensure the transition would be harmonious. The tantrums, of course, got worse.

"That's because she's two years old and still sucking a fucking boob!" my husband exploded, hurling his familiar refrain to explain why our daughter—now a full-blown Terrible Two—was throwing tantrums daily. He and I had opposing philosophies on the subject: his, that Izzy was old enough to deal with her emotions herself and that we were approaching freak show territory with the nursing; mine, that our daughter had been on earth for only two short years, and that she was dealing with anxiety about her new sister on the way and was still too little to "sort things out" without the comfort of her mommy. To compromise, we had attempted to place limits on her nursing, saving it for morning, naptime, and bedtime. But clearly, the approach wasn't working. At every outburst, she would scream, "MILK-Y! MILK-Y! I WANT MILK-Y!" then launch herself toward my breast for consolation.

We agonized over the situation. Why were we putting her through what was, to her, a premature termination of breastfeeding? In the grand scheme of things, would a few extra months of nursing really make a difference? Were we permissive parents, ignoring cultural norms that seemed to work perfectly fine for everyone else? But just how "normal" were those norms in reality?

Save for the terrible twos, we knew our daughter to be a wonderful child—compassionate and confident, bright and beloved by all who knew her. It appeared we were doing *something* right. After the heat of a tantrum had passed, Matthew usually agreed.

But inevitably we would go through a week of particularly bad tantrums or a string of sleepless nights when, for whatever developmental reason, Izzy would awake at four in the morning shrieking for MILKY! at the top of her lungs. Then the battle about the breast would start all over again.

SUDDENLY, WITH THE BIRTH OF OUR SECOND DAUGHTER MIKA, our family was four. I was becoming reconciled to the fact that I would be simultaneously breastfeeding a newborn and a Terrible Two in full tantrum mode, an arrangement known as tandem nursing (it's called that without the tantrums, too). How I would explain this to the curious, the naysayers, and even the appalled was another thing altogether. As it turned out, even when friends and family members didn't ask outright, I could feel their whispers at my back.

My own mother put it bluntly: "How can you possibly breastfeed two kids at the same time?"

"I have two breasts, Mom," I responded, as though this was something any observant individual could surmise.

"But it's like *Out of Africa*," I would catch her later whispering to my brother (clearly she had not seen that movie at all). I noted the two of them shaking their heads conspiratorially.

My closest mommy friend, a bit more supportive, seemed concerned about the logistics of it all. "How do you put them both down for a nap at the same time?" she wanted to know, probably envisioning pre-nap nursing as some kind of circus contortion act.

This time, I had no defense at the ready. Just home from the hospital, I'd barely had a chance to consider that scenario or any of the other practicalities of breastfeeding two children at the same time. I had read online that women in "other cultures" often nursed their children well into toddlerhood and even nursed multiple children at once, but just which cultures were these exactly? There wasn't a whole lot of information out there.

In a mommy blog online, I came across one touching account of a tandem-nursing mother whose toddler and newborn baby lovingly held hands the first time they nursed together. Lost in that lovely image, I figured all would be OK. After all, what did women do in the Olden Days? I guessed that a pioneer woman with two hungry babies probably didn't have bottles with neatly mixed formula standing by. *I* was not a pioneer woman, however; I was the wife of a television writer in urban Los Angeles. What the hell was I getting myself into?

Settled in at home with a child at each breast, I had a lot of time to think. If what the lactation consultant had said was true—that at one time, nearly *everyone* remembered being breastfed—then maybe what I was doing was considered "normal" from a biological perspective. One thing was undeniable, though: In the modern industrialized world (and more and more in the developing world, too, I would discover) we had come to view breastfeeding—a biological process as essential to our survival as eating, sleeping, or procreating—as a choice, and a controversial one at that. But what had women naturally done throughout most of human history? What did they do in the corners of the world where instinct still prevailed? I longed to know, as though their stories would somehow bolster my own sense of purpose.

Moreover, I wondered: How did we get to a state where parents preferred to feed their babies corn syrup solids over breast milk, even while it was becoming more evident that our industrialized food system was wreaking havoc with our national health? After all, the science in favor of breastfeeding was sound, and virtually no one (including the formula companies themselves) now claimed that formula was superior to or even the equivalent of the nutritional and immunological value of breast milk. Why would we want to possibly commit our babies to lifetimes of health struggles? And if we had come to discover that so many components of breast milk were not only vital for physical health and development but also essential to human bonding, why was it that mothers around the globe clamored for formula rather than rely on the life-giving nourishment that flowed so naturally from their breasts? Could we blame the formula companies? Could we blame modern life?

At first glance, the story of breastfeeding—of how we lost our connection to what is one of our most essential biological functions—mirrors what happened to other essential facets of our human existence during the twentieth century.

It mirrors what happened to birthing, which became a strictly controlled medical procedure; it mirrors what happened to the eating of real food, which morphed into the ingestion of processed foodstuffs; and it mirrors whatever has become of meaningful human interaction, which is being replaced so steadily by social media and texting that we prefer to use our smartphones even in the midst of one another's warm and human company.

Some may argue that when it comes to feeding our young, breakthroughs such as infant formula and breast pumps have, respectively, saved lives and allowed working mothers to give their babies the nutritional advantage of breast milk when those mothers are absent. But are our lives and, more important, are our children's lives better as a result? Are these advances benefiting us, or are they benefiting other entities? And, if the latter, do we really want to hand these entities the future of our children and the future of our health while we distract ourselves with controversy? If we are going to do that, shouldn't we first ask ourselves: *Why?*

Sitting there on the couch, with my two babes cuddled up in my arms, I hadn't yet discovered the quest that would send me to the ends of the earth and back in pursuit of the answers to those questions. But there it was, the beginning of my journey, waiting for me just over the fence of my own backyard.

two

What Would Baby Jesus Drink?

And it came to pass, as he spoke these things, a certain woman of the company lifted up her voice, and said to him, Blessed is the womb that bore you, and the breasts which you have sucked.

—LUKE 11:27

When I first met Baila, she was thirty-nine years old and six months pregnant with her ninth child. Her first child, the eldest of her four daughters, was born when Baila was nineteen. This may sound shocking if, like me, you live in one of the cities on either coast of the United States and many women you know have delayed parenthood until their midthirties. (At the tender age of thirty, I was one of the first of my friends to have a baby; my marriage at twenty-five was considered downright old-fashioned.) Yet, to me at the time, Baila's story seemed typical for Beverlywood, the Orthodox Jewish neighborhood of Los Angeles where I lived for over a year. Although I should say that Baila's situation was typical only with respect to the number of children she bore. As I would find out later, there is nothing commonplace about Baila and her story.

If you want a glimpse of what motherhood might have been like in days of yore, Beverlywood would be a good place to start. Less than a mile south of where Beverly Hills' well-preserved Lululemon-clad mommies lunch on chiffonade-cut kale salads, the Beverlywood area just below Pico Boulevard is home to one of the largest Orthodox Jewish populations in the country. In Beverlywood you'll find more than twenty synagogues within a two-mile radius.

The neighborhood is a fascinating blend of tradition and modernity. Men drive by in *kippot*, their long beards flying as they shout into iPhones and speed recklessly through intersections. Hunched-over Persian grandmothers haggle over fruit prices with the Mexican immigrants who work in the local Israeli market. Teenage boys' *tzitzit*—the tassels on their tallit prayer shawls—bob and waft in the breeze as they zip down sidewalks on their Razor scooters. And mothers in head scarves and long skirts hustle their large broods off to school, spandex underneath and Nikes in place for their morning constitutionals.

Nowadays, it is without doubt a stereotype that all Orthodox Jewish women marry young and raise very large families. There are successful Orthodox women surgeons, professors, Wall Street warriors, and even lactation consultants (see the previous chapter). Many have successful careers *and* families, but the reality is that Orthodox women do indeed give priority to motherhood and many of them don't just have families, they have whole *flocks* of kids—or at least they did in my former neighborhood. In fact, if the Chevy Suburban was the enduring symbol of the 1990s soccer mom, the full-size passenger van could rightfully epitomize the *ima* (that's the Hebrew word for mother) of Beverlywood. There were three of those vans parked on my block.

Clearly, one reason why so many of the moms in my former neighborhood have a large number of children is that they have a head start. In 1990, the average age of marriage for an American woman was twenty-three. Now it's twenty-seven, and that number continues to climb every year. In Beverlywood, however, where Baila also serves as a matchmaker for the community, twenty to twenty-four is more the norm, according to her. ("After twenty-four, they start to get worried a little bit. That's sad," she said.) But aside from starting young, a driving force behind these large broods may also be that Orthodox Judaism values motherhood and family in a way that modern secular life does not. After all, says the orthodoxy, men can cook and clean, but they can't necessarily create the home environment that a woman can. The Talmud (the sacred text that forms the basis for Jewish law) calls this *binah*, a deep understanding—in this case, a deep understanding of family that only women possess.

It had proved a bit tough for me to make friends in this tight-knit, faith-based community; though Matthew and I are Jewish, we are semi-observant. We had moved there the year after Mika was born, looking for a little more space for our family of four, and had fallen in love with a beautiful bottom-floor 1930s duplex for just a little more rent than we had been paying previously. Only this apartment was so large it could have comfortably lodged a sizable Orthodox family. In fact, a unit across the street from us housed a family with seven children. But before we moved in, I didn't know just how many Orthodox families lived in the neighborhood. It was only after we unpacked our boxes that I realized we were outsiders.

For months, I had been working up the nerve to introduce myself to Baila, my next-door neighbor. Daily, the sound of happy mayhem wafted over the sizable fence between our backyards. Her voice sounded so cheerful, corralling her brood, and I really wanted some friends for my girls. But admittedly, I also wanted to meet my next-door neighbor for another reason: I had already begun to organize my ideas for this book and had been looking at breastfeeding in other cultures and time periods. I wondered if Baila could give me a glimpse of what mothering was like in an earlier time in our history.

Though I knew that the Orthodox lead twenty-first century lives, I also knew that in their family life they adhere closely to tradition, with many of the laws and cultural practices of Orthodox Judaism drawing directly from the ancient Talmud, which was compiled between the second and fifth centuries. The roots of the Talmud can be traced back even further. Many scholars believe that the document is the written form of what, in the time of Jesus, was referred to as the tradition of the elders. My thoughts spun with the idea of the possible connection: What did the Talmud say about breastfeeding? Could my next-door neighbor provide a virtual "firsthand" account from the biblical ages? Through the fence, it sounded like she had a *lot* of kids, and I wondered whether she had nursed every single one of them. And if so, for how long? Would she even tell me if I asked?

Finally one day I found myself on her doorstep, nervously ringing her doorbell. When she came to the door, she was wearing the customary head kerchief and a long, drapey housecoat of sorts. Her face was free of makeup. So kind and open, it made me realize that I had no reason at all to be apprehensive about stepping into her world. We were both just mothers.

I told Baila that I was researching a book about motherhood and breastfeeding and asked if she would be willing to talk to me. She invited me to stop by the following week for a longer visit. So the following Tuesday, dressed in my most modest skirt and armed with kosher bakery cookies, I found myself on her front porch again, hoping for a glimpse at the intersection of ancient and modern worlds.

Baila welcomed me in. Considering how many children I had guessed she had, I was amazed at the tidy scene inside. The house was small and well worn, but everything was tucked neatly out of the way. What little furniture I saw—including one leather couch, a small desk, and a tall bookshelf—was pushed flush against the walls, leaving the whole front of the house as a clearing I assumed was designed to prevent scampering children from smashing into the furniture. At the rear of the house, Baila ushered me around a banquet-length dining table and through a door that led to a cozy backyard. There, we seated ourselves on a porch swing in front of a leaf-littered trampoline.

I found out shortly that Baila was the child of Russian immigrants, although she had grown up in Melbourne, Australia. She still had a tinge of an Aussie accent. Surprisingly, she hadn't been raised religiously.

As we talked, her son, who looked to be about three, the same age as Izzy, bounced from one end of the porch glider to the other, swinging on the support posts. "I want to watch an episode!" he announced.

"Chayim, honey, we're not watching anything today," Baila countered.

"I'm just telling you," he said sweetly.

She looked at me. "We have a movie night," she said a bit defensively. I was relieved to discover that even a highly religious mother was as self-conscious about her children's TV-watching habits as I was about Izzy and Mika's.

"He sounds exactly like Izzy," I told her.

I also discovered that, just like me, Baila was a child of divorced parents. In fact, her parents had separated when she was a baby, and she grew up not in a large family like the one she had created but as an only child in Melbourne, alone with her mother. In those days, Baila had been singularly focused on her training to become a professional ballerina. I also found out that Baila wasn't her original name. Born Bella, she changed her name after joining the Chabad sect of Orthodox Judaism. The Hebrew name Baila is derived from the name Bilhah (one of the six matriarchs of the Jewish people), but it also is similar to *bailar*, which means "to dance" in Spanish. She chose the name in homage to the professional dancing career she had to give up once she became an Orthodox Jew, since there are laws against touching the opposite sex and dancing in front of men.

But before she had a chance to tell me more of her story,

an older boy of about ten with tightly wound blond curls appeared at the back door. "I barfed in school," he said.

"Ugh, maybe you and *Abba* have the same thing," Baila said. "Go lie down."

I told her I was happy to come back some other time, but she waved me off.

"My two girls are always catching something," I offered. "But you're probably used to that, with . . . with . . . how many do you have?"

She paused, anticipating my reaction. "We have eight and one on the way."

"Wow!" I said, quickly adding *B'sha'ah tovah!* from the back of my brain.

She thanked me for my good wishes, and I couldn't help but confess, "I've had a hard time adjusting to life with two. I can't even imagine . . ."

"Well, it *is* hard," she admitted. "The first is hard, and then two is hard because you're juggling both. Three is hard—just to warn you—but after that, it gets easier."

I said I supposed it probably depended a good deal on how children were spaced, but she said, "Mine are every two years. I have one who's three or four years apart from another, but it's an average of two years. I nurse, I get pregnant, I'm done nursing. That's about it. I'm a big believer in nursing."

Bingo.

AT THAT POINT IN MY OWN LIFE, PEOPLE WERE GENERALLY ASTONISHED (or appalled) that I had been breastfeeding my girls for nearly four years straight. But by my calculations, Baila—

who had her first child at nineteen and was just five years my senior—had been nursing for close to *twenty* years, interrupted only midway through each pregnancy when her milk supply dwindled, which made breastfeeding too uncomfortable for her to continue.

I, on the other hand, had found nursing Izzy through my pregnancy with Mika only mildly uncomfortable, so I had breastfed all the way through and was still nursing both girls. Yet interestingly, my way of doing it was probably not how it was done in antiquity, according to Katherine Dettwyler, whom I had rung up hoping to get a better picture of breastfeeding in biblical times and perhaps even the time that came before. Dettwyler, a University of Delaware anthropology professor who has conducted extensive research on the biocultural aspects of breastfeeding, was just the person to talk to. She told me that Baila's pattern (give birth, breastfeed for at least two years but even as many as seven, conceive, wean) was more the norm. It was a pattern that even the earliest humans may have followed.

"Around the world it's pretty typical that there is some sort of rule about spacing the kids out. [That's why] you don't end up with very much tandem nursing anywhere other than in modern industrialized countries," she said.

And since no one I knew in the modern world had even *heard* of tandem nursing let alone done it, my guess was that I was in a very slim minority. Dettwyler explained that because, biologically, babies are geared to nurse very frequently, including through the night, it is probable that in the age before food was secure, women's bodies may not have had the calorie reserves to nurse a newborn and a toddler simultaneously and have them both survive. So civilizations developed cultural beliefs to avoid that scenario. Some cultures dictated that a mother would wean once she got pregnant, much as Baila had done on her own. Others, like the Dani people of highland New Guinea, naturally developed postpartum sex taboos. "They nurse their kids for two years, but after the birth of a child they don't have sex with their husbands for *five* years," she declared a bit dramatically.

"Wow," I said.

"Yeah," she agreed.

People throughout the ages also had nature to thank for generous spacing between children, since ovulation is naturally suppressed by hormonal shifts that occur during breastfeeding. Known as lactational amenorrhea, this phenomenon is not accepted by most modern medical professionals as a reliable means of birth control, but it did largely succeed over the course of history, providing humanity with a natural means of child spacing and population control. One of the reasons breastfeeding as birth control doesn't work as well in modern times is because modern mothers don't ordinarily nurse according to the ancient pattern: letting babies breastfeed at will, co-sleeping and nursing frequently at night, and not introducing solid foods until after the age of six months. But it could also be because we're better nourished now (most would say too well nourished given our epidemic of obesity), which allows for a faster return to ovulation.

"Having access to fire to cook food, having access to domesticated animal milk, having access to grain, [and having] less physical activity—all of these things add to the ability of healthy well-nourished women to have children closer together than every six or seven years, and still have most of them survive," noted Dettwyler. "The additional improvements in children's health from clean water, sewer systems, antibiotics, and immunizations add to the survival of children born close together." After all, she quipped, "Look at the Duggars!"

Of course, women have long attempted to tweak their natural fertility. Ancient Egyptian women used pessaries made with crocodile dung and honey as contraceptive devices. And while it was only in the twentieth century that the milk-stimulating hormone prolactin was identified as responsible for suppressing ovulation, people throughout the ages were well aware that it was difficult to conceive while nursing. Before the advent of infant formula, those wishing to get pregnant more quickly either hired a wet nurse or else stopped breastfeeding and "dry" nursed their babies a dangerous pap of animal's milk or water mixed with bread crumbs and often sugar.

Even in those early days, women were making choices about birth and breastfeeding, and culture had already begun to play a role in those decisions. As I saw it, Baila's nine-child, two-years-of-breastfeeding-each scenario could be a glimpse into an earlier time period (it certainly wasn't representative of what most modern women I knew were doing). It might even be a glimpse into biblical times. But did it take us all the way back? Short of having a time machine, can we see what breastfeeding might have been like for our metaphorical Adam and Eve, at the very dawn of human history?

Dettwyler said my best bet would be to look at modern hunting and gathering societies. "Humans lived as hunters and gatherers for most of the time that humans have existed," she said. "It's only in the last eight to ten thousand years that people started growing their own food and settling down in permanent locations. Among hunters and gatherers, of course, *everybody* nurses; if you don't, the baby dies."

The click language–speaking !Kung people (the "!K" sounds like the pop of a cork being pulled from a bottle) are one of those existing hunter-gatherer societies with a direct link to our primordial past. For at least the last twenty thousand years, the !Kung have made their home in the Kalahari Desert of southern Africa. And their link to the earliest humans may extend even further: Recent genetic research suggests that all modern humans are descended from similarly small groups of hunter-gatherers who first appeared in this area during the Pleistocene, the geological epoch that lasted from about 2.6 million to 11,700 years ago.

In very recent years, the !Kung have begun to incorporate small-scale farming and cattle raising into their hunter-gathering ways, but they have held fast to their eons-old ways of mothering. !Kung women maintain constant skin-to-skin contact with their babies, carrying them naked in a leather sling during the day and allowing them to nurse from their uncovered breasts at will, up to several times an hour. At night, babies sleep next to the mother on her kaross (leather cape) and nurse frequently throughout the night. Prechewed meat and sweet vegetables are introduced at the age of six months, but nursing continues until a new pregnancy is established. The average age of weaning is anywhere between twenty-eight to thirty-five months.

Thirty percent of !Kung children have no following siblings, though, and these nurslings are allowed to breastfeed much longer, typically self-weaning around the age of four, although sometimes continuing to nurse until the age of five or even six. But just as children in our modern world love to tease their peers, these "big babies," too, wind up taunted by other kids for continuing to suckle, and the breastfeeding eventually ends. It is weaning, well into our modern-day equivalent of the kindergarten years, that marks the end of infancy.

THE YOUNG BAILA, OF COURSE, DIDN'T KNOW ABOUT THE !KUNG or that—like most women throughout history—she would wind up spending much of her entire adult life breastfeeding. She foresaw none of this when her quiet, meditative life as a ballerina began to crack open at the age of eleven. It was in that year that a friend of her mother's took the young Baila and her mom to the community's Chabad house on Yom Kippur, the Jewish holy day of fasting and atonement. Mother and daughter had cursorily observed Yom Kippur in previous years by attending a local synagogue, but Baila's only memory from that time is of her mother publicly breaking the fast to buy her an ice cream cone, much to the horror of the religious Jews outside the shul.

But celebrating that evening at the Chabad house with a warm community and kids her own age, Baila suddenly felt as though she had found home. She became attracted to the Chabad way of seeing the world, which likes to spin the negative into the positive, and she soon found herself heading down the path to a religious life. Unbeknownst to her, however, an entire continent away, her father—whom she had been estranged from since she was a baby—had been introduced to a Chabad community in New York City and was also transitioning to life as a religious Jew. And not long after her eighteenth birthday, her father arrived in Melbourne to see her. He had finally located his daughter after searching for her for many years.

"There he was, with the black hat and beard," she said, clearly moved by the memory. "We hit it off right away."

Baila told me she hadn't been happy in Australia with her mother for some time, so she decided to move to New York to live with her father, where she immersed herself in her new Jewish life. Shortly after that, she met her husband Mendel (now a rabbi). The young couple lived first in the Crown Heights neighborhood of Brooklyn and then moved on to New Jersey, where at nineteen and about to give birth to her first child, Baila became friendly with a group of Orthodox women who were home birthers and La Leche League enthusiasts. Initially, she had a difficult time nursing her first daughter, Esther. But by her second child, she and her newfound friends were very close.

Baila recounted how it was the Blizzard of 1996—a monumental nor'easter that paralyzed the East Coast for three days and buried it under mountains of snow—that was her final stepping-stone to committed nursing mother. Listening to Baila's story, I marveled that, at the time, I was just a junior in high school excited to miss a week of school due to the deluge. But here was Baila, just past the teenage years herself, in the hospital in the midst of the storm and struggling with the birth of her second child. The doctor was trudging back and forth in the snow, waiting for her to dilate. Because of the influence of her newfound friends, she had opted for birth sans medication and had refused to artificially speed up her labor with the drug Pitocin. When the doctor pressured her to let him break her water to move things along, she found herself having a baby in a hospital with a skeleton crew. So, as it happened, there were no hospital staff members around to interfere with mother-child bonding after the birth.

"With my first one, in those days, they just took her away to the warmers, and I didn't even know enough to say I needed to keep her in my room," Baila said. But with her second baby, in the middle of a record-setting blizzard, there was no choice. "There was no one around to take the baby!" she exclaimed.

So after her second child, Rivka, was born, the doctor placed the baby on Baila's chest and departed—and Rivka nursed. "It was like one of those baby kangaroos that just know [where the pouch is]," she said. "I fell in love with nursing with my second one."

I, TOO, HAD LOVED BREASTFEEDING MY TWO GIRLS. I COULD blame it on oxytocin, the "love" hormone secreted during lactation, but every time they nursed, I felt an incredible sense of well-being. And I loved how being that close to their tiny faces gave me the constant opportunity to relentlessly cover them with kisses. Still, any way you look at it, making my breasts available to my two nurslings twenty-four hours a day was physically a *lot* of work, especially once they had gotten older and I was lugging around a twenty-two-pound toddler while I was trying to cook dinner, feed them both, put them to bed, and then return to my laptop in the hopes of meeting book deadlines. Yes, I had the slim figure to show for it, but at the end of each day, I was also completely wiped out. And, admittedly, I sometimes had a pretty short fuse, trying to handle it all. Yet I had only *two* kids; I couldn't help wondering how Baila had managed to nurse *eight* children thus far, each for two years! This raised the even bigger question: How had so many women nursed so many kids for so long throughout human history?

When I phoned Rabbi Jill Jacobs, executive director of the human rights organization T'ruah, to learn more about what breastfeeding may have been like for the ancient Jews, she brought up an interesting point. Breastfeeding and raising children in earlier times were respected for what they truly are: hard work. And the laws and texts of ancient Judaism reflect this. "There's the principal business in the Mishnah [the oldest collection of Jewish oral law] that breastfeeding is one of the jobs that a woman does for her husband," said Jacobs. "I think there's actually something feminist about that; that it's considered work, not just sitting around. Because it *is* work."

Jacobs knows a thing or two about work and breastfeeding. The mother of two daughters, she breastfed her older child until she was two and a half, and Jacobs was still nursing her eighteen-month-old when she and I spoke. What's more, she has continued nursing while sustaining the more than full-time work schedule of a CEO, regularly traveling around the United States and Israel (breast pump in tow). Last year, she even found the time to get herself arrested at a human rights demonstration in New York.

Yet apparently, in the old days, a mother would never have been expected to handle that much work on her own if she didn't have to. And although ancient Jewish mothers were not jetting around the world, their many responsibilities dictated by Hebrew law included cooking, laundry, weaving, *and* breastfeeding. But if the family had the financial means to bring in a servant, the mother would be allowed to delegate one or more of her jobs. It is interesting to note which jobs often fell by the wayside first.

"There's one mishnah that says if [a mother] brings two maidservants into the marriage, she doesn't have to cook and she doesn't have to nurse," said Jacobs, explaining that one of the servants would act as a wet nurse and breastfeed the child. (Baila concurred that no Orthodox mother raising a brood can do it all. She had been managing a dance school until a couple of years before we met, and she said that in her world help is a must. Modest though their house was, she had found a way to have a housekeeper come by regularly to clean, so she could focus on her kids.)

In certain instances, Jacobs said, a mother could even be financially compensated. Since breastfeeding was considered a marital obligation, a divorced mother was no longer obligated to comply with marital laws, and the father would be required to hire a wet nurse. But Jacobs related one eye-opening tale from the Talmud about a divorced mother who appealed to the rabbis for permission to stop nursing her child before the minimum eighteen months required by law (remember, these were the days when a child would die without being breastfed for at least that long). Maybe, like many single parents in our own time, she was overwhelmed trying to do everything on her own; we'll never know. But the rabbi considering the case feared that the baby, who was at that point old enough to recognize his mother, would refuse milk from a hired stranger and thus would starve. So to see if the baby did indeed recognize her, the rabbi carried the child through a gauntlet of women that included the mother. She tried to turn away, but not before the rabbi noticed the child reaching for her. So he ruled that the mother breastfeed her son but be compensated by the father for continuing to nurse him, essentially making the mother her own hired wet nurse.

The rabbi in the parable—and Rabbi Jacobs, too—brought to light an important point: the ancient Jews seemed to possess a certain wisdom about the effort required and the commitment involved in breastfeeding, one that is entirely absent in modern-day American society. This is evidenced, not the least, by the conspicuous fact that the United States is the only advanced country (and one of only a smattering of countries in the entire world) that does not provide paid maternity leave. Is it right—or even realistic—to expect all women to bounce back to work full-time mere weeks after giving birth and keep up the commitment of breastfeeding a newborn? If the government, especially, wants American women to breastfeed exclusively for the six months it is recommending, shouldn't we be "paid" by receiving adequate maternity leave?

I couldn't help but marvel at the irony of our current situation here in this country when I went to visit Rabbi Nicole Guzik, at Sinai Temple in Los Angeles. Sitting across her desk from me, Guzik, then a mother of two young ones herself, excitedly told me how, in the Talmud and the Torah (known to non-Jews as the Old Testament, or the first five books of the Bible), breastfeeding isn't only deemed work; it is also seen as a wondrous miracle. In the book of Isaiah, God himself is compared to a mother who could never forget her nursing child. In Exodus, breast milk is compared to the manna that falls from the heavens to sustain the Israelites wandering the desert for forty years after fleeing from slavery in Egypt.

And in Genesis, Sarah, ancestress of Israel, miraculously proves her motherhood at the age of ninety by disrobing and revealing her two breasts "pouring out milk like two jets of water." Even one of the names by which God is known in Hebrew, *El Shaddai,* may come directly from *shadayim*—the word for *breasts*, Guzik suggested.

Yet the rabbi also shared how attached she had become to her breast pump after the twelve weeks of her (luckily, paid) maternity leave were over. "Pumping was more my life than nursing," she admitted. She had a positive take on it, though, viewing her pump as a connection point to her babies. (She also said she was thankful that she had a big private office to pump in.) Still, I couldn't help but wonder: How could Sinai Temple, arguably one of the wealthiest congregations in the country with a preschool and top-notch K-8 private school on its campus, not offer its own working mothers on-site day care? Why was someone in Guzik's esteemed position resigned to toting her breast pump to work every day and leaving her nursing children behind? I wondered how we might bring back some of that eons-old reverence for breastfeeding and see once again the mother-child connection as the stuff of miracles—a mind-set that was certainly not exclusive to ancient Judaism.

Prehistoric statuettes uncovered from the Stone Age reveal buxom figures providing the promise of plentiful milk. Fourteen hundred years ago, the divine calling of a Muslim mother to nurse her child for at least two years was spelled out in the Koran. Ancient Egyptian statues show the goddess Isis offering her breast to her son Horus. And cult figures of the Greek goddess Artemis uncovered from second-century Ephesus (in modern-day Turkey) are adorned with grape-like clusters of breasts affixed to her torso.

Sadly, though, it seems that breastfeeding has lost its sacred aura. For if you look at the modern-day symbols for Christianity—primarily the cross, but also the ubiquitous Christmastime crèche of the holy family lovingly gathered around the manger—it's fascinating to note that a most fundamental aspect of the picture appears to have been edited out: namely, how baby Jesus was fed.

We know that Christ wasn't fed infant formula, and it wasn't likely that Mary and Joseph hired a wet nurse, either, since the family was of humble, if not downright meager, means. So where are Mary's breasts? Evident or not, we can easily deduce that Mary did indeed breastfeed Jesus herself. As a matter of fact, in at least one passage in the Gospel of Luke (11:27), Mary's contribution as a breastfeeding mother is on par with her sacred pregnancy: "Blessed is the womb that bore you, and the breasts which you have sucked."

We can also be fairly certain that Jesus, born a Jew, was likely nursed well into toddlerhood, since we know that was dictated by ancient Hebrew law. According to Christian theologian Charles John Ellicott, the stages of Jesus's Jewish childhood were clearly marked, and the young boy transitioned to wearing the traditional fringed *tzitzit* only after being weaned at the age of three. Oh, and one more thing: the baby Jesus probably didn't sleep in that cradle. Like most ancient peoples, in all likelihood he slept on the ground close to his mother (maybe on a nice, soft clump of hay), so he could nurse throughout the night.

It would appear, though, that modern Christianity has forgotten all these realities of Jesus's time. Yet earlier Christians were not only very much aware that baby Jesus was breastfed, they, like the ancient Jews, regarded breastfeeding as the ultimate miracle. In fact, for most of the Middle Ages and much of the Renaissance, it wasn't the crucifixion that served as the ultimate symbol of God's love for humanity, it was the Virgin Mary's lactating breast. We have this on excellent authority from art historian Margaret Miles, professor emerita at the Graduate Theological Union in Berkeley, California, and author of *A Complex Delight: The Secularization of the Breast 1350–1750*.

As it happens, the very idea for her book arose when she kept coming across paintings of the Virgin Mary with one breast bared, Miles told me one morning from her home in Berkeley. She began to wonder about it, especially since there was so little textual evidence from that era to support the images she was finding.

"Historians are limited to the remains of historical cultures, and the people who nursed infants are seldom the ones who left an historical record!" she noted wryly.

But as she unearthed more clues, she also discovered that

these works of art held tremendous meaning for our ancestors. At that time in history, she explained, the nursing breast signified provision and nourishment, life and health. In other words, in an age when people regularly dealt with severe food shortages and recurring waves of pandemic plague (when in Florence, for instance, between the years 1340 and 1427, the average life span plunged from thirty to twenty years), breastfeeding and breast milk, with all its life-giving properties, was something people probably cared about quite deeply.

To my untrained eye in the present day, scanning the glorious color plates of Miles's book, I decided that the art from this period ranged from the creepily captivating to the breathtakingly beautiful. In Ambrogio Lorenzetti's *Madonna del Latte*, which dates from before 1348, a Virgin in profile gazes at her infant Jesus suckling on her highly placed, unnaturally round breast (a stylization from the time period), while the child pointedly stares out at us. Around 250 years later, the image of the baby Jesus tenderly caressing the Virgin's neck as she offers her breast in Artemesia Gentileschi's *Madonna and Child* is so intimate and naturalistic, it takes your breath away. (Artemesia was one of the few and certainly most famous female painters of the period. Maybe personal experience inspired her work?)

As I sat on the floor thumbing through page after page of nursing madonnas, Mika, then two, pushed me out of the way to get a closer look. "Mommy, Mommy, baby loves Milky! Baby drinking Milky!" she said excitedly, pointing to a Franceschi *Nursing Virgin* from the fifteenth century.

Miles laughed when I recounted the story. "Well, she would understand those pictures perfectly," she chuckled.

And so would the people from the time period, for whom breastfeeding openly was a normal facet of daily existence, she said. That's why the works were often placed in parish churches that were visited many times weekly, if not daily, by those who lived in the communities their entire lives. In troubling times, the images of Mary nursing the baby Jesus were meant to comfort and to reinforce faith.

But the paintings may have been meant to deliver another message, as well: to admonish mothers about the dangerous practice of wet-nursing. At that time in Renaissance Florence, the practice was becoming widespread, even among middle-class families. And the babies sent out to the countryside to be nursed by a *balia* (not to be confused with Baila) were often "overlaid" by their nurses—a catchall euphemism covering a range of fatalities, including accidental smothering and death from poor care. Depictions of the nursing Virgin reminded women, daily, that breastfeeding was not only an important job but a holy one. Unhappily, this sentiment didn't last forever, Miles discovered. By 1750, religious paintings of a breastfeeding Mary had all but vanished, replaced by artwork that represented the breast as primarily medical or sexual. (Sound familiar?)

Yet when it comes to re-embracing breastfeeding as a symbol of religious beauty and of a mother's revered role, there have indeed been stirrings in the Catholic Church, at least. In 2014, Pope Francis encouraged mothers to nurse their babies in the Sistine Chapel, advising "If they are hungry, mothers, feed them, without thinking twice. Because they are the most important people here."

TURNS OUT, IF I HAD BEEN LOOKING FOR MY FRIEND BAILA'S STORY TO offer a direct connection to breastfeeding in biblical times, I was misguided. True, like Baila, most women of all faiths at that time in history breastfed however many children they birthed. For the ancients, that was in all likelihood for a minimum of twenty-four months, just as it had been for Baila in the twenty-first century. And a biblical-age mother might have turned to baking bread to distract herself from the pains of labor, as Baila did, baking challah during labor. (I learned about this when an animated Mendel knocked on my door to borrow an egg during Baila's home birth of Devorah, their ninth child.)

But after I came to know Baila and her family, I saw the truth about how she lived, birthed, breastfed, and raised her children: Baila was half devout Jew, half granola home-birthing mom. Her mothering choices weren't made *because* she was a religious Jew who observed laws and customs that dated quite possibly to the time of Christ. They were made as a result of the home-birthing La Leche mothers she had befriended back in New Jersey. Like me, she had had a spiritual epiphany about breastfeeding not in temple, but in a hospital.

I saw another truth, as well. As it turns out, while Orthodox Jews continue to value motherhood, modern-day Jews as a whole have forgotten the breastfeeding part of that picture, just like most of the modern world.

Baila told me that at Nessah, a Beverly Hills Orthodox synagogue where Mendel is one of the rabbis, the community is largely Persian, and the women like to really dress up. "I see a lot of bottle-feeding going on," she said. "I don't think anyone there is saying, 'Oh, I'm going to wear clothes that I can nurse in.' "

Then there's the issue of breastfeeding in public. She told me that, technically, she's allowed to pray in synagogue and nurse at the same time, even if she is completely uncovered. In practice, though, there's no doubt that the modesty laws (covered hair, knees, and elbows) that are so integral to an Orthodox Jewish woman's life do indeed have an influence on her breastfeeding practices.

"Listen," she said. "A lot of Orthodox people have kids, and a lot of them nurse. But most of them probably wouldn't feel comfortable nursing in public. At Nessah, if I'm nursing, I'm not going to be nursing in front of anybody. I'll go find a private spot."

A few weeks before we moved out of the neighborhood and into our new home in another part of town, I saw Baila find such a spot. It was the last night of Chanukah. Matthew was working at the studio, and the girls and I went over to Baila and Mendel's house to light the menorah candles and eat homemade *sufganiyot*, the powdered sugar doughnuts that are traditionally eaten on the holiday. I had grown fond of Baila and her warm, lively family over the course of the year-plus that they welcomed us over for Jewish holidays and stuffed us with plate after plate of poached fish and schnitzel, Israeli salad, and home-baked spelt challah, all while Mendel held us spellbound with sermon-esque stories in the way only a truly special rabbi can.

On this last night, we all stood together as Mendel helped his children and mine light their collection of menorahs in the window of the front room of the house as we said the prayers. Mendel and Sarah, his eldest daughter still at home, put their arms around each other and sang while I tried to keep my rambunctious girls from knocking over what seemed like a hundred lit candles and burning down their house. But out of the corner of my eye I saw Baila, awash in the glow, sit down on the couch, gently push aside her blouse, and draw her seven-month-old baby Devorah close to her breast.

It was the first time I had actually seen Baila nurse. Mother and baby, serene, looked like that glimpse back in time I had been hoping all along to capture, and I thought: What would it take to reconnect with the ancients who viewed breastfeeding as the ultimate symbol of God's life-giving manna in the wilderness? What would it take to re-embrace that image of Mary, transferring through her breast the love for all mankind?

For starters, we might need to uncover the miracles that even now remain hidden. Our ancestors came to worship breastfeeding because they knew only two things: that the babies of mothers who weren't able to nurse usually died and that, amazingly, babies were able to thrive nourished solely by a miraculous substance. Yet what may be most astonishing is that countless centuries after the Pleistocene, after the ancient Jews, after the birth of Christ, after the time of Lorenzetti, we still don't know much more about breast milk than they did.

three

Milk Mysteries and Maternal Duty

I think there is no nurse like a mother.

—BENJAMIN FRANKLIN

It was a ninety-two degree March day in Los Angeles when I phoned Katie Hinde, who was holed up in her Boston laboratory as the city was less than four inches away from its all-time snow record. At the time, Hinde was assistant professor of human evolutionary biology at Harvard University and director of the school's Comparative Lactation Lab, which has conducted some of the most groundbreaking lactation research in the country. (She and her lab have since moved on to warmer weather and more trailblazing research at the School of Human Evolution and Social Change and the new Center for Evolution and Medicine at Arizona State University.)

I wanted a crash course in the miracle of milk. Today, when women in the developed world could choose to bottle-feed and know that their children would survive, I wanted to find out: Would they choose differently if they discovered that breast milk actually ensured much more than basic survival? I was pretty sure Hinde would have some answers for me.

I also was fairly certain that whatever enlightening information she had to impart, she would be entertaining, as evidenced by her thoughtful yet highly amusing blog *Mammals Suck . . . Milk!*, where she peppers extrapolations of her own and other researchers' findings with games like Mammal March Madness and with YouTube links to Monty Python bits. I had become a regular reader, and I told her that her relatable yet often wacky posts sounded delightfully unscientist-like for a scientist of her standing. She chuckled, "I have been accused of having an overabundance of personality!"

Hinde is my age, thirty-five, and in less than a decade since completing her dissertation in anthropology at the University of California, Los Angeles (UCLA), she has become a leading expert in the science of lactation. This may be partly due to her boundless enthusiasm for the subject ("I wake up in the middle of the night thinking, *Oh! I wonder how this affects breast milk!*"), but it may also be because up until very recently, breast milk has been unabashedly ignored by the scientific community.

Hinde first became aware of this hole in the literature while pursuing her master's degree. As an undergraduate, she had studied primate growth and development at the University of Washington and had worked on an honors thesis (which she never published) revealing that pigtail macaque females who were ill as youngsters were at higher risk for losing their pregnancies once they reached reproductive age.

But after entering the graduate program in the anthropology department at UCLA, she wanted to take her research to the next step: Once those monkeys were finally able to sustain a pregnancy to full term, how did their prior illness affect their milk? So Hinde dove into the literature and discovered that there had been just two studies conducted—*ever*—on nonhuman primate milk synthesis.

The omission was striking, since humans are primates, and nonhuman primates are our closest living biological relatives. Monkey and ape mothers naturally nurse their young very much the way that humans have evolved to do. (Note that I say *evolved to do* and not simply *do*, since the discrepancy between our innate biology and the cultural influences on our practices is pretty much the basis for this whole book!) Like humans, other primate mothers ordinarily give birth to a single infant at a time and intensely nurture that baby through childhood. They maintain skin-to-skin contact, allowing their offspring to suckle frequently and at will. And the great apes—including chimpanzees and bonobos, with whom we share 98.8 percent of our DNA—continue to nurse their babies for several years.

Yet it wasn't only the primatologists who had turned a blind eye to uncovering the secrets of milk. In 2008, the US National Institutes of Health (NIH), one of the world's foremost medical research centers, set out to map the human microbiome, the vast colonies of microbes found in the human body, which have only recently been discovered to play a critical role in our health. To accomplish this feat, the NIH spent $115 million over the course of five years and examined more than five thousand samples from over three hundred human volunteers. These specimens included blood, feces, skin, vaginal secretions, cord blood, amniotic fluid—basically, everything indispensable to human life—except breast milk, the lifeblood that has sustained mankind for millions of years. Apparently, breast milk didn't make the cut.

Lactation may have been long overlooked because of the one-time misconception among scientists that human breast milk is sterile. (It is not; a human baby consuming twenty-seven ounces of breast milk will receive anywhere from one hundred thousand to ten million bacteria and the like *each day.*) But Hinde gave me another, more practical, explanation, at least when it comes to conducting research with primates. Up until recently, the way samples were collected—essentially by capturing a monkey mom and her baby—made it very difficult to obtain anything. The mother would be stressed-out and wouldn't let down her milk.

"One of my really wonderful mentors gave me what he thought was the best advice," Hinde recalled. "He said, 'Don't even bother studying milk in monkeys. You won't get any samples, and if you do, you won't find anything interesting!' "

Hinde, of course, ignored that helpful suggestion. She met a research technologist at a primate research center, and the two devised a method wherein the monkey mother (Hinde now works with rhesus macaques) wears a little Velcro jacket that prevents her from nursing for a few hours but allows her to sit calmly with her infant while her milk accumulates. The mother is then briefly sedated, and Hinde is able to obtain a large milk sample before reuniting mom with baby. This method doesn't replicate the natural suckling intensity of the infant ("All milk studies have necessary constraints," she conceded), but it provides a measure that's biologically meaningful and allows Hinde to compare milk synthesis among mothers in a standardized way.

Now granted, rhesus macaques aren't humans. But their mammary glands have much in common with our own mammary glands. Perhaps more important, as with human mothers, monkey mothers play a vital role in each infant's neurodevelopment after birth. In fact, the interaction that babies have with their mothers through breastfeeding is one of the ways they learn and grow. According to Hinde, short of conducting research with human babies (which is difficult given that most American mothers aren't too keen about allowing their infants to be subjects of experiments), rhesus macaques are currently our best available model for understanding the behavioral biology of human lactation. *Behavioral* is the key word here since our twentieth- and twenty-first-century assessments of mother's milk have been incredibly one-dimensional, focusing on milk for its nutritional benefits only.

"Human breast milk is food [but it's also] medicine; it's hormonal signal," said Hinde. "But most formula is really oriented around being a food."

This is changing, she maintains. Hormones in milk (the good, human kind) are going to be the next point of focus in terms of how mother's milk—and even newer infant formulas—influence infant physiology, especially in light of the discoveries she found through the milk samples of the monkey mothers. It was using the Velcro jacket method last year that Hinde and her team were able to measure levels of the stress hormone cortisol in their milk. What they uncovered was profound: The hormone cortisol acted as a messenger from mother to child, affecting babies' growth and even their *personalities*. Simply put, first-time monkey mothers had milk with higher levels of cortisol, yielding babies with more nervous temperaments than the children of more experienced mothers. (I wonder if the "precious firstborn syndrome" we observe in so many new human parents may have more of a physiological basis than was previously thought.)

But this isn't just a case of a high-strung oldest child. Higher levels of cortisol in a monkey mother's milk were also associated with greater weight gain in the infant. In fact, the more nervous temperaments of monkey babies born to less experienced mothers may serve an important purpose at a time when a young macaque mother's mammary gland is still ramping up to full capacity, signaling to a nursling to prioritize growth over playing and to quit, well, monkeying around.

Other research has been pouring in. One recent study found that female pigs not exposed to the hormone relaxin as piglets via their mother's milk had smaller litter sizes as adults. (Relaxin activity in pig milk is similar to that in humans.) Yet another study, this time among humans, revealed that lower concentrations of leptin—a natural hormone suspected to play a pivotal role in breastfed babies' intuitive appetite control—in the milk of Filipino mothers perhaps programmed their babies, especially their baby daughters, to gain more weight.

Hormones, however, are like Facebook status updates, Hinde explained. A hormone is received only by "friended" tissues that have the right receptors. In an interesting parallel to Hinde's cortisol study, another research team out of the University of Illinois at Urbana-Champaign recently examined these cortisol receptors that develop in intestines of human babies. What they found is that nonbreastfed babies may be, quite literally, missing the message. The glucocorticoid receptor gene in breastfed babies had five times the expression than that of formula-fed babies, suggesting that a good deal more "docking sites" for cortisol develop in the guts of breastfed infants.

Why is this important? Well, although cortisol may be only one type of glucocorticoid, it is the most essential one for human life, playing a pivotal role in gut development, enzyme expression, and overall immune function. Anyone who has ever rubbed over-the-counter hydrocortisone cream onto a bug bite can understand the powerful anti-inflammatory role that glucocorticoids play in the body.

As it happens, "Formula feeders' immune profiles tend to skew toward more inflammation," said Sharon Donovan, a professor in the Department of Food Science and Human Nutrition at the University of Illinois at Urbana-Champaign and the lead author of that study. I had called her to find out more about the health implications for her work and shared that I had been one of those exclusive formula feeders as a baby. She told me that she has also been looking at the balance of T cells in the gut immune system of formula feeders versus breast feeders. "Those are ingredients that we're not going to be able to mimic in formulas, because they're so unique to human milk that we can't isolate them from another source."

Still, these studies are the tip of the iceberg, and they focus solely on hormones—one small aspect of a staggering number of human breast-milk factors that have yet to be fully explored. As for commercial infant formulas, they contain only about nine components, although that's an estimate since much of that information is proprietary to the companies that produce them. By contrast, there were once thought to be more than two hundred components in breast milk—including (to name a tiny handful) immune and growth factors, fatty acids crucial for brain development, antiproteases that may play a role in preventing allergic reactions, hundreds of species of microbes, and the newly discovered oligosaccharides, which are complex sugars that may have evolved partially to feed many of those beneficial microbes. It now appears that there are hundreds of variations of each and every one of those hundreds of previously identified components.

"When all is said and done, when we [construct] a comprehensive library of breast-milk composition, I think we're going to be talking in the thousands," said Katie Hinde. Or possibly more. Recently, a research team that included Hinde at the Genome Center at the University of California, Davis, used a new type of molecular analysis to examine just one component—proteins—and discovered more than 1,600 distinct types.

And therein may be what is most astonishing. It is 2016, we finished sequencing the entire human genome more than ten years ago, yet we still don't have a comprehensive library of what's in breast milk?

"It's kind of scary sometimes that we know so little about the first food a mammal is adapted to consume," Hinde admitted. "It's convenient for those of us who are researching it because there's lots to find out. But it's also very problematic that this hasn't been a research priority."

Of course, there has been considerable work done in the field of public health, attempting to understand what breastfeeding means for infant and maternal well-being. It was these types of studies that uncovered the connection between not breastfeeding and catastrophically high rates of infant mortality in developing countries lacking sanitation. And such studies continue to yield findings about the higher risk of gastrointestinal and respiratory illness in nonbreastfed infants in every part of the world, along with the higher risk of obesity, type 1 and type 2 diabetes, sudden infant death syndrome (SIDS), and childhood leukemia, not to mention higher risk for ovarian cancer and certain kinds of breast cancer for the nonbreastfeeding mother.

But the flip side of these epidemiological studies—which essentially look at different populations and then try to trace the cause of different health outcomes—is that many of the results have been all over the place: "Breastfeeding Past Two Months Lowers Obesity Risk!" "Breastfeeding May Not Reduce Obesity Risk!" "Breast-Fed Babies Are Smarter!" "Breast Milk Is Not Why Babies Are Smarter!" (The emphasis is mine, but these are some actual headlines from the past two years.) Unfortunately, such confusion played out in the media has led a lot of well-meaning parents to assume that breastfeeding doesn't always offer a distinct health advantage over formula feeding.

But as Donovan explained: "These studies look at a twenty-, thirty-, fifty-year-old and then try to go back and say, did it matter whether they were breastfed or formula-fed?" Yet one of the main issues, she pointed out, is that researchers don't always clearly define what breastfeeding *means*, which reduces its potential benefits. "When you look at the studies, sometimes it's exclusive breastfeeding for six months but sometimes it's half breastfeeding and half formula, which is very common today," she cautioned.

Hinde cited another issue with our perception of these studies—we often fail to recognize that our long-term health outcomes are very multifactorial. "There is no silver bullet, no magical thing that you can do to ensure perfect human health throughout the life span. Seeing that breastfeeding can shift that needle in a healthier direction is very important, but thinking it can fix all the ills is an unreasonable expectation."

So here's the big question: If human milk is admittedly still a mystery, if our understanding of how it fully affects our health continues to be imprecise, if even our greatest minds are still working to figure all of this out, then why the endless back and forth about breastfeeding versus formula feeding in the media and on message boards? How can we be arguing about that of which we know so little? What are the mommy wars *truly* about?

Hinde, for one, is all too aware that the messaging may be as important as what she finds in the milk. She's worked very hard to communicate her findings in a way that's accessible, and as the daughter of a folk musician raised in a family of artists and performers concerned about social justice, she may have a leg up over other scientists. (Hinde quipped, "The joke in my family is that I ran away from the circus to join the science.") But it's clear that navigating the mommy wars is something she still struggles with.

"There's this perception that breast milk isn't special and

that formula is an effective replacement. And in many cases it's a perfectly acceptable replacement balanced against all other things, like being able to earn a paycheck, right? That's really, really important. And so it's tricky, because how do you create messaging about how incredibly magical and amazing breast milk is, without undermining women who can't breastfeed for a variety of reasons? And how do you convince Congress to create funding mandates for breast-milk research when many [politicians] don't have an understanding of the complexity of lactation biology? All of these things are a complicated socio, historical, political, economic context for breastfeeding and formula feeding. But somehow, it almost always gets messaged as, 'a mother's personal choice.' "

In other words, it may be less about the facts and more about our long-conflicted feelings about what is and isn't our maternal duty.

EVEN BEFORE THE ADVENT OF COMMERCIAL INFANT FORMULA, mothers were making personal choices about how to feed their babies. Nearly all children may have been breastfed, but they didn't necessarily have to be breastfed by their own mothers.

In prehistoric times, when bands of hunter-gatherers roamed the earth, a kinswoman might have been called upon to nurse a child in the event of a mother's absence or illness, or more tragically, her death. But later—as humans grew in number, societies organized, and there were more lactating women to go around—breastfeeding mothers began to outsource more formally. Mothers (or fathers, since they were often the ones put in charge of an infant's feeding needs) could hire a wet nurse, another lactating woman who was paid to feed their child.

Next to prostitution, wet-nursing is perhaps one of the world's oldest professions for women; nearly every advanced civilization employed some version of it. There's the earlier story about the divorced ancient Jewish mother who wanted to procure a wet nurse for her son instead of nursing him herself, but there are countless other examples: a Sumerian lullaby from 3000 BC makes mention of a nursemaid suckling; King Tut built a lavish tomb to honor his own wet nurse; Islamic law views two children having suckled milk from the same woman as a lifelong form of kinship equal to that of a blood relative; ancient Romans could bring their hungry infants to the Columna Lactaria for a nursing; and in the medieval kingdom of Castile, wet nurses for royal children were hired for one or two decades and became governesses after weaning. In fact, it wasn't until I began work on this book that I realized that Mammy—the house slave character in Margaret Mitchell's *Gone With the Wind*, the film version of which I've seen at least a dozen times—wasn't just the servant who raised Scarlett O'Hara; Mammy had been Scarlett's wet nurse. (More on that conflicted arrangement in a moment.)

From antiquity through the Middle Ages, a wet nurse was often a convention only for royalty or the very wealthy; most healthy women breastfed their own children. Of course, wet nurses were also employed for abandoned children or when a mother died and left a nursling behind or when she couldn't nurse for medical reasons. (If you ever have a day when you feel like a bad parent, consider the case of Greco-Roman

Egypt, where unwanted babies were often tossed on trash heaps and you could snag one for a cheap slave by "saving" it and hiring a wet nurse to feed it.)

By the Renaissance, the wet nurse as status symbol had begun to trickle down to the merchant classes. Employing a wet nurse became so commonplace by the seventeenth and eighteenth centuries in certain parts of Western Europe that a mother feeding her own child was considered strange except among the very poor. Sometimes, even wet nurses themselves hired other wet nurses; they would hire themselves out to a wealthy family and then send their own babies to a less expensive wet nurse out in the country, living on the difference.

Still, just because people were perpetuating the practice of wet-nursing didn't mean everyone was OK with it. For many, the biological predilection to feed one's own offspring seemed obvious, and in second-century Rome and Greece, philosophers including Pliny and Plutarch spoke out against the practice of wet-nursing among the wealthy. They called attention to the severed bond that resulted between a natural mother and her child, and they even believed that a child could imbibe the physical and mental qualities of the wet nurse via her milk. (This belief persisted through the nineteenth century. In light of Hinde's study, which revealed that baby monkeys' personalities were altered by the cortisol they absorbed from their mother's milk, perhaps the ancients weren't too far off the mark.)

Preachers and physicians of the Middle Ages advocated maternal breastfeeding, calling attention to the deep connection and love that developed between a nursling and whoever suckled him—even if that woman was not his birth mother.

And later, in Colonial America, the Puritan Reverend Cotton Mather implored women to nurse their own children, admonishing them not to become "one of the Careless Women, Living at Ease." (Never mind that he himself was wet-nursed, as were some of his fifteen children.)

Although most Puritans as well as most women in the northern colonies breastfed their own babies (the former viewing it as their duty not just to their children but to God, as well), wet-nursing in Colonial America was certainly common enough to elicit Mather's opposition. Wealthy New World settlers from Spain and France, accustomed to hiring wet nurses of lower social status in their home countries, turned to Native American women, who were viewed as inferiors, to serve as wet nurses. The city of Boston and its surrounds became a thriving market for women seeking employment as such. By the eighteenth century, breast milk was the most frequently advertised vendible in Colonial newspapers.

The wet-nursing business wasn't a boon to everyone, of course. In the South, the maternal bond turned maternal shackle in the role of "Mammy." On the plantations, black slave women were stripped of all reproductive rights and exploited to suckle the children of their white masters. The breastfeeding was almost always at the expense of the enslaved women's own children, who either were brutally confiscated or else died as the result of their mothers not being able to feed them regularly. Those slave children who did survive were allowed virtually no connection with their mothers, and weaning was forced early so that slave women could conceive additional slave children (often upwards of fifteen in a lifetime) for their master. Whether it's conscious or not, the emotional scar of this unfathomable history could be one of the reasons why African American women have the lowest breastfeeding rates in the country. And the health of African American children continues to suffer as a result. Black babies are twice as likely to die before their first birthdays as white babies, and as older children, black youth suffer markedly higher occurrences of obesity and asthma.

Yet perhaps nowhere else on earth at any point in history did wet-nursing reach the degree it did—where Mather's "maternal duty" was turned more on its head—than in eighteenth-century France. There, the business of wet-nursing became so rampant, so nearly universal, that a Parisian police official, Lieutenant General Jean-Charles-Pierre Lenoir, was placed in charge of supervising the referral bureaus parents used to find wet nurses.

Lenoir's comprehensive 1780 survey of the twenty-one thousand babies born in the city that year shows that only about 3 percent were breastfed by their own mothers. Another 3 percent or so were fed by hired wet nurses in the homes of the wealthy, with a greater minority of privileged children nursed near their parents' homes. But the vast majority of wet-nursed tots, either castaways or those born to the middle and lower classes (some fifteen thousand infants in that year alone) were placed in foundling hospitals or were shipped off mere days after birth to the countryside, to be nursed and ostensibly nurtured by a stranger who likely corresponded with the birth parents only a few times before returning the child upon weaning years later—or who would send but a note in the event that the child had died.

And there were many, many deaths. Registers from the

Bureau of Wet Nurses of Paris during the years 1770–1776 show that of the 66,529 nurslings placed by the department, more than twenty-one thousand died in the care of their rural wet nurses. (An astounding number when you consider that at nearly the same time in history an ocean away, roughly twenty-five thousand American patriots died in active military service during the Revolutionary War.) Still, a mortality rate of around 32 percent would have been a miracle for the other group of babies: the foundlings, or the thousands of infants abandoned each year. For them, the situation was far bleaker, since foundling hospitals attracted only the poorest and least employable wet nurses and there simply weren't enough breasts to go around. As many as 90 percent of these innocents did not make it to their first birthday.

For the scant number of Parisian babies who were breastfed at home by their mothers, or for babies born in other parts of France where mothers were more likely to nurse their own children, the infant mortality rate was strikingly lower: 18 to 20 percent. Aristocratic children who were wet-nursed under supervision in their parents' home had very similar survival rates. It could therefore be concluded that it wasn't the act of wet-nursing itself that was killing so many babies, but the sloppy care that many nurslings received once removed from the watchful eye of their parents.

Many infants didn't even survive the journey out to the countryside to the home of their wet nurse. And the ones who made it were often switched from the breast to porridge much earlier than the minimum twelve to eighteen months of nursing recommended at that time, leaving the children more vulnerable to disease and death. Still others may have been inadvertently smothered when their nurses took them into bed at night. And in the summer months, the worst time for neglect because wet nurses were needed to help with the harvest, babies were left unattended in the fields or else alone at home, abandoned to the very real and all-too-common fates of being devoured by pigs or crawling into the fire.

Why would any mother willingly send her child off to such a precarious destiny? Even if a weaned child were returned to her birth parents alive and well, she would no doubt have suffered emotional trauma, torn from the only mother she had ever known—her wet nurse—and abruptly dropped back into a family she perceived as strangers. I'm also guessing that a mother who hadn't seen her child since birth might not have felt much of a connection, either. Was breastfeeding so abhorrent that it obliterated the normally overpowering maternal instinct to keep one's child alive?

The answer is manifold, but it's one that may perhaps sound familiar to modern mothers. As it turns out, the decisions eighteenth-century French mothers made regarding breastfeeding had less to do with breastfeeding itself and more to do with those mothers' individual struggles. Certainly, cultural preferences played a role. The corsets, plunging necklines, and often-exposed nipples from the time of Marie Antoinette made it clear, at least among the aristocracy, that breasts were viewed as erotic and not for feeding babies. The French nobility's reliance on wet nurses was also a method of increasing a mother's fertility that dated back to medieval times. (Remember that no breastfeeding equals more babies.)

But the vast majority of parents caught up in the wet-nursing whirlwind of eighteenth-century France weren't aristocrats; they were working folk—artisans, shopkeepers, tradesmen, and even domestic servants—who felt they had no economic alternative at a time when rents were high, incomes were low, and half of a family's meager budget was allocated for food. Both men and women of those days had to work to survive, and if a mother had to give up her work to nurse a new infant, the family might very well perish.

It was a cruel catch-22 in an era without modern birth control. Women were having more and more babies that cost the family more and more money to send out to wet-nurse, and in the end, those babies were more and more likely to die. In fact, the average middle-class woman gave birth to anywhere from twelve to sixteen children in her lifetime. Of those, perhaps two or three survived to adulthood. I wonder if any of these mothers ever took a step back and wondered: Just what is all this *for*?

That kind of self-reflection may have been what the Swedish taxonomist Carl Linnaeus was hoping for when, in 1735, he made a very bold move. He named the class of animals that defines humankind *Mammalia*, which comes from the Latin *mammae*, for our milk-producing breasts. Only half of all mammals—the females—actually suckle their young, but as Linnaeus was vehemently opposed to the widespread wet-nursing practices of his time (along with Enlightenment moralists such as Jean-Jacques Rousseau and the famous French physician Jean-Emmanuel Gilibert), the message embedded in his science was very clear: To nurse one's own children is part of our nature, a part of our inherent biology. To act against that would be an aberration.

THE MIRACLE OF MILK MAY BE EONS OLD, BUT OUR SENSE OF maternal duty, apparently, is not as steadfast. Or rather, maternal biology is often back-burnered by whatever maternal choices we're given in the time in which we live.

It's easy to look at eighteenth-century France and say that parents were caught up in a bizarre cultural bubble and simply lost sight of what was intrinsically most important. But were the challenges they faced—economic uncertainty, social inequity, a lack of reliable information as to how to best care for their children—all that different from the ones we face today?

True, life was cheap then. Most of us could never dream of shipping off our precious babies to endure the level of widespread neglect and dangerous methods of caretaking that many wet nurses of that era employed. Today, we would view that practice as child abuse.

Yet of the twenty million children under the age of five today in the United States, 12.5 million are in full-time childcare. Seventy percent of babies under the age of one are regularly cared for by someone other than their parents. Combine that with the fact that infants of full-time working mothers are fed either infant formula or pumped breast milk, by bottle, by someone else (unless you have on-site day care at your office and can take breaks to breastfeed, which is quite rare), and what we have in the United States today is a modified version of wet-nursing on a grand scale.

Maybe a historian of the future will look back on us, siphoning the milk from our breasts via electrical pump as we gaze at our laptops, and wonder why we didn't come up with a better solution.

four

Industrial Age vs. the Breast

First, we must teach regularity, the cultivation of accurate habits in the baby; make a machine of the little one. Teach it to employ its various functions at fixed and convenient times.

—DR. P. J. EATON

After the failure *énorme* of France's experiment in massively organized mammary swapping, the professional wet-nursing business died down a bit, although it never vanished completely. In China and other Asian countries where cow's milk wasn't part of the traditional diet—and the only substitute for a mother's breast was *another* woman's breast—the practice continued through the first half of the twentieth century. Meanwhile, American children's hospitals, recognizing early on that human milk meant the difference between life and death for premature and sickly infants, regularly employed wet nurses through World War II. (And if you accept my earlier definition of pumping as a form of wet-nursing, then the practice of wet-nursing continues in hospitals in the form of the human-milk donations and high-tech human-milk-derived fortifiers that are considered crucial for a preemie's survival.)

Even now, just a couple of miles from my home in Los Angeles, there's a staffing agency that advertises wet nurses for Hollywood celebrities and other too-wealthy-to-wean types alongside its cadre of butlers and vegan chefs.

Still, after the tragic fate of so many babies shipped off to wet nurses in eighteenth-century France, many parents undoubtedly realized that maybe it was a good idea to keep one's progeny closer by. Not surprisingly, by the mid-nineteenth century, *live-in* wet nurses became the preference for the wealthy families who could afford them—not just in France, but in Britain, Scandinavia, and parts of America and Australia as well. The problem was that live-in wet nurses were tough to find, expecially later in the century after the pasteurization of cow's milk was widely adopted in Europe and many wet nurses switched to bottle-feeding their charges. (Though this was regarded as a dangerous last resort. More on that in a moment.)

The new generation of live-in wet nurses also wasn't as experienced as the rural mothers who took nurslings into their own home for supplemental income in days of yore. Nineteenth-century married women, unless truly desperate, weren't willing to ditch their own families for more than a year to move to the city and nurse someone else's child. That meant the prime candidate for a live-in wet nurse was either an untried first-time mother whose baby had just died and whose milk supply was questionable (not to mention her feeding and childcare knowledge) or a "fallen" woman who had surrendered her own illegitimate child so she could be employed as a wet nurse.

In Victorian Britain, for instance, wannabe wet nurses could, for a flat fee, unload their newborns on a baby "farmer," who would take care of the infants for payment (or, more often than not, neglect or even murder them). Whether an upper-class Victorian mother hiring a live-in wet nurse acknowledged it or not, she faced quite the moral dilemma—trading the life of her wet nurse's baby for the life of her own child. At best, she benefited from another mother's misfortune; at worst, she was one of countless Britons complicit in mass infanticide.

With all this talk about wet-nursing, it may sound as though very few nineteenth-century mothers were actually breastfeeding their own babies, but it's important to keep in mind the big picture: Throughout history, wet nurses were employed only by the most elite members of society, or when an infant's mother had died. The extreme cases of Victorian Britain, eighteenth-century France, and others were just that—extreme cases in very isolated pockets. Even as late as 1900, mothers worldwide almost universally breastfed their own children, and nursed them on average from two to four years.

Yet in the hundred years prior, the Industrial Revolution had uprooted mankind—and motherhood—in a manner unprecedented since arguably the last Ice Age. Whereas in 1800, only 3 percent of the world's population lived in urban areas, by 1900, that figure had surged to 14 percent. (Today, more than half of the world's population is urban; by 2050, three-quarters of us will live in cities.) And the mothers in those big cities became stranded in a way that sounds all too familiar to many of us today. They lived in strange new places, leaving generations of family and female know-how about birthing, breastfeeding, and child rearing behind them. They worked in factory jobs where they could not keep their babies with them and went back to work, on average, just one month after giving birth. Even more privileged mothers were increasingly expected to fulfill societal duties outside the home, leaving their children in the care of others. So a lower-class woman could risk destitution by quitting her job to nurse her own child at home. And a woman of privilege could smile sweetly as she passed the potentially infanticidal stranger suckling her child in the nursery, Or, these mothers could start experimenting with feeding alternatives.

The problem was there *were* no viable alternatives to breastfeeding. The reason why so many cultures throughout history practiced a form of wet-nursing or, at minimum, cross nursing among kinswomen and friends, was because—extreme factors aside (ahem, eighteenth-century France)—it worked, at least when you're looking at infant survival. Granted, babies raised at another woman's breast might not have bonded with their birth mother as they could have with early, prolonged exposure to her "mothering" hormones (oxytocin and prolactin). And there may have also been other as-yet-unknown repercussions to being suckled by another, since the research of Katie Hinde and other lactation scientists has revealed that a mother's milk is specifically tailored to the needs of her own infant. Nevertheless, the babies still *lived*.

Breast milk was immutable. A living fluid, it had evolved over millennia to meet the distinct survival needs of the human infant. Put another way, nearly every human who had ever lived on earth past infancy had been reared on human milk. Any attempt throughout history to replicate it artificially via "hand feeding" or "dry nursing" proved overwhelmingly fatal.

One telling clue to the inadequacy of such methods is that when archaeologists uncover what are believed to be feeding bottles from thousands of years ago—often teapot-like pottery vessels or constructed from horns with leather nipple-like contraptions attached—they're frequently found alongside the skeleton of a poor little child who didn't make it past infancy. We also know that in certain societies where wet-nursing or cross nursing was never practiced, the chance of an orphaned infant's survival was known to be so slim that these babies were often preemptively abandoned or even buried alive.

Historically, experimentation with artificial feeding happened only in the face of abject desperation. For instance, in eighteenth-century French foundling hospitals, when there was a severe shortage of wet nurses, or in the case of diseased infants with congenital syphilis who were feared to spread the disease to their wet nurses, the babies would be fed with animal milk. Some hospitals, creatively, even trained goats to straddle the cribs so that the babies could suckle away. (In case you're concerned about the fate of the goats as well as a newborn with a hoof in its face, goats can't contract human syphilis.) But such experimentation didn't go well. In Béziers, France, 75 percent of infants fed animal milk didn't survive to their first birthday. In Ireland of the same era, the notorious Dublin Foundling Hospital dealt with its epidemic of abandoned babies and shortage of wet nurses by feeding infants a pap of bread and water mixed with a little animal milk (plus regular dosing with a strong opiate). The mortality rate was an unfathomable 99.6 percent.

Without the immunological defense load conferred by mother's milk, artificially fed babies simply had no protection from the microbes that came their way. Substitute mixtures made from various iterations of bread, sugar, and animal milk (even butter or meat broth) were breeding grounds for bacteria, as were the feeding apparatuses themselves. After all, widespread acceptance of germ theory and routine sterilization wouldn't arrive until well into the nineteenth century. And given the vast unknowns of the miracle of breast milk that persist even today, there was a lot more missing from these humble mixtures than just immune protection. Mushy bread-water simply wasn't enough for babies to grow.

True, there were some rare instances in which, from about the fifteenth century onward, and for now forgotten reasons, it became the custom *not* to breastfeed. But these aberrations occurred in mostly colder climates, such as Germany and Scandinavia, where bacteria were slower to take hold and contamination of feeding bottles was marginally less of a concern. Still, up to half of all infants in these circumstances died.

In fact, infant mortality rates teetered around 40 percent in the Finnish-Swedish border parish of Nedertornea (now part of Sweden) near the Arctic Circle, where for unknown cultural reasons, babies were reportedly left to scream in their cradles all day with propped-up feeding horns dispensing soured milk as their only comfort. It wasn't until the nineteenth century, when a Swedish doctor arrived in town, took stock of the horrifying situation, and conducted a pro-breastfeeding campaign with the help of a midwife that the infant death rate halved.

How could a Nedertornean bury infant after infant and not realize that something was amiss? Apparently, the populace accepted such tragic circumstances as readily as the Parisian mothers who had shipped their babies off for wet-nursing two hundred miles away and never saw them again. Still, when you consider that in these times people died in the same home in which they were born, likely never venturing beyond the radius of their own tiny town, the cultural bubble becomes easier to accept. Isolated from the rest of the world and cut off from whatever larger culture they might have known, the Nedertorneans and others simply forgot their breastfeeding history.

DESPERATION. DISEASE. HISTORICAL AMNESIA. THESE WERE THE instances in which mothers had been willing to risk their infants' lives by forgoing the ingrained human knowledge that feeding babies anything other than human milk meant probable death. And at the dawn of America's Industrial Age, there was the perfect storm of all three—the ideal environment that would spawn the great infant-feeding controversy of the next 150 years.

If you wanted to go back in time and see where the breast-versus-bottle debate began, 97 Orchard Street on the

Lower East Side of Manhattan would be a very good place to start. Now the site of New York City's Tenement Museum, the century-and-a-half-old dwelling sports an adjacent slick glass-encased gift shop, but the block still reverberates with the ghosts of thousands of immigrants who lived throughout the building's residential history from 1863 to 1935.

The museum has painstakingly reconstructed the apartments of real families who lived there, including the Sicilian-born Baldizzis, who put on a brave face for their two young sons through the Great Depression by adorning their tenement windows with lace-trimmed curtains. There were also the Russian-Jewish Levines, who like my own great-grandmother escaped the pogroms at the turn of the last century. They turned their tiny home into a garment shop.

But at the center of it all is the story of Agnes Mary Moore, a five-month-old baby girl who died at 97 Orchard Street on April 21, 1869. Her Irish immigrant parents, Joseph and Bridget (née Meehan), had two older daughters, both alive when the Moores moved to the apartment shortly after Agnes was born. With Agnes, however, something went horribly wrong. Listed on her death certificate are the causes marasmus and scrofula. In modern-day terms, a tubercular-like infection had caused the pathological swelling of her lymph nodes (scrofula), making it increasingly difficult for her to swallow and leading the way for her little body to waste away (marasmus).

There's something about the death of a child that transcends even centuries. I can close my eyes and superimpose my own face upon the images in Bridget Moore's story. I can see myself as Bridget, at seventeen, crammed among throngs in steerage for weeks on the ship to America. Later, I can watch as a thick layer of grime builds on her skirt hem while she perpetually hangs laundry and mops filth from the tenement floor at 97 Orchard, pausing only to trudge up and down the stairs to haul up pails of water from the backyard. I can imagine these things. But when my eyes first scanned the date her third child died, I could *feel* my own throat tighten. Maybe that's because a child's death is every parent's worst nightmare, or maybe it's because the five-month mark is a time I vividly remember from my own girls' babyhoods when they were so deliciously giggly and tender, eagerly exploring the world around them—Izzy scooting across the floor and Mika crawling everywhere. I thought of my own little girls, and I couldn't get Agnes's story out of my head.

Neither could the Tenement Museum researchers. Several years ago, when they began piecing together what would become the Moore family exhibit, they were stumped by one pivotal part of the story: What, specifically, had led to Agnes's death?

David Favaloro, now director of curatorial affairs for the museum, was a researcher working on the Moore history. He told me that, intriguingly, the team kept finding death records of other young children who had perished in the building from the 1860s through the 1880s. Like Agnes, the causes of their deaths were also marasmus, or else diarrheal diseases such as cholera infantum. Were the living conditions of the day (no ventilation, no indoor plumbing) so deplorable that these kinds of illnesses were a matter of course? Or had Agnes and the others consumed something tainted?

Favaloro consulted a number of present-day physicians, but "it was difficult for them to make heads or tails of some of this," he said. The researchers also contacted public health officials. The officials' consensus was that there was no way to definitively determine that the cause was contaminated food or milk. That's when the researchers decided to consult a historian.

"Actually, it was easy to tell it was tainted milk, especially given the death rate of infants from diarrhea at that time," said Jacqueline Wolf, professor of the history of medicine at Ohio University. Her voice was tinged less with *I told you so* and more with the empathy of a mother who had felt the same pangs at Agnes's story that I had. "It's really tragic," she sighed.

At the time I scheduled our interview, I hadn't realized Wolf had been brought on, Poirot-style, to solve the medical mystery of 97 Orchard Street. I had originally contacted her after reading her book *Don't Kill Your Baby*, which sounds like an inflammatory pro-breastfeeding diatribe from the modern-day mommy wars but which is actually a historical account of the decline of breastfeeding in Chicago in the late nineteenth and early twentieth centuries. The book title was lifted from an actual poster designed in 1910 by the Chicago Department of Health to warn women about the very real dangers of bottle-feeding.

As it turns out, death by artificial feeding was one of the greatest public health issues of the early twentieth century. The city of Chicago was teeming with poster-carting health care crusaders beseeching mothers to breastfeed. By the 1910s, Chicago city officials estimated that *fifteen* bottle-fed babies were dying for every *one* breastfed baby. And the grim statistics weren't limited to Chicago. A decade earlier, the 1900 US census had revealed that 13 percent of US babies were dying before their first birthday; the majority, from diarrhea caused by contaminated milk. Even the phrase "artificial feeding" was meant as a warning cry, noted Wolf. It was coined by doctors of the day who—accurately, given the statistics—viewed *not* breastfeeding as a form of infanticide.

In truth, Wolf was surprised at what she had uncovered. As a graduate student at the University of Illinois at Chicago, she had planned for the book (which began as her dissertation, after she had become interested in breastfeeding after the birth of her daughter) to focus on the time when women stopped breastfeeding and switched to bottle-feeding. That era, she assumed, was the 1940s and '50s. I always thought that was when mothers had made the switch, too, since I had just assumed it was the formula companies, with their Madison Avenue advertising and too-convenient-to-resist inventions, that first led the movement away from the breast.

Evidently, I was half a century off. So was Wolf. "I just kept going back in time, back in time, back in time until . . . wait a minute, *when* did this happen?" she said, still incredulous at the memory. The book finally ended up focusing on the late 1800s and early 1900s, when America first industrialized and women began working long, demanding hours away from home or, like Bridget Moore, suddenly found themselves an ocean away from their mothers and grandmothers, who would have nurtured them in the weeks after new motherhood and taught them to breastfeed. It was at *this* time, remarkably, that women began experimenting with their own breast-milk substitutes. Wolf's research revealed a truth that perhaps we mothers—especially the ones who are all too quick to demonize the formula companies for today's abysmal breastfeeding rates—have been rather willing to forget. The formula companies weren't the driving force; *we* were.

"The formula was a *response* to women not breastfeeding," Wolf said, pointing out that many of the initial turn-of-the-century formula ads seemed overly apologetic for their product. "They were the opposite of the hard sell: *If you must formula-feed, try us. Your baby might not get* too *sick.*" She acknowledged the jokey paraphrase but emphasized that formula companies in the early days were all too well aware that mothers were turning to them out of desperation and that formula was an inferior product. Then there were the doctors. "I mean, the pediatricians were frantic because they were the ones who had to save all these dying babies, and it was very obvious that it was a reaction to what the women were doing."

So what *were* the women doing? What were they feeding their infants? The first commercial infant formula, Liebig's Soluble Food for Babies, had been invented two years before Agnes's death by the famous German chemist Justus von Liebig and would spur the creation of twenty-seven other patented artificial foods by 1883. Condensed milk—canned milk concentrated via evaporation and preserved into a sweet, sticky substance with the copious addition of sugar—was another alternative that had appeared in the United States a decade before Liebig's formula.

But the majority of women not breastfeeding in the late nineteenth and early twentieth centuries concocted their own more cost-effective animal milk–based formulas at home or fed their babies pure cow's milk, though perhaps *pure* is the wrong word here. The cow's milk in cities at the time was so contaminated, so rife with bacteria and adulterants, that it's a miracle babies survived at all. (Adults were sickened, too, but infants, with their immature immune systems, were far more vulnerable.) Prior to urbanization, families may have milked their own cows to feed their children, but the milk Bridget procured for baby Agnes had likely come from a pushcart near the family's tenement, ladled from an open vat of milk that had been spoiling for days after being transported for miles via unrefrigerated wagon or railcar.

This was before routine pasteurization, which took a longer time to gain widespread acceptance in the United States than it had in Europe (the first commercial pasteurizer was made in 1882; New York City didn't mandate pasteurization until 1911). The raw milk controversy that preoccupies the media today raged even then, with many believing it to be a healthier and more "vital" food than its pasteurized cousin.

That may have been the case with the milk Bridget procured for baby Agnes, had this milk been anything like milk at all. This foul potion, however, had not only bred millions of pathogenic bacteria on its days-long journey to the mouths of babes; it had also quite likely been cut with chalk to make it look whiter, or tinted with yellow dye to give the appearance of butterfat. It may have been laced with formaldehyde to keep it from spoiling, or altered with soda, salt, ammonia, and water to mask an alcoholic odor, common because cows were routinely fed distillery waste as a way to cut costs. The cows that consumed such garbage literally rotted away, and the resulting "swill milk" could harbor bovine tuberculosis, as well as the deadly nontuberculous mycobacteria (NTM)—two likely causes of the scrofula infection that killed Agnes.

Of course, mothers didn't set out to kill their children, and most didn't want to artificially feed. The vast majority of them actually started out breastfeeding, and in an original June 1898 issue of *Babyhood* magazine (the *Parents* of its day) that I purchased off of eBay, a doctor's column warned about the higher risk of diarrhea in the summer months (food-borne bacteria grow fastest in hot weather). Curiously, he noted that "the disease is one of infancy, but not of the earliest infancy"—not making the connection that very young babies were protected because they had yet to be weaned and thus moved to substitutes for breast milk.

But weaning would come soon enough. By a baby's third or fourth month, American mothers began mysteriously complaining of insufficient milk. Like a nineteenth-century version of *The Twilight Zone*, women across the country started writing in to *Babyhood* and the like, claiming their breast milk had run out. By 1889, New England doctors proclaimed that more than half of all mothers could not nurse their young. "It looks very much as if nursing of the infant will, in the not distant future, become a lost art," wrote one Dr. E. G. Morse in the *Annals of Gynecology and Pediatry*. The idea was even floated around at health care conferences of the day that our *Mammalia* classification was no longer: the inability to lactate could be the next phase in human evolution.

Sitting on my patio, flipping through the pages of *Babyhood*, and imagining I was a well-heeled nineteenth-century mother (*Babyhood*'s target demographic) desperate for advice about how to raise little Walter, I could see that "parenting" of the day was essentially hand-wringing about the infant-feeding issue. There were pages filled with ads for bottles, rubber nipples, sterilizers, and various proprietary infant foods offering free samples, plus one ad that boasted "Swan Gin" as a beneficial tonic during the nursing period (perhaps to help baby and me forget our lactation woes?). There were also paragraphs of instructions contributed by a mother sharing an elaborate home formula recipe and sterilization method that I'm guessing took an hour every time she had to feed her starving baby.

And everywhere there were tales of digestive woes. "My little girl, now thirteen months old, has been troubled with 'wind colic' . . . ever since her birth," wrote one mother. "As he is obstinately constipated, I add from 1 to 1½ teaspoonfuls of milk of magnesia to each bottle," shared another. "Nature has deprived me of nourishment for my little one," one mother wrote in another issue, referring to her inability to breastfeed. "Her only difficulty is constipation, which I've heard is a usual occurrence with bottle-fed babies."

As it happened, the problem of constipation was so extensive that *Babyhood* published a special-edition book by its medical editor, Dr. Leroy Yale (the aforementioned doctor dispensing diarrhea advice), devoted entirely to the issue, entertainingly titled *Constipation in Children and Its Domestic Management*.

It could be easy to make light of a generation of backed-up babies, but there are other anxious letters to Dr. Yale that reveal not only the true gravity of the situation but also just how much insane feeding experimentation was going on:

> *My baby is between five and six weeks old. He is small . . . and cries but little. We are obliged to feed him*

on condensed milk. It seems to agree with him and satisfies him. I prepare it by using six tablespoonfuls of boiled water, three of lime-water, one and a half teaspoonfuls of milk, and a little salt. He takes this portion from a cup at intervals of three hours (excepting at night), six times during the twenty-four, making in all about a quart of the prepared milk. Yet he does not grow. He weighs no more now than when one week old (seven pounds).

Of course, these mothers weren't using insufficient breast milk as an excuse not to breastfeed. Who would let their child starve on a concoction of condensed milk and limewater? Many truly were having serious nursing problems. "But it really was all a response to women's new habits," said Wolf. In short, they just weren't spending enough time with their babies to maintain their milk.

The rule of lactation, if you remember, is that demand equals supply. Even today, my new parent friends have a hard time believing just how continuously babies—and even toddlers, I can attest—need to nurse. (*But our doctor/baby book/iPhone app said I only needed to feed him every three hours!*) Yet the wealthier *Babyhood* readers were regularly turning their infants over to immigrant servants. And if those immigrant servants were mothers themselves, they couldn't bring their own babies on the job; they also couldn't bring their babies to the factories or the sweatshops, two other primary employers of immigrant women at the time.

Instead, immigrant mothers often left their babies at home with older female siblings, some as young as eight.

These "little caretakers" became so common, said Wolf, that public schools began teaching girls about bottle-feeding so they could properly care for their brothers and sisters. Of course, they relayed the information to their mothers, who accepted it willingly and perpetuated the artificial-feeding cycle. "It was part of the acculturation of being an American," said Wolf.

There were other factors that took babies out of the proverbial nursing sling. For the first time in history, people began marrying for love instead of security or parental approval, and children took a back seat to their parents' romantic relationship. Then, too, there was the acceptance of germ theory, which later proved crucial in convincing cities to clean up their milk supplies but which also taught women to mistrust their own bodies. ("One has only to do a little regular visiting among these [poor, rural breastfeeding] mothers to find such an ignorance of sanitary laws and of hygienic principles that one would gladly see exchanged nursing power and all for the degeneracy of culture and luxury and a good clean bottle of milk," wrote one *Babyhood* reader a few pages after a giant ad for Listerine.)

But if you want something bigger to blame, there's another reason for the widespread lactation failure that at first sounds so farfetched you might think I've had a few too many. As it turns out, so had nineteenth-century America.

"America had a real drinking problem," said Wolf, who noted that alcoholism was the other massive public health issue of the day. She pointed to the saloons on every corner in her hometown of Chicago as relics of our former addiction. *That's* why swill milk cows had all that whiskey mash to munch on.

Desperate to reclaim all the absentee fathers and halt the rampant boozing, the Woman's Christian Temperance Union (WCTU) began promoting the theory that alcoholism was caused by "vicious feeding" in infancy—in other words, when a mother "gave in" to her baby every time he wanted to breastfeed. If women wanted to prevent their children from becoming alcoholics later in life, the WCTU warned, they had to curb their children's instinct for pleasure early on. "Teach [babies] restraint, that they had to wait to be sated," said Wolf. (This is an idea that persists. The week I was writing this chapter, Mika bumped her head and wailed, and I offered her my breast. Matthew asked me if I thought it was a good idea to give in to her cries for "Mommy milk" every time she got hurt.)

But above all else, what may have altered our breastfeeding relationship forever was another unforeseen consequence of America's industrial progress: the advent of the railroads. Before then, said Wolf, no one paid attention to the mechanical clock. There weren't even time zones. Yet almost overnight, farmers had to know exactly when the railcars would arrive to pick up their goods. Suddenly, everyone had to pay attention to the clock, she said. And at the same time, parenting manuals and doctors began completely changing their advice.

Throughout the ages, common sense had told mothers to nurse their babies whenever they, um, seemed hungry. But now, in the newly regimented age of the railroads, mothers were advised to curtail breastfeeding sessions to twenty minutes or less, or they were informed that healthy infants didn't need to be fed at night. Even the Chicago health campaigners trying to discourage artificial feeding inadvertently hurt their own cause by advising breastfeeding mothers not to nurse a baby more than every four hours, for fear of overfeeding the baby.

" 'Start your babies off early, don't spoil them; put them on a schedule young so they'll be prepared for factory work,' " Wolf echoed their advice, and then sighed. "It guaranteed lactation failure."

The pursuit of progress moved quickly, and the mothers' disconnection from their innate feeding wisdom was equally swift. In 1862, President Abraham Lincoln signed the Pacific Railway Act, commissioning the Union Pacific and Central Pacific railroad companies to build the first transcontinental railroad, linking the existing East Coast rail network with two new lines that would be built toward each other from Omaha to Sacramento. Just seven years later, the additional 1,777 miles of track laid by hand were complete, and the final spike was driven in Promontory, Utah, forever linking east and west in ways wholly new to our world.

The date was May 10, 1869—just three weeks after the death of poor baby Agnes.

WHY HAD BRIDGET MOORE CHOSEN NOT TO BREASTFEED HER third daughter? We'll never know if she had tried to adopt the rigid feeding schedules of the day and found herself with insufficient breast milk, or if she had been overwhelmed taking care of three small children with her family thousands of miles away and turned to the German immigrants in her new neighborhood for artificial-feeding advice. It appears as though Bridget hadn't been forced away from breastfeeding because of factory work, since she was listed in the 1870 census as "keeping house" (although she may have taken in laundry as an extra source of income).

But one clue may be that Bridget—who no doubt experienced cultural isolation in her new homeland—was unwittingly willing to gamble her baby's life because of the second and third elements of the perfect storm of America's Industrial Age: disease and, ultimately, desperation. Bridget would herself die young, at the age of thirty-six, from a condition referred to at the time as "fatty degeneration of the heart." This was before doctors understood disease causation in the way we do today, said the Tenement Museum's David Favaloro, but it's possible that Bridget had been ill for some time—too ill, in fact, to breastfeed Agnes. Nor would she likely have breastfed the five additional daughters she bore in the thirteen years before she died, of which only two survived past the age of five. It's not clear if those little ones' deaths, too, were linked to a lack of breastfeeding, but the polluted living conditions of the time, unimaginable by today's standards, no doubt played a role.

Over the next several decades, cities and public health officials would work tirelessly to forestall the hundreds of thousands of infant deaths caused by contaminated milk. They cleaned up their milk supplies while simultaneously trying to promote breastfeeding, but the consequence of the now safer milk product—pasteurized, bottled, and refrigerated in Chicago by 1920—was that more mothers felt confident about choosing the artificial alternative. Meanwhile, formula companies, in concert with physicians, endlessly experimented with different formulations that would lessen gastrointestinal anguish while minimizing the risk of formula-induced nutrient deficiencies and malformations such as scurvy and rickets. But there would be many miscalculations and calamities in the century to come.

The women who opted (*opted*—a choice for the first time in human history!) to breastfeed were given increasingly regimented instructions about how to prepare for and conduct an act of biology that once came instinctively. By the 1920s, a few astute physicians had started to see the connection between nursing schedules and breastfeeding failure.

But it was too late. The modern woman had lost her way, and she had a new authority to guide her.

five

Doctor Knows Best

"It is easier to control cows than women."

—DR. EDWARD BRUSH

The week I was supposed to be writing this chapter, Mika came down with a vicious stomach flu. With her home from preschool for the first half of the week, I put work on hold and distracted her, between retching fits, with episodes of *Yo Gabba Gabba!* and plenty of "Mommy milk." The boob plus boob tube has been my go-to routine for comforting my kids during the many gastrointestinal bugs they've encountered throughout their early childhoods (yes, breastfed kids do get sick although, thankfully, mine always bounce back faster than I do). However, knowing how to console my poor barfing babies wasn't instinctive at first. Hanging out on the couch with Mika that week and wedging the family's metal Farberware "throw-up bowl" between us, I had a flash to the first time Izzy came down with gastroenteritis. She was ten months old, and I was so frantic seeing her sixteen-pound body expel what seemed like quarts of liquid across the room that I threw her in the car and sped over to my hospital's urgent care clinic.

"Have you been giving her any food or liquids since she started throwing up?" the pediatrician asked.

"Just breast milk," I said, glancing at Izzy in the baby carrier, her hot cheek squished up against my chest, eyelashes crusted with tears. She had bawled all the way to the hospital, conking out mere minutes after grabbing my nipple to her mouth, pacifier-style, in the waiting room.

"Oh no! No dairy," said the doctor. "Just small spoonfuls of Pedialyte once her stomach has an hour to rest after each bout of vomiting."

That advice seemed strange to me. No *dairy*? Was I a Holstein? I was also puzzled as to how this doctor thought I could easily avoid nursing my baby. I was supposed to watch her puke and then push her away from her only comfort? *Sorry sweetie, the doctor says Milky isn't a good idea right now.* Izzy couldn't even talk yet, let alone understand that kind of reasoning.

The pediatrician sensed my reluctance. "Don't worry, you can go back to breastfeeding once she's feeling better. But when you do, make sure you only nurse her for a minute at a time so her stomach doesn't get irritated and cause her to vomit again."

Back home, I quickly realized the doctor was clueless. Izzy took one whiff of the Pedialyte and knocked the spoon out of my hands and onto the floor. After she threw up again, I tried distracting her from clawing at my chest for a heart-wrenching thirty minutes (half of the doctor's recommended wait-to-feed time). Then I decided enough was enough. Poor thing. At that point, it would have been easier to wrench a two-by-four out of a vise than to tear her off my breast after his recommended one minute of nursing. So I did what mothers no doubt did in the centuries before Pedialyte and vomiting-recovery timetables: I let my baby nurse whenever she felt like it. Izzy threw up a few more times, and then it was over.

I was right to be surprised by the doctor's assertion that breast milk is a dairy food. Despite recent distasteful novelties like breast-milk ice cream, human milk is *not* a dairy food and is rapidly digested by a nursling. It also contains antibodies as well as innumerable still-mysterious molecules and compounds that appear to be critical in fighting gastrointestinal pathogens, which is why WHO names exclusive breastfeeding as one of the essential factors in preventing infant deaths from diarrheal illnesses worldwide.

The pediatrician had insisted on Pedialyte because he had been concerned about dehydration. Yet breastfed babies rarely become dangerously dehydrated from the stomach flu; in fact, that recommendation for Pedialyte and other oral rehydration solutions is meant for *formula*-fed babies with gastroenteritis. Not coincidentally, Pedialyte is made by Abbott Laboratories, the very same company that makes Similac infant formula.

That's what the doctor apparently didn't know. Yet what *I* didn't know about the doctor at the time was that it wasn't his fault he was misinformed. His knowledge of formula feeding, not breastfeeding, was so deeply ingrained it had become primary protocol. As it turns out, pediatric medicine owes its very existence to the advent of artificial formula.

In fact, prior to the twentieth century, the specialty of

pediatrics didn't exist. A family doctor would have treated an ill child, but everything else—birthing, feeding, infant care, child rearing—had long been the realm of womenfolk. But by 1908, it was estimated that infant feeding and related pediatric issues made up *half* of a family physician's practice.

As we saw in the last chapter, it may have been Industrial Age mothers who led the initial march away from the breast. Having moved to the cities to pursue work, they no longer lived near female family members who, in generations past, would have shown them how to breastfeed. The new regimented breastfeeding schedules touted to help them keep up with the demands of both work and modern mothering inadvertently caused an epidemic of insufficient milk production (a dilemma that persists today). Yet the doctors tasked with saving the lives of thousands upon thousands of artificially fed babies in the early twentieth century—methods for which were wildly experimental, at best—were quick to discover a whole new market of patients. "For one woman whose baby's life he has saved will give him more advertisement in the community than a full page ad in his county paper," wrote Dr. W. Nicholas Lackey, a rural Tennessean health official, in 1913.

These early infant-feeding specialists had to ensure adequate growth for the first generations of formula-fed babies in human history, closely monitoring the babies' height and weight (ever wonder where those growth charts came from?). But many specialists became fixated on researching and inventing feeding substitutes themselves. Dr. Joseph Brennemann of Northwestern University conducted years of experiments with formula in the early twentieth century and discovered that commercial infant formula was more digestible than raw cow's milk, thanks to the help of a bulimic man who could handily sample different concoctions and then vomit up the results. Brennemann also confirmed that limewater increased the tolerability of cow's milk by altering its pH to more closely resemble breast milk. (Breast milk is alkaline, whereas cow's milk is acidic. Modern-day formula achieves this alchemy via the addition of sodium citrate.)

Then there was Harvard Medical School's Dr. Thomas Rotch, who, in the late nineteenth and early twentieth centuries, advocated breast-milk substitutes precisely tailored to each infant via his "percentage" method of feeding. His approach became wildly popular, and it was a good one, at least in theory, since we now know that breast milk, unlike formula, isn't one size fits all; every mother makes her own "recipe" that is ever changing, according to her baby's needs and even according to her baby's gender.

In practice, however, percentage feeding was a mess. With varying proportions of cream, milk, milk sugar, limewater, and boiled water, "milk laboratories" synthesized concoctions according to doctors' prescriptions, using Rotch's intricate percentage-feeding calculations. At home, mothers could whip up their own percentage formulas in a jiffy with the help of a complicated algebraic equation. Later, of course, the bottles of pricey laboratory-recipe milk were found to vary drastically from the original written orders. And doctors got fed up with all the math, which finally became so complex one physician commented that the whole lot of percentage feeding began to resemble astrophysics. By the second decade of the 1900s, doctors began turning to simpler, less costly alternatives.

Even so, in the twenty years that the percentage method dominated the medical establishment, two ideas took hold: one, that infant feeding was a problem that required a scientific solution; and two, that the scientific solution should be determined not by mothers, not by companies, but by men of medical science.

The formula companies shrewdly acquiesced to the pediatricians' new realm of expertise. As early as the 1860s, companies began advertising in medical journals and sought physician endorsements, inviting doctors to visit their facilities. In 1912, Mead Johnson & Company created Dextri-Maltose, the first commercial formula developed in conjunction with a pediatric researcher, which it unveiled at a meeting of the American Medical Association. The company cleverly packaged the formula without feeding instructions so that parents wanting to use it would have no choice but to head to their doctors for guidance. Other formula companies followed suit, taking the labels off their cans, as well.

Under the doctor's watchful eye, more babies survived. Physicians such as Brennemann and Rotch had always championed breastfeeding, but as they involved themselves in fixing the artificial-feeding problem, many became enamored with the results. And many soon came to see formula as preferable in an era when doctors believed that breastfeeding could only be successful under ideal conditions: if the mother had ample daily exercise; if she drank prescribed quantities of water; if she followed a plain diet; if she abstained from tea, coffee, and alcohol; if she wasn't stressed in any way. The bottle, unlike the breast, was predictable and measurable.

"It is easier to control cows than women," wrote Dr.

Edward Brush in the *Journal of the American Medical Association* in 1904. "Human mothers are often emotional, excitable, indiscreet, sometimes hysterical, and not always able to control themselves."

In 1888, the American Pediatric Society was founded. From 1900 to 1915, ninety papers on the "science" of artificial feeding were presented at its annual meetings. By the 1920s, the doctor-recommended addition of orange juice (vitamin C) and cod liver oil (vitamin D) to the diets of formula-fed babies eliminated the dangers of scurvy and rickets, respectively. On June 23, 1930, the American Academy of Pediatrics was founded. Chicago physician Dr. Isaac Abt, who had once predicted that more and more women would lose their ability to breastfeed due to lactation failure brought on by "the progress of civilization and the stress of modern life," became the first AAP president. The medical establishment that had once equated artificial feeding with infanticide now saw no reason *not* to bottle-feed a baby, provided that baby was physician supervised.

Breastfeeding percentages started to plummet. In 1920, the vast majority of American women nursed for at least a few months after giving birth (and remember that prior to the twentieth century, women worldwide routinely breastfed their children for two to four *years* or longer), but by 1930, one-quarter of Boston mothers were switching to the bottle within a month. And by 1948, one year before my father's birth, more than half of American hospital-born infants were either weaned by the time of discharge or already receiving supplemental bottles. Considering that around this time, more than 90 percent of white babies and 58 percent of "non-white" babies (an unfortunate designation of the time period) were born in hospitals, the shift to bottle-feeding had been both swift and stunning.

By 1958, 63 percent of babies would never taste a drop of breast milk. Many of the doctors who cared for them had never known it any other way.

ONE OF THESE PHYSICIANS WAS DR. LAWRENCE GARTNER, WHO had graduated from the Johns Hopkins University School of Medicine that very year. When I called him up at his seven-acre ranch in the hills of San Diego County, I was hoping the semiretired Gartner, now eighty-two years old, could give me a vivid picture of what it was like to be a doctor in those days. After all, Gartner graduated from medical school at a time when breastfeeding in the United States was well on its way to extinction. Yet curiously, he had gone on to enjoy an illustrious and enduring career as one of the world's foremost medical authorities on breastfeeding and neonatal jaundice. Now a frequent lecturer and breastfeeding advocate, he was the founding chair of the breastfeeding section of the AAP as well as a founder and past president of the Academy of Breastfeeding Medicine. Gartner is also professor emeritus of pediatrics at the University of Chicago, from which he retired in 1998.

One of the first things I asked Gartner, who amiably asked me to call him Larry, is what he was taught about breastfeeding in medical school. I anticipated a slight pause as he searched his memory back more than half a century.

"Nothing," he answered at once, pouncing on my question with perfect comedic timing. "Wasn't even mentioned."

With a voice that belied his age by at least two decades, Larry Gartner explained that his interest in breastfeeding had been sparked only during a rotation as a fourth-year medical student at Johns Hopkins. He had been assigned to a follow-up clinic for infants and children, and on one particular day, a mother came in with her three-month-old child. As Gartner began taking down the patient's history, the baby became fretful and started to cry. So the mother put the baby to her breast. "The child quieted down immediately," Gartner recalled. "And I had actually never seen a baby breastfeed before. That was literally the first time I had ever even *thought* about breastfeeding."

The mother wasn't bottle-feeding, Gartner explained, because she was a recent European immigrant. Blissfully unaware of the importance of that moment, she was completely at ease nursing her baby in front of the awestruck young doctor. "It simply opened my mind to this remarkable thing I'd never seen before," he said.

He began to research breastfeeding on his own and, before long, became an intern at Johns Hopkins, just as his own wife was expecting their first child. By that time, he had come to see breastfeeding as important, and the two agreed she would nurse their newborn son. But after two months, the new mother ran into trouble. Gartner—along with their son's doctor, a renowned pediatrician of the day—had no idea what to do about it. "He was a wonderful guy, but he didn't know anything more about breastfeeding than I did!" Gartner laughed then turned serious. "Between the two of us, we failed at helping my wife breastfeed successfully."

I asked him if, in retrospect, he knew what knowledge

they had lacked. "Oh, all the simple routines of getting a baby into successful breastfeeding and the mother into producing adequate milk," he said, pointing out that they didn't know anything about latch and positioning and didn't know to suggest more frequent feedings. "Had I known what I know now, she wouldn't have had any problems breastfeeding," he said matter-of-factly.

After about two months of trying what they could, he and his wife switched their son to formula. "He became a very fat, *overly* fat little—infant," Gartner said pointedly. I thought he was going to say something like "pudge ball," but he paused and chose his last word carefully, not wanting to blame his son for the sins of his father.

Gartner was so open and engaging that I began to wonder who else I knew of that generation who would share a breastfeeding (or nonbreastfeeding) experience with me. I realized sadly that I had never gotten the chance to hear those stories from my own older family members, who have long since passed away. Over the years, however, I have heard the tale of how my mother and aunt were bottle-fed and how my aunt was brought into the world in 1950. My grandmother felt the first twinges of labor, went to the hospital, and woke up with a baby. (My mother was born three years later in Phoenix, then a "cow town" according to my grandmother, who was quite surprised to discover that the hospital there didn't offer the "modern" medicated delivery she had experienced with my aunt in Cincinnati. She was obliged to give birth to my mom the old-fashioned way.)

And indeed, we can't possibly talk about the medicalization of infant feeding without understanding the radical transformation of birthing in the twentieth century. Whereas in 1900 virtually all women delivered their children at home and without pain medication, mothers of the 1930s through the 1960s handed over their birthing experience to science—or rather, *men* of science, since very few women were doctors in those days. For many women like my grandmother, giving birth was, in fact, one event they didn't experience at all. Given first an injection of morphine to heavily sedate them throughout their labor and then the amnestic scopolamine to erase their memory of pain, women were anesthetized into "twilight childbirth," leaving doctors to completely take over delivery of the baby.

The drugs had numerous side effects, not the least of which meant that medical personnel often had to bind a mother's arms to the bed to curtail her thrashing, and doctors frequently used forceps to physically extract her baby from the birth canal. Not surprisingly, the babies as well as their mothers suffered serious repercussions. Morphine is a heavy respiratory depressant, and newborns were sometimes so oxygen-deprived that they were born blue. My father, born in 1949, had been one of those blue babies. He was lucky to survive.

If you've seen the episode of *Mad Men* in which Betty Draper goes to the hospital to have her third child, Gene, you've caught a glimpse of childbirth 1950s and '60s–style. While her husband, Don, drinks Scotch in the waiting room, Betty hallucinates about her dead parents during the "managed" delivery, only to awake from her drug-induced fog with a fully swaddled stranger in her arms.

It goes without saying that breastfeeding against the backdrop of "scientific" birth wasn't exactly intuitive. Mothers were robbed of their primary emotional connection to their babies—the very memory of the moment their child entered the world. The heavy medication also depressed the natural release of the "love" hormone oxytocin, essential not only for bonding with their babies but for the letdown reflex necessary for successful lactation. Then—regardless of the method of birth—mothers were physically separated from their infants, who were cared for in the nursery by medical staff and brought to their mothers only at prescribed intervals. ("Rooming-in" would come only later and even now is practiced by a mere one-third of US hospitals.)

We now know that early and maintained skin-to-skin contact between the mother and newborn, as well as nursing on demand, is essential for the successful establishment of breastfeeding. It's not surprising that while my grandmother recounted that she had breastfed, it must have been for only a very brief period of time. I haven't seen them, but my mom told me she has pictures of my grandfather bottle-feeding her as a tiny infant.

And everywhere, *everywhere*, formula was at the ready to step in. In an era when very little was known about the biology and benefit of breast milk, "it was easy enough to promote the idea that this nice, clean, industrially made product was better than anything coming out of the mother's breast," said Gartner. Hospitals were stocked with free samples. Formula-company detail men swarmed the floors, delivering gifts to nurses and doctors. They were intimate with interns and residents as well as university faculty, Gartner recalled. "They would take us out to lunch and dinner, providing free formula, delivering to your door any amount you wanted," he said. Doctors of the era were also courted with luxurious vacations, all expenses paid. And in many cases, the formula companies themselves designed the maternity wings. "Ross Laboratories had a program where they would do the architectural drawings and work with you on designing your nursery," Gartner added.

In later decades, as formula companies expanded their marketing to third world countries, they also sent female representatives dressed up as nurses into hospitals to consult with mothers and hand out samples. These "milk nurses" proved quite effective at persuading mothers to try their product. Global breastfeeding rates collapsed. In Singapore, for instance, the breastfeeding rate for low-income three-month-olds plunged from 71 percent to 5 percent between 1951 and 1971. And millions of infants died or suffered malnutrition as a result. These were regions of the world where the water supplies used to mix infant formula were—and still are—nearly always contaminated. Few women could afford adequate stores of formula, so they often dangerously stretched supplies by over-diluting the product.

These sales tactics and the detrimental effect they have on breastfeeding are well known, which is why in 1981, two years after I was born, WHO ratified the International Code of Marketing of Breast-Milk Substitutes. The code includes the ban of milk nurses, as well as formula advertising to the public, the distribution of free formula samples to mothers, formula promotion in hospitals, and gifts to health care workers. To date, 165 out of 199 countries have translated the code into a national measure or legislation, but the United States still has taken no official action. In fact, save for milk nurses, what's banned by the code is simply the formula companies' routine way of doing business here in the US. Considering that two of the Big Three formula manufacturers in the world are American companies (Abbott Laboratories and Mead Johnson are American; Nestlé is Swiss owned), it should come as no surprise that, back in 1981, the US was the only country in the world to vote against the code.

What's not so obvious is how formula companies intricately insinuated themselves into the medical community, advancing their cause in the name of science. Stories of unethical conduct abound. One doctor and public health researcher told me that shortly after she graduated from medical school in 1975, Ross Laboratories representatives assisted her with reference searches for a breastfeeding-related paper she was writing, then offered to write entire articles for her, with only her signature required. She declined.

But in earlier decades, the relationship between doctor and formula company was decidedly more genteel. "Ross Laboratories had the most knowledgeable, well-educated detail men that you'd ever want to meet," said Dr. Ruth Lawrence, a pediatrician, neonatologist, clinical toxicologist, and professor of pediatrics and obstetrics and gynecology at the University of Rochester School of Medicine and Dentistry.

At ninety-two, Lawrence was a decade older than Larry Gartner and unbelievably just as peppy when I spoke with her by phone. She told me she had received her medical degree from Rochester in 1949 and was the first female doctor invited to do her residency at Yale–New Haven Hospital. There, she learned about natural childbirth and breastfeeding under the tutelage of Dr. Edith Jackson, who at Yale had created the first rooming-in maternity unit in the United States.

Quite the revelation in the age of formula and twilight childbirth, natural childbirth was something Lawrence got to experience herself when she gave birth to her own first child at Yale in 1951, while her husband was overseas in Korea. They went on to have nine children, the majority of whom Lawrence breastfed for eighteen months to two years. And eight years shy of a hundred, she is still practicing medicine, teaching, conducting research, and running Rochester's Breastfeeding and Human Lactation Study Center. She was a real hoot to talk to. "Oh, I've got stories!" she exclaimed halfway into the first of what would be three very lengthy phone conversations. "I've got a million of 'em!"

After finishing her residency at Yale–New Haven, she brought what she had learned about natural childbirth and breastfeeding back to the University of Rochester's Highland Hospital and ran the nursery there, later becoming chief of pediatrics, creating that hospital's first rooming-in maternity unit, and working her doctor's schedule around her own babies. She did rounds at the hospital in the morning while her own infant napped and her older kids played at home with the babysitter. Then Lawrence would come home around noon, breastfeed her baby, and answer calls for the university's poison control center, which she also helmed for fifty years. That way, she could be with her kids from early afternoon through bedtime. (This work-life balance was a lesson she learned early on from one of her male obstetrical colleagues whom she noticed was never available for a meeting after one o'clock in the afternoon. She thought he was working hard seeing patients but later discovered he was actually out playing squash. "Guys run their lives the way they want to," she said. "The trouble with us women was we were always making excuses; we were always apologizing—*Oh, I'm sorry I have to go. I have to go get my baby.* Yeah, right. Keep your mouth shut.")

Still, when the formula detail men wanted to talk, it was on her terms, though the relationship was cordial, even cozy. Knowing what we now know about aggressive—even illegal—formula marketing tactics, it's hard to imagine Lawrence willingly interacting with the very people who were trying to derail her pro-breastfeeding work. But she explained that while the formula companies may have been trying to sell formula, they were also funding important research of the day, especially investigation into improved (that is, less injurious) infant formulas for the then epidemic of women who either couldn't or wouldn't breastfeed.

In the 1920s, researchers had already rendered cow's milk more suitable for human infants by removing the animal fat and substituting vegetable oils, along with adding some vitamins and minerals. In the 1930s, formula was boosted with additional protein, since it was believed that human milk was higher in protein than cow's milk. (It wasn't until 1962 that the opposite was discovered to be true and formula was rejiggered. Oops.) Iron was included in 1959. Other recent additions to the mix since my formula-fed infancy are the building blocks of DNA known as nucleotides, the amino acid taurine, and fatty acids such as DHA (the first ostensibly to aid the immune system, the others to promote brain development, but the jury's still out as to whether this supplementation is even effective).

"[Formula at the time] was better than evaporated milk and Karo Syrup," said Lawrence, referring to the homemade version she was taught to make in medical school. Ironically, though, many of the formula-company men were all too aware that they were selling an inferior product. "All of the detail men I knew, when they had young kids, had a garage full of formula, and their wives were breastfeeding," she quipped.

One of those Ross Laboratories detail men, Dewey Sehring, used to stop by Lawrence's home quite regularly, delivering his pitch from the kitchen table while she ironed. She would hand him a basket of socks to match while they talked. Small world that it was in those days, Dr. Larry Gartner also knew Sehring and later interviewed him in 2009 for an AAP oral history interview project, funded by—who else?—a donation from the Abbott Nutrition Division. (Abbott acquired Ross in 1964.)

When I called Sehring, now eighty-five and still living not far from the Abbott Laboratories plant in Columbus, Ohio, I was betting that he would hang up on me near instantly once I told him I was writing a book about breastfeeding. But Sehring not only took my call graciously, he told me he had separated himself early on from the detail men and their unscrupulous sales tactics and had directed the Ross Laboratories conference division for twenty-six years.

Established in 1950 as the Ross Conferences on Pediatric Research, the program began with a conference organized to determine what role formula feeding played in the development of megaloblastic anemia (it was discovered that a lack of vitamin C in formula, preventing the proper synthesis of folic acid, was the culprit). It then expanded over the years to encompass hundreds of health issues and to include the participation of thousands of physicians. One early conference that Sehring organized around erythroblastosis fetalis—a disorder in which a mother's antibodies attack her baby's red blood cells—would even help save his own children's lives when it was discovered that his pregnant wife was Rh-negative and thus predisposed to the immune reaction. Recently tackled topics include the role of inflammation in chronic disease and a transcultural approach to curbing the global diabetes epidemic, two issues that researchers now believe may be directly attributable to the rise in formula feeding. It would seem that the formula companies have been quicker to address their shortcomings than we have been.

Sehring had first wanted to be a doctor, and sounding like a wistful grandfather, he told me about the relationships he had fostered with leading physicians and researchers over his forty-year career. He had even received the Vermont "Great Guy" award. I may have been hoping to find a whistle-blower in the ex–detail man, but it was hard to find fault with Sehring, who insisted, "I never said a bad word about breastfeeding." He regularly included breastfeeding advocates and La Leche League leaders in his Ross nutrition roundtables. He himself had been breastfed; his five children were breastfed; his own children went on to breastfeed his grandchildren.

Yet according to Gartner, the pro-breastfeeding stance was actually a sales tactic the formula companies encouraged. Gartner had told me about his visit to Ross Laboratories'

Similac facilities in Ohio in the 1960s, when Dave Cox, then president of the company, revealed that women who initiated breastfeeding but failed after a few months would ultimately buy more formula than mothers who had formula-fed from the get-go. Whereas an exclusively formula-feeding mother would buy a few months' supply of formula, soon realize the high cost, and switch to regular container milk, mothers who breastfed at first but then proved unsuccessful would buy formula through the entire first year of life out of guilt, to overcompensate for their feelings of failure.

This is a marketing strategy that persists today. *Breastfeeding is best, but just in case it doesn't work out, we're here*, goes the theme of most formula ads. "It's a fragile enough situation that those hints were often enough to encourage women to stop early and [those hints] implied that breastfeeding wasn't all that important," Gartner added ruefully. ("We know breastfeeding is best for babies," stated an Abbott spokesperson, adding that there was no way to confirm that Gartner's account was true. "We market our Similac formulas to compete with other brands of infant formula, not to compete with breastfeeding.")

Sehring had no memory of this particular strategy, and politely and patiently answered my questions as I continued to press him. It was clear that he viewed his role at Ross and later, Abbott—helping the physician help his patients via access to cutting-edge research—as separate from the self-seeking sales tactics of a Fortune 500 company.

After a few more questions about the inner conflicts he may have had about his work, I sensed our call was coming to an end. "Write what you like, Jennifer," said Sehring. "But I'll leave you with a quote someone once said about me: 'Dewey would have made a wonderful politician, but he's too honest.' "

AND THERE'S THE RUB. THE WORLDWIDE MEDICAL CONSENSUS may now be that breast is best, but can this stance exist independently of the long intertwined history of pediatricians and infant formula? And what, if anything, has changed since formula man Dewey Sehring sat around folding socks at Dr. Ruth Lawrence's kitchen table? The answer is not much. Just last year, for instance, the AAP—the largest organization of pediatricians in the United States—received more than $2 million in contributions from the Big Three formula companies, making them the academy's biggest contributors. (The academy ignored my requests for this information, but I was able to obtain a newsletter that thanked Abbott, Nestlé, and Mead Johnson for their support in the top-tier "$750,000 and above" category.)

Some may argue that these contributions haven't prevented doctors from taking a strong stance on breastfeeding. After all, the academy recommends six months of exclusive breastfeeding, along with a year or more of continued nursing—a goal that, currently, few American women are able to achieve.

Yet unlike mothers in the 1950s, nearly 80 percent of American mothers today start off breastfeeding their babies. Why is it, then, that around half of all new mothers move to formula (either fully or partially) within just four weeks? In an era in which most of us can no longer turn to our mothers and grandmothers for breastfeeding advice, one contributor to our high rate of breastfeeding failure may be the very "feeding experts" we have come to rely on: our well-meaning doctors. As late as 2004, one study found, 45 percent of pediatricians believed breastfeeding and formula feeding were *equally acceptable* methods for feeding infants. Pediatricians, after all, spent the past century devoted to improving the health of artificially fed infants. Perhaps that history has been tougher to shake than we anticipated.

But what may be more to blame for our abysmal breastfeeding success rate is that most doctors are still simply unequipped to offer breastfeeding help to new mothers, who in the modern world almost always experience problems with latching, pain, insufficient milk, or all the above, when they set out to breastfeed their babies. Astonishingly, little more about breastfeeding is taught in medical schools today than when Larry Gartner and Ruth Lawrence graduated in the decade after World War II.

My daughters' own pediatrician (not the one in my opening tale) had learned that breast is best, but her residency focused on the management of formula feeding, since the hospital's lower-income Latino patient population almost exclusively bottle-fed as a result of the government-sponsored free formula available through the federal WIC program (more on that later in the book). My sister-in-law Sarah, a nurse-practitioner (NP), said that in the eighteen months of her graduate program, she took just a single class on the practical aspects of breastfeeding. With tongue in cheek, one professor I know offered this about her medical school: "We're an extremely baby-friendly, breastfeeding-friendly medical school. Our students get three hours of exposure."

The result is that not if, but *when* a mother runs into breastfeeding trouble, many OBs and pediatricians are ill equipped to do anything other than reassure her about switching to formula. Lactation consultants can be wonderful, but not every hospital employs them, and they're not always covered by insurance once mom and baby return home. I had issues with severe breastfeeding pain after Izzy was born, and I credit the Kaiser Permanente hospital where I gave birth with my ultimate breastfeeding success. There, mothers are given unlimited access to free follow-up visits with lactation consultants. Later, with Mika, I gave birth at a different hospital where mothers, once home, have to pay out of pocket for a lactation consultant or rely on their OB or pediatrician for breastfeeding assistance. If I had been a first-time mother then and encountered the same kind of pain issues, let's just say you probably wouldn't be reading this book.

The status quo is changing. The Academy of Breastfeeding Medicine, which Larry Gartner and Ruth Lawrence helped found, has successfully lobbied to include more breastfeeding questions on the pediatric and OB/GYN board exams. (*This* academy does not accept funding from formula companies or any violator of the International Code of Marketing of Breast-Milk Substitutes, although there has been some pressure to accept funds from certain pump manufacturers.) The organization includes a growing specialty of physicians who are trained in the field of human lactation and can delve into the treatment of breastfeeding problems with more depth than a lactation consultant can, including screening for hormonal imbalances and insufficient breast tissue. It's estimated that only 1 to 5 percent of all women have medical conditions that truly inhibit lactation, yet struggles with insufficient milk are unbelievably prevalent. Still, to date, the Academy of Breastfeeding Medicine has only eighty-eight members. By contrast, the Mayo Clinic alone has teams of doctors—endocrinologists, cardiologists, neurologists, urologists, and psychologists—devoted to treating erectile dysfunction.

There is a glaring gap in the medical research as well, said Laurie Nommsen-Rivers when I called her from a working family vacation to hear her thoughts on the medical establishment and the modern mother's breastfeeding woes. Nommsen-Rivers is assistant professor of pediatrics at Cincinnati Children's Hospital Medical Center, as well as a lactation scientist, and as I sat with my cell phone cupped to my ear and a silencing breast in Mika's mouth (she had woken up early from her nap, what else is new?), I found myself nodding in agreement at the unfairness of it all. "We have hundreds, maybe thousands of clinical studies on how men's physiology affects erectile function," she said. "And yet we have virtually nothing on how a woman's physiology impacts her ability to make milk." At the time, she was conducting a study (since published) that revealed that women with diabetes during pregnancy are at a markedly higher risk of low milk supply—a pivotal connection in a country where diabetes and prediabetes are epidemic. That these very real issues are only now coming to light is evidence of how "women's issues" like breastfeeding have been pushed aside and trivialized by a medical community long dominated by men.

While a new specialty in breastfeeding medicine is a huge advance, some physicians still see their role in breastfeeding as secondary. "It is not the doctor's role to put the baby to the breast," said Lawrence, who emphasized that she and other doctors and lactation consultants are now filling the void of two generations of lost cultural knowledge about how to breastfeed. Lawrence herself learned how to breastfeed from her own mother.

Indeed, it was women who first fought to reclaim their place as the rightful infant-feeding experts when in 1956 a group of seven breastfeeding mothers from Illinois met in a living room and founded La Leche League. Gartner met with the group shortly after its founding to discuss his findings about breast-milk jaundice, which he discovered to be a natural and protective phenomenon in breastfed babies. "That's where I learned about breastfeeding," he said.

With all the talk about women as rightful breastfeeding experts and the male-dominated medical establishment as breastfeeding trivializers, it may be surprising, then, that there is at least one more male physician (other than Gartner) who has decided to buck the establishment and make breastfeeding the very cornerstone of his pediatric practice. In fact, his work has raised more than a few eyebrows and has even prompted many to label him a quack. I, for one, looked forward to my meeting with Dr. William Sears.

six

Extraordinary Attachment

In Mongolia, though babies might cry for many reasons, there is only ever one solution: breast milk. I settled down on my butt and followed suit.

—RUTH KAMNITZER

The office that houses one of the most famous (or notorious, depending on whom you ask) pediatricians of the twenty-first century would be best described as nondescript. Situated off a quiet commercial road in the upscale but laid-back seaside hamlet of Capistrano Beach in Orange County, California, I had to make a U-turn three times before I spotted the Spanish new-construction building bearing a plastic green-and-white banner with the words I had been looking for: Sears Family Pediatrics.

Inside, the office was decidedly old school. Behind a generic laminate front desk, open shelves displayed hundreds upon hundreds of neatly stacked color-coded files. Two kindly looking middle-aged women stood in front, jotting down notes and taking calls. As I walked up to introduce myself, a lean man in his seventies walked in briskly from the back, wearing bright blue scrubs and gym shoes.

I recognized Dr. William Sears at once from his book covers, not to mention the controversial 2012 *Time* magazine cover story that had first put him on my radar. He seemed much more vigorous in person. I glimpsed the name inscribed on his scrubs: Dr. Bill. It was what all his patients called him, his son Matt had informed me when I set up our meeting. Like the sign outside the entrance to the office, Sears Family Pediatrics is very much a family affair. Dr. Bill and his wife, Martha, a nurse and breastfeeding consultant who has coauthored twenty-five of Sears's more than forty books, have eight children, three of whom are doctors. Dr. Jim Sears (of the CBS show *The Doctors*) and Dr. Bob Sears practice in Capistrano Beach alongside their father. Matt handles media relations for the family.

Given that the elder Sears is semiretired now and sees patients in the office just two afternoons a week, I was expecting the office to be a zoo. For now though, it seemed curiously calm. No one was even waiting in the waiting room. As my eyes darted out the window toward the parking lot to see if maybe a line had begun to form outside, Sears leaned in to greet me with a cheerful handshake. "Hello, Jennifer! Are you ready?"

Sears turned seventy-six this past year, but it was easy to see why he was so fit. Before I could even pull my tape recorder out of my bag, he dashed off to the room where his first appointment was waiting. "It's checkup time!" he announced as he burst through the door where a young mom and dad sat quietly with their preschool-age son and baby daughter. "Vincent, give me five!" he said to the little boy and looked down at his chart. "Now, Vincent here was breastfed for seven months—"

"No, twenty-one months," the mom interrupted.

Sears glanced down at the page again. "Here we go: He self-weaned because you were pregnant. It's your fault!" he joked to the little girl. Everyone laughed as she gazed at him with her bright blue eyes.

"Now *she's* going strong at nine months," the mom added proudly.

Sears turned to me. "The first thing you notice about these two kids is how attentive they are," he said. "They're engaging, they have eye contact." The two beamed at me, each one held securely in a parent's lap. "Let-'em-cry-it-out babies, they're fearful, because that's what they learn. Now, the very first thing a child learns about being breastfed is trust."

IF STARTING OFF A THREE-YEAR-OLD BOY'S CHECKUP WITH A TALK about breastfeeding and trust sounds somewhat unusual, thirty years ago, it was downright radical. "It was *There's that crazy pediatrician who wants all his moms to breastfeed*," Sears recalled of that first year after he moved his office down to Capistrano Beach from Pasadena back in 1985, after serving as associate professor of pediatrics at the University of Toronto and completing a prior residency at Boston Children's Hospital. The doctor himself had never imagined this was the path his career would take. But back in Toronto in 1972, on his first official day of practice as a pediatrician, he was confronted by a slew of concerns from new moms he hadn't anticipated: *Doctor, how important is it to breastfeed my baby? I'm having trouble latching on—how do I do it? He wakes up every time I put him in his crib! Where should he sleep?* "Here I am, a so-called expert in all these diseases, and I'm getting questions that I have no clue how to answer!" Sears chuckled. "I came home that night and said [to my wife], 'Martha, I've got to go back to school!' "

Sears's top-notch training had taught him a lot about how to treat sick babies. As for what created a happy, healthy, *normal* child? That, he said, he knew next to nothing about. So Sears decided to "go back to school," only this time using his pediatric practice as his laboratory and classroom. He surrounded himself with children he liked, with moms he thought were smart, with babies who seemed bonded, and with teenagers who were well disciplined. And he took copious notes. "They thought I was writing in their chart? No, I was writing little cue cards that I'd go home with at the end of the day [and study]," he said. Years later, that drawer, filled to the brim with notes, led to his first book, *The Baby Book*. Published in 1992, the book's revolutionary "new" brand of child rearing forever changed the course of parenting in America.

Sears called it attachment parenting, and at its core is the simple belief that mothers and babies have a biological need to be close to each other. Now dubbed "AP" by its ardent followers, the philosophy has been refined throughout Sears's now fifty-year career as a pediatrician and father, but the gist of it is this: Children who are nurtured intensely early on are more likely to become self-sufficient, caring adults later in life. Attachment parents do this using a set of "tools," as Sears outlined for the purposes of his books, but really, the tools are the traditional methods that have been used to care for babies over millennia, including breast-feeding (on demand and for as long as possible), "wearing" baby (in a sling or baby carrier), and sleep sharing (Sears prefers this term to co-sleeping; it encompasses bedding with or even close to baby). (The AAP cautions against bed-sharing for safety reasons, although the organization is evidently revising its recommendations given the prevalence of the practice and given newer evidence that it may actually be *protective* against SIDS, something Sears has long maintained. For parents nervous about putting baby in bed with them, he recommends the use of a co-sleeper, a bassinet that attaches to one side of the bed.)

There are those who have misinterpreted the tools in Sears's books as mandate, assuming attachment parenting means a mother has to literally be *attached* to her child all day. But in person, Sears is far more moderate and realistic about the challenges of twenty-first-century parenting than his critics claim. He stressed that attachment parenting isn't an all-or-nothing approach. He has patients who exclusively bottle-feed but sleep share, and he has lots of office moms with children in day care who pop their baby in a sling and nurse when they get home from work.

In fact, his own eighth child, Lauren, was adopted; she was artificially breastfed for less than a year using a nursing supplementer (a device that carries expressed breast milk or formula via thin tube to a baby's mouth while nursing). Lauren was fed pumped breast milk from Martha, along with donated milk from other moms in Sears's practice. Breastfeeding on cue, responding to the infant's cries, providing lots of physical touch by carrying the baby—these are merely practices that have facilitated mother-baby bonding throughout the ages and are arguably more important than ever before in a technologically distracted world, where a frustrated parent can hand a kid an iPhone to play with and call it a day. "Kids need relationships, not stuff," he said.

Indeed, over the course of human history, most children were neither put to bed in cribs with video monitors nor pushed in Bugaboos. Keeping babies close to their mothers ensured their survival not only by keeping them out of the reach of predators but by allowing them unrestricted access to their only calorie source, the breast. And in the time before modern medicine, when food was often scarce, ongoing breastfeeding—for anywhere from two and a half to *seven* years—was not only "normal"; it was fundamental, providing children with a biologically perfect source of nutrition and immune protection. Lactation research has been largely focused on these two latter aspects, but the psychological significance of the breastfeeding mother-baby dyad has been harder to quantify scientifically.

Here's what we know about the science of attachment as a whole: A baby is born with one hundred billion neurons, yet by the age of three will have formed hundreds of *trillions* of connections between these cells, firing information within the brain and on to every part of the body. (Around half of these synapses will be permanent; circuits that are used will remain.) How such exponentially rapid brain development is achieved in so short a span of time is still largely a mystery, yet the latest science is showing that what may be more crucial than anything else in forging these connections are the core human experiences in childhood: Love. Affection. Family. Interestingly, all these interactions are associated with increased levels of oxytocin, the "bonding" hormone that floods a mother's body during breastfeeding to trigger milk letdown. And as it turns out, the window for these interactions to make their impact may be the very breastfeeding years that Sears endorses.

In one pivotal study that looked at impoverished four-year-olds, markedly lower IQs were correlated with an upbringing in the homes most lacking in nurturing. In another more famous study, EEG scans of eight-year-old Romanian children who had been abandoned as babies and placed in the country's state-run institutions revealed significantly lower brain activity in children who had not been moved to caring foster care families before the age of two. Those who were rescued early enough showed normal brain scans; those who remained behind were missing white matter (a part of the brain that affects learning ability and mental health) forever.

These studies focused on children who were *deprived* of love, as did the work of British psychologist John Bowlby, whose studies with orphans in the mid-twentieth century formed the basis of attachment theory, the psychological model to which Sears's style of parenting owes its name. But what about someone like me, who as an infant was bottle-fed and slept in a crib but was raised by a loving and devoted mother? Was my emotional growth somehow stunted? Had I sacrificed neural pathways? These may sound like silly questions to generations of parents who can point to their bottle-fed or stroller-pushed children and attest that they turned out just "fine," but the truth is no one has ever extensively studied these issues.

Sears, for one, told me he could spot an attached baby within seconds. Like the little boy Vincent and his sister, these babies are more alert and focused; as older children, they're more caring and empathetic than other kids their age, their parents say. There was something unusual about Sears's office, too. I had sensed it when I first arrived and it took me a while to figure it out, but when I did, it was startling. Unlike the tearful mayhem of my conventional pediatrician's office, Sears's office was practically silent. "You won't hear the crying, frantic babies here," he said.

In the modern world, many have come to accept wailing babies as simply a normal part of parenthood to be "dealt with" or ignored. But in fact, prior to the past hundred years or so, an infant's cries for nourishment, love, or security—the very connection between mothers and babies—were rarely called into question. It was only the more modern advice of ill informed doctors and self-appointed "baby experts" that dismissed the notion of that profound bond.

There was Dr. L. Emmett Holt at the turn of the last century, who in *The Care and Feeding of Children* mandated rigid feeding schedules for infants and claimed that crying was "the baby's exercise." (This no doubt contributed to the epidemic of insufficient breast milk in the Industrial Age, since the ignored and starving babies were also denied the ability to stimulate their mothers' milk production.) There was the psychologist John Watson in Sears's generation, who admonished parents to greet their children in the morning with a handshake instead of a kiss. And there are the "tough love" proponents of today, who insist parents should get their infants sleeping through the night as early as possible, even if they have to do it by letting them "cry it out" in their cribs. Of course all parents want more sleep, but many don't realize that nightwaking is not only normal, babies are actually *wired* to rouse—and nurse—at night. This pattern not only helps a mother maintain a strong milk supply, researchers now believe it has developmental benefits for the baby. Sears warns parents to beware of these baby trainers and to believe that their baby's cries are a fundamental form of communication, not manipulation. "All I've done in a nutshell is validate a mother's and father's own basic instinct. Period."

Hold your baby. Breastfeed. Respond to his cries. With this kind of urging, it would appear that Bill Sears is an expert who is imploring us to ignore the "experts" and reclaim our innate knowledge. Yet there is a deep controversy surrounding Sears and attachment parenting that goes far beyond disagreement about the safety of co-sleeping. For many women who have had to "relearn" how to breastfeed after generations of lost mothering knowledge, it seems this supposedly elemental way of raising children is anything but instinctive.

The 2012 issue of *Time* magazine that featured the cover photo of Jamie Lynn Grumet breastfeeding her three-year-old son also included a scorching story on Sears and his "demanding" brand of attachment parenting. It described weary mothers who tended to and nursed their babies round the clock, and who were reluctant to ever put them down or let them cry for fear of brain damage. (On his website, Sears says that excessive crying could be harmful, and he cites research that babies who are left to cry may suffer higher rates of ADHD, as well as lowered IQ.) Sears said he was blindsided by that *Time* article and the media frenzy that ensued. "Controversy sells," he said. "Everyone knows it's just pure old common sense to pick up your baby when he cries, to breastfeed your baby. [Humans] wouldn't exist right now if those things weren't true."

Controversy may sell, but the suckling preschooler on the *Time* cover did take many in the Western world by surprise. I've now nursed two children past the age of three, and I can tell you that the pose in that photo—with the boy perched on a toddler chair—is not representative of the way older children breastfeed. When I cuddle up with Mika to let her nurse before bedtime while I read her a story, she looks as sweet and cozy as a toddler snuggling with her Binky. Except in this case, I'm the Binky. (Interesting how a lot of us have forgotten where the need for pacifiers and thumb-sucking comes from.) But the truth is that few Americans have seen an older child nurse up close, in any position. That picture was *designed* to elicit gasps, and the exploitative shot only exposes our Western belief that breastfeeding past infancy is bizarre, despite the fact that a prolonged period of breastfeeding is not just biologically normal and highly beneficial to the health of both mother and baby, it is utterly commonplace throughout much of the world.

In fact, there seems to be no issue more inflammatory around the subject of breastfeeding than the question—*how long?* Only a fraction of American women breastfeed for even one year, yet there is an obsession with those who are inclined to continue.

Before the *Time* magazine media frenzy, a 2006 British documentary entitled *Extraordinary Breastfeeding* explored the tiny minority of UK mothers who breastfeed their children past the age of two. The month I wrote this chapter, photos of an Aussie woman still breastfeeding her six-year-old child (featured in another "extreme breastfeeding" documentary, this time for the Discovery Channel) met some very ugly backlash. Commenters labeled her an egomaniac and called the pair "disgusting." The *New York Times* wrote that the girl was "latched onto [her mother's] breast like an enormous baby." And in reference to the story, one prominent New York pediatrician even had no problem brushing aside WHO's recommendation that children be nursed for two years or beyond. She was quoted as saying that her mom patients who breastfed their children past the age of two "had other mental illnesses." (Call me crazy.)

But does our culture truly believe that breastfeeding through toddlerhood is nuts, or do we believe that it's merely nuts to do so *in our culture*? Many of us have seen the stereotypical photos of bare-breasted women in Africa nursing much older children, yet those images don't set off tirades on the message boards. Yes, breasts are overly sexualized in our culture, but what *else* was it about Jamie Lynn Grumet (a blonde, educated white woman) choosing to continue breastfeeding her older son that lit a match to the mommy wars? What is it about Sears teaching us how to relearn traditional parenting methods that provoked such a visceral reaction? Perhaps the guilt-inducing headline that accompanied Grumet's *Time* cover photo provides a clue. "ARE YOU MOM ENOUGH?" it shouted in bright red letters.

In the modern world, where 64 percent of US mothers with children under the age of six work, maybe we've been conditioned to believe that the separation of mothers and babies is the way things have to be; labeling Sears and his followers as extremists and scoffing at "attachment" as something best left to overzealous mothers.

ON THE CEASELESS, WINDBLOWN STEPPES OF MONGOLIA, A LANDlocked nation wedged between Russia and China, *attachment* would be a superfluous descriptor for parenting. There, one in three Mongolians lives in poverty, and 42 percent of the population resides in rural areas, half still living the seminomadic lifestyle that Mongolians have followed since the time of Genghis Khan—herding livestock in the nonwinter months and holing up in their *ger* (yurt) to survive the unfathomably frigid winters. It's not surprising, then, that infant formula is an option only for the very few: 93 percent of babies are breastfed within one day of birth, and nearly 65 percent of children are still nursing at the age of two.

But what *is* surprising is the zeal with which Mongolian mothers (and grandparents—hold on, you'll see what I mean in a second) breastfeed their children, who are commonly nursed not just through the early walking and talking years but through kindergarten. In fact, breastfeeding and breast milk are so revered that there's an oft-repeated expression, said Ruth Kamnitzer: the best wrestlers are breastfed for a minimum of six years. Considering that wrestling is the national sport of Mongolia, this isn't a statement to take lightly.

Kamnitzer is a Canadian biologist and writer who, with her husband and young son, once called Mongolia home. Her Scottish husband, also a biologist, had been conducting a wildlife study in Mongolia during their three-year stay. But when I caught up with her, she had been living in Oman for four years, accompanying her husband on yet another study and working with the government to produce educational materials on the local wildlife. Her time in Mongolia was now nine years past, although she wasn't all that surprised that I had contacted her. Before moving to Oman, she had penned a short article about her experience living in Mongolia for *Mothering* magazine, and the piece had gone viral. Her recounting of the enthusiastic breastfeeding culture there was so singular, and stands in such stark contrast to our adamant Western views about how and how long it's "appropriate" to nurse, that people all over the world still e-mail her about it.

It's easy to see why the curiosity persists. In remembering Mongolia, Kamnitzer may as well have been describing Mars, complete with tales of a friend who recalled being weaned at nine (that's *years*, not months), adults who downed bowls of expressed breast milk as "treats" (welcome relief for engorged mothers), and both grandmothers and grand*fathers* who routinely offered their own flabby breast when a mother was absent (no milk, but still comforting). She said that since tandem nursing isn't common, most kids wean between the ages of two and four, when a mother is pregnant with her next baby. But the youngest child in a family will often nurse far longer, hence nine-year-old nurslings and well-fortified wrestlers.

In Mongolia, no one ever questions the biological and emotional need a child has for his mother's breast. There's no rush to grow up, yet interestingly, the average Mongolian child is far more independent than his helicopter-parented American counterpart. "Even young children often have responsibility for younger siblings and help with chores such as herding," Kamnitzer said.

Early one morning, she Skyped with me from Muscat, Oman's capital. For me, it was night the day before in Los Angeles, but our connection was clearer than I usually get on my cell in the city. The Toronto-born Kamnitzer sounded just a little bit homesick. "Your accent has that really familiar sound," she said. "I feel as if I know you." She told me that Calum, the baby boy she had nursed through blizzards in a *ger* three hours' drive from the Mongolian capital of Ulaanbaatar, was now ten. She also now had a daughter, age five, who was raised in the United Kingdom and Oman and had since been weaned. She didn't have a lot of memories of nursing her daughter in Oman because as a foreigner in a Muslim culture where local women wore the *abaya*, she didn't have many opportunities to do so comfortably out in the open. (Omani women do breastfeed in public, albeit modestly. Remember that the Koran says a baby is entitled to breast milk until the age of two.)

But about Mongolia, her memories are vivid, and maybe that's because the breastfeeding culture there was the complete opposite of Canada, where she had lived for the first two weeks after Calum was born, and the United Kingdom, where they had lived for three months before moving to Mongolia. Back in the UK, she had once gone for coffee with a mom from her baby group who nervously asked her if they would be "allowed" to nurse at a local café.

In Mongolia, she said, no one is shy about breasts, where their singular purpose is to nourish and comfort children. Once, a fellow-expat friend of hers went on stage for a brief performance and handed off her fussing baby with his pacifier to a Mongolian mom backstage. When the expat mom returned, the child was calm. The other mother had breastfed her baby! Kamnitzer recalled another night when she went out leaving Calum with a babysitter and came back to find him sleeping on the babysitter's shoulder, his hand stuffed down her shirt. "She had quite big breasts, and she had gotten him to fall asleep [that way]. But she was just absolutely fine with that!" she laughed.

By that point, Kamnitzer didn't have a problem with it, either. It would seem the mommy wars had no place in Mongolia, and it was easy to become acclimated in a culture where everyone she encountered was like her personal breastfeeding cheerleader. Taxi drivers gave her the thumbs up in the rearview mirror when they spied her nursing. Grandmas in the park regaled her with tales about the children they had nursed and adored. People everywhere said, "Oh! You're breastfeeding—that's so great! It's the best thing for your baby!"

"It was really great to have so much positive feedback, and not just in terms of breastfeeding," she said. "As I'm sure you know, it's really tiring being a mom, and you don't normally get people telling you that you're doing a good job."

One reason Kamnitzer elicited comments (albeit unbelievably positive ones) was because she was a foreigner. The

Mongolians she met largely had the impression that Westerners bottle-feed their babies, and they were thrilled to see her doing it "the Mongolian way." But the other reason was that unlike a lot of Mongolian mothers, Kamnitzer was actually *seen* out and about. As an expat with only one child, no full-time job, and no herd to tend to, she was free to explore as her family split their time between their *ger* in the countryside and an apartment in Ulaanbaatar. "Mongolians spend a lot more time at home, especially if they're mothers," Kamnitzer explained. "They don't take young babies out."

It's this reality, though, that unfortunately may be responsible for the current state of breastfeeding in Mongolia. Kamnitzer was surprised when I told her that breastfeeding rates have declined sharply since she left, as Mongolians' traditional way of life is being threatened not only by changing economics but by climate change. Much like at the dawn of the Industrial Revolution in America, more mothers in this traditional agrarian society are now being forced to head to the city to find work.

Kamnitzer recalled that, during her time in Mongolia, sometimes a mother would have to leave her children in the countryside to work in the city for a few months, but another breastfeeding relative or friend would step in and nurse the child. Looking at the country's recent statistics, though, these cross nursing arrangements might be increasingly hard to find. According to the United Nations Children's Fund (UNICEF), the number of Mongolian babies exclusively breastfed for six months dropped from 60 percent to 50 percent between 2010 and 2013 alone.

Not surprisingly, formula advertising in Mongolia is on

the rise. Young moms working in the city and separated from their families back home in the countryside are especially susceptible to the extensive displays of formula cans lining city supermarket shelves (breast pumps are uncommon and too expensive for most Mongolians). Kamnitzer didn't doubt this recent turn of events. She said that while she had never seen bottle-feeding in the countryside, a mother in Ulaanbaatar once approached her and asked her to translate the English directions on a can of formula. The mom said her baby was crying a lot, and she was worried that she didn't have enough breast milk. "She didn't have her parents around," noted Kamnitzer, who—thanks to the open-minded culture in Mongolia and the unflagging support she received there—continued to breastfeed Calum until he was just past the age of four. She tried to pass along some of that same encouragement to the anxious young mother, but Kamnitzer will never know if the woman, disconnected from the attachment parenting wisdom Mongolian parents have always possessed, followed her advice. "It was kind of interesting that she didn't have anyone."

AMERICAN WOMEN, ON THE OTHER HAND, HAVE BEEN DISPLACED from our traditional parenting heritage for well over a century now. Our Industrial Revolution sent us to work in cities away from our own mothers; it sent us to factories and later to offices, where we had to leave our own children behind. But for most of human history, women didn't have to choose between their babies and their livelihoods. Mothers have always worked, but prior to the twentieth century, they didn't have to be separated from their children to do so. In the old days, one's world encompassed a much tinier circumference. People didn't drive fifty miles on a freeway to their job every day. People didn't hop on flying machines and travel to the other side of the world for business meetings.

In the 1975 book *The Continuum Concept: In Search of Happiness Lost*, which influenced Sears's views on attachment, the American writer Jean Liedloff wrote about how her years living among the Yequana and Sanema tribes in the jungles of Venezuela opened her eyes to the extreme disconnectedness of modern American life—and in particular, American parenting. In the tribes, babies were kept in close physical contact with their mothers from birth until the babies could crawl, breastfeeding on demand and even being held securely in a sling as the women navigated their way down a precarious mountainside several times a day to gather water. Infants rarely cried, and older children—given the freedom to explore and do "adult" work alongside their parents yet seldom harshly disciplined—never argued. Liedloff came to believe that in the modern world, where we no longer experience that physical security as children, we are left emotionally empty. "Loss of the essential condition of well-being that should have grown out of one's time in arms leads to searches and substitutions for it," she wrote.

The anthropologist Katherine Dettwyler, who conducted extensive research on breastfeeding in West Africa in the 1980s, had told me that in Mali, a nation of agriculturalists and pastoralists where people also hold "regular" jobs in banks and offices and restaurants, babies often stay with a working mother throughout the day. In fact, Dettwyler was breastfeeding her own first child during her initial years of research there. "The women are out in the field planting millet with the baby tied to their back," she said.

Even moms who worked as schoolteachers or nurses would bring their babies along, breastfeeding as needed. Sears advocates these types of work arrangements, encouraging mothers to arrange alternative work schedules, start home businesses, or reduce their hours. And indeed, this was the case with some of the moms I saw that day at his office. One young new mother, holding tight to her tiny bright-eyed six-week-old baby, told me she probably wouldn't return to her job as a lawyer recruiter after her maternity leave ended. "It's amazing how babies can change things," Sears said to me with a knowing smile. I had felt that way after Izzy was born, but I also hadn't had all that exciting a career in those days. What about women who loved their children but also loved their work? Why was it fair to make them choose?

In reality, the majority of Sears's moms work away from their babies. They use extended breastfeeding, baby wearing, and sleep sharing as ways to reconnect with their children in the off-hours. One CEO attachment mom travels all around the world for her job, FedExing cases of breast milk back to her baby wherever she goes. This obviously isn't easy, and in fact, Sears is often criticized for promoting a model of parenting that would best suit stay-at-home mothers or "privileged" parents like Yahoo! CEO Marissa Mayer, who paid to have a nursery built next to her office so she could breastfeed and then banned her employees from working from home. But Sears pointed out that even in his early days as a poorly paid intern, he and Martha (who as a nurse then made five times his salary) would juggle both their schedules so she could breastfeed between shifts. She managed to balance work and breastfeeding with all their eight children, he said. "The greatest multitasker in the world is the mom," he said. "That has never changed."

But are we multitasking, or are we just torn in a million different directions? Is it fair to expect all moms to be supermoms? The fact is there's an ugly, ugly truth that has been long ignored in the mommy wars: the United States is the only industrialized country in the world where the law does not provide for paid maternity leave.

What's more, an overwhelming number of *developing* nations—including Mongolia, as well as countries like Algeria, Bangladesh, Uzbekistan, and Costa Rica—provide mothers with 100 percent pay for the minimum fourteen weeks established by the Maternity Protection Convention of the United Nations' International Labour Organization. A survey of 167 countries found that nearly half also offered paternity leave, with Slovenia and Iceland giving fathers ninety paid days to be with their children. (Women may breastfeed, but fathers play an essential role in attachment, too, notes devoted dad Sears.) Although US law now guarantees new parents their jobs for twelve weeks after the birth of a baby, this is unpaid and applies only to mothers and fathers who work for companies with fifty or more employees.

Putting maternity leave—something the rest of the world now views as an essential human right—in the hands of US corporations to offer at their discretion has proved an abysmal failure. A scant 12 percent of US private-sector workers have access to paid maternity leave through their employer.

And on-site day care, which allows a mom to bond with and breastfeed her baby as needed throughout the day, is provided by only 7 percent of US companies, even though it has been shown to improve worker productivity. One-third of women have no time off at all, and the average woman who takes leave is back to work just ten unpaid weeks after giving birth. Are we surprised, then, that one-third of mothers give up breastfeeding mere weeks after returning to work? Maybe it's time we forget the mommy wars and instead band together for a Million Mom March on Washington to demand meaningful maternity leave legislation.

What the US government now mandates—free of charge, thanks to the Affordable Care Act—is a sad, lonely substitute for the love and time spent with a newborn: a breast pump. To some, Bill Sears's attachment credo may sound demanding, even crazy. But it may not be any more demanding than what the typical American mom going back to work full-time after giving birth endures.

TWELVE WEEKS AFTER THE C-SECTION BIRTH OF HER DAUGHTER, my sister-in-law Samantha went back to work as director of sales at her digital advertising tech firm. Here's the rundown of her typical day at the time: She would wake up, nurse the baby, pump an extra bottle of breast milk to add to her day's supply of frozen breast milk, pack it up together with bottles and diapers and clothes, and drop everything off at day care along with her daughter. Then she'd head to the office for a day jammed with client meetings, darting off to the break room four times to pump (or sometimes pumping during a

Skype call with a client, positioning the camera so she could be seen only from the shoulders up) and disassembling and reassembling the pump each time to clean it thoroughly. At six, she'd leave the office to pick up her daughter from day care and head home, where she'd cook dinner, clean all the bottles for the next day, put the baby to bed, and (finally) collapse in bed herself, knowing she'd be woken up twice during the night by her daughter's cries. And each time, she'd shuffle into the baby's room to breastfeed, head back to bed herself, and then have to start the whole ridiculous cycle again the next morning.

Now Sam was expecting her second child, and she confessed she had hated breastfeeding the first time and was dreading it this time around. But upon further thought, she said it was really the *pumping* she hated. Before her maternity leave ended, she loved how close she felt to her daughter when she was nursing. But back at work, she and her fellow new moms so despised the pumping that as they got more relaxed about seeing one another unclothed, they would all meet for "happy hour" in the pumping room and chug down wine to make the boredom of it more bearable. "The alcohol doesn't hit your milk supply if you drink while you're pumping," she claimed. (Alcohol peaks in a mom's blood and milk anywhere from thirty minutes to an hour after drinking, although this varies from person to person.) After she started traveling across the country again for work, pumping became truly unbearable. When my niece was eight months old, Sam gave up nursing altogether. "I can't tell you how many *disgusting* airport bathrooms I've pumped in," she quipped.

Then there's my brother's wife, Sarah, the nurse-practitioner. In order to complete the requirements of her nursing school scholarship, she had to go back to work at a community health clinic outside of Boston when her son was three months old. Overscheduled with patients from the time she arrived until the time she left, she was not only prohibited by her employer from scheduling time to pump at work but also not provided with a private place to express breast milk, even if she had been able to find the time. Both of these things are illegal, ostensibly. Since 2010, the federal Fair Labor Standards Act has required employers to provide reasonable break time to nursing mothers in order to express breast milk, along with a place to pump (other than a bathroom) that's shielded from view and free from intrusion. Unfortunately, there are a ridiculous number of exemptions to the law, and Sarah, being a salaried "learned professional," was one of these exempt employees. (Seriously? How can we expect health professionals to encourage their patients to breastfeed if we don't even provide *them* with a place to pump?)

Even so, given the number of new-mom NPs and doctors who worked at the clinic, Sarah and the others could have banded together and raised the issue with management. But no one dared. So Sarah had no choice but to keep her endless line of patients waiting while she squeezed in a fifteen-minute pump session in an exam room—which she said is an even grosser place to pump than a bathroom. "It's like pumping in a hospital, with MRSA everywhere. I would lay paper down everywhere I put my bag and supplies because I was so nervous germs would get all over his milk."

One day when Sarah had to pump, a new male medical assistant made the mistake of revealing to her restless patients the real reason they were kept waiting. He was Somali and had different cultural views about breastfeeding. He thought that it would appease them to say that the NP was "pumping her breasts." "That was the term he used," said Sarah. One patient, enraged, ran to the room Sarah was in and started pounding on the door. "Stop pumping your breasts!" she screamed. Not surprisingly, Sarah was unable to let down any milk in the midst of being verbally assaulted. So she stopped the pump and came out into the hall, where the woman continued to scream at her in front of everyone in the clinic. But instead of having the unruly woman escorted out by security, management apologized profusely to her and whisked her to a provider in another office. "I started crying at work, I was so upset about it," Sarah said. "I was going to quit. Except I had three weeks left on my contract."

THE REASON I'M SHARING OTHER MOTHERS' STORIES, RATHER than my own, is that admittedly I have no such workplace horror stories to share. I became an attachment parent by default after Izzy was born, long before I ever read one of Bill Sears's books or even knew what "attachment" was. I was a work-from-home freelancer, with a husband who had only recently gone back to work after a very long stretch of unemployment. We had no money. My only choice was to keep baby Izzy with me while I was writing. And we had a small one-bedroom apartment, so for more than a year, she slept next to me at night, in a borrowed baby hammock at first and then in her crib. (I sleep very deeply and was too nervous to bring her into our bed, though Sears says that even having her in the room close to me is a form of sleep sharing.)

But after I finally got the hang of breastfeeding, I realized that I liked having my "assistant" at my side, or rather, on my chest, in a wrap carrier. I got some of my best work done when she was snuggled up against me, and when I was out running errands in our walkable neighborhood, I worked off a lot of the baby pounds by keeping her in there while I carried my groceries. As I quickly realized, breastfeeding on demand, in a carrier, is a multitasking mom's dream—available boob, quiet baby, free hands. I was offered two different full-time editing jobs shortly after Izzy turned one, but I turned both of them down. Matthew and I decided we would rather scrimp and save than have me miss this special time with her. (Well, he wasn't entirely convinced, but now, in retrospect, he says he's glad I was around for those early years.)

Sears calls this feeling being an attached parent, and if that's the case, I was hooked. So as the months, then years, went by, I just kept up the routine, even after Mika was born and I had to figure out a truly insane writing schedule around their staggered naps and tandem-nursing sessions. I'm not going to pretend that I had it all figured out or that it was easy. Izzy was what Sears would call a "high need" baby (and toddler, and preschooler) who was insatiable at the breast; Mika started walking at nine-and-a-half months and soon after enjoyed climbing up on our dining room table and swinging from our chandelier.

Despite everything we tried (short of "cry it out"), neither of them slept through the night until well past age two, and of course as the breastfeeder and the one who didn't work late nights, I was the bleary-eyed one forever shuffling into their room. (I wish I had read Sears's books earlier and realized I would have gotten a lot more sleep if they had just been in bed with us!) And after Izzy weaned, I became the lopsided bleary-eyed breastfeeder, since Mika got used to nursing from "her side" and refused to go near the other. But the advantage was that I always had at least one magic orb at the ready to quell any tantrum, and to lull them quickly to sleep at night so I could go put my feet up and have a glass of wine. That, and that I deeply, deeply loved my girls, in a way I wasn't sure all parents did.

So basically, I didn't have a clue what it was like to be a real working mom. And in four years, I hadn't spent more than a day—and most of the time, more than a few hours, later when they started preschool—away from my kids. (This wasn't because I had to be available to breastfeed, since nursing a toddler is far more flexible than nursing a baby. This was because we had neither the finances nor the family around to allow us to take a vacation!) And then one day, I opened up my e-mail in-box and saw an invitation waiting for me for a weeklong press trip to Taiwan.

My first thought was to turn it down. I was already well into working on the manuscript for this book, and I was still nursing Mika, who had just turned two. She was showing no signs of losing interest in "Mommy milk," as she called it, and I wasn't ready to wean her. Even if she had been ready, I certainly didn't want to do it by saying, *See ya!* and hopping on a plane to the other side of the world. That would have been traumatic. Still, what was the harm of Googling *Taiwan* and *breastfeeding* to see if something interesting popped up? And that's when I came across an intriguing blog post by a Taiwanese American journalist named To-wen Tseng.

WHEN I MET TSENG ONE MORNING AT AN INDOOR-PLAYGROUND café in the trendy kid-crawling enclave of Larchmont in central Los Angeles, she looked every bit the stylish attachment mommy. Slim and pretty, with sleek shoulder-length black hair, she rushed in with a two-year-old boy planted serenely on her hip. "Say hi, Jade-y," she implored, intoning something to him in Mandarin before reaching out to shake my hand. I told her I was sorry my girls couldn't join us; they both were at home with colds (as usual, I had negotiated with Matthew to go to work an hour late so I could zip across town for the interview). "He'll warm up," she said. "So sorry I'm late. The traffic coming up from San Diego was so bad."

We grabbed a couple of teas from the counter, then sat down to talk in the tree-muraled kids' play area. Jade seemed more interested in sitting on Tseng's lap than in exploring the wooden slide or any of the colorful toys scattered around, so she rocked back and forth on a Wheely Bug to demonstrate how fun it would be for him to play (and allow us to talk, undistracted). This was not how she had originally pictured her life as a journalist, as I soon found out.

She also never imagined she would become a breastfeeding advocate, not to mention one at the center of a highly publicized lawsuit about the rights of women breastfeeding in the workplace. In fact, Tseng had been working for the Taiwanese-owned *World Journal* for only one year when she found out she was pregnant with her first child. "People had told me my company didn't have a good policy about breastfeeding, but I was like *Who cares? I'll just feed my son formula.*" After all, she, like me, had been formula-fed, and becoming a mother was never high on her list of life goals. In fact, it wasn't on her list at all. She loved her job as a reporter on the crime and disaster beat (she had previously worked for Asian-language TV station LA18 for nine years, which is also owned by *World Journal*'s parent company), and her husband was deeply involved in his career as a computer engineer. They had spent the first five years of their marriage shuttling between Los Angeles and San Diego, spending time together only on the weekends, and had made the decision not to have children.

But they decided to go through with the pregnancy, and when she gave birth to her son, Jade, after an exhausting twenty-hour labor followed by an emergency C-section, the moment he latched on erased all of Tseng's former plans. She fell in love with breastfeeding and being Jade's mommy and decided to scrap her original plan to formula-feed him once she returned to work. But while her views had changed dramatically over the course of her three-month maternity leave, *World Journal*'s anti-breastfeeding environment had not. She returned to an office with no lactation room and resigned herself to pumping in the restroom. "I had no knowledge about labor law," Tseng said, explaining that while California law mandates break time and a reasonable space for all breastfeeding employees to pump that is *not* a toilet stall (unlike the exemptions permitted by federal law), she didn't know where to turn.

The situation wasn't ideal, she said, but it was manageable. What was untenable, however, was what would happen after she pumped, when she went to the office kitchen to wash out the machine's parts. "People would say, 'Don't wash your dirty panties here,' " said Tseng, still visibly angered by the memory. She reported the harassment to HR, but they did nothing.

Then, two months into her return to work, the newspaper—the largest Chinese-language newspaper in the United States—published an article with the title "Breastfeeding Photos Embarrass Chinese-American to Death." It was about the "disturbing" trend of sharing breastfeeding photos via social media, and it described breastfeeding in public as "disgusting." There was a public backlash, and the paper received hundreds of letters of complaint. But not long after, the paper published another anti-breastfeeding piece, this time about the unfeasibility of employers providing nursing rooms for their employees.

"I got really upset," she said and described how she sat down to talk with her editor and also, finally, HR. Her editor said she was taking the whole thing way too personally. HR had a more creative response. "They said, 'No one ever breastfed in this company,' " Tseng recalled. "I was like *Really? You add something in your water? Nobody pregnant?!*" she laughed incredulously. Fed up and facing a dwindling milk supply from all the stress at having to pump amid such hostility, she quit. And then, with the help of California's nonprofit Legal Aid Society–Employment Law Center, she sued the company for sex discrimination.

The suit was settled in her favor, and in addition to an undisclosed monetary sum, *World Journal* was ordered to provide lactation accommodations for breastfeeding employees, which the company implemented in 2014. But Tseng turned down half the sum in exchange for her right to talk and write about the experience. She now writes a blog aptly titled *I'd Rather Be Breastfeeding*, along with a Chinese-language version, and contributes to the million-member MomsRising website, among several others.

Though her experience with the US-headquartered but Taiwanese-owned *World Journal* was unfortunate, she told me that *in* Taiwan, a lot had fortunately changed in the past several decades. The government had worked hard to create breastfeeding-friendly workplaces and had even passed a strict law fining anyone who tried to oust a mom for nursing in public. Breastfeeding rates had skyrocketed since her formula-fed childhood living there. All in all, it appeared Taiwan was doing something right.

Could a culture change that quickly? I wanted to know more. I felt myself moving one step closer to accepting that trip. But would Mika want to nurse when I came back, after my being away for so long? *Maybe we can all go and just make it one big family adventure*, I thought. But the thousands of dollars on extra plane tickets aside, I saw the flash in my mind of how Mika had sprinted away from me at the farmers' market the previous week, hysterically laughing as I almost lost her. What if that happened in Taipei in the midst of speeding scooters and Mandarin-labeled street signs? Forget never nursing her again, we would likely never *see* her again. I shuddered at the thought and decided she would definitely be safest if I left her *if I left her* back in Los Angeles.

Tseng must have been reading my mind because at that

moment she decided to tell me about when she once had to leave Jade, then fifteen months, for a business trip to Austin. "When I came back, he went back to nursing, although it went down to only the morning and bedtime sessions," she said.

"How long were you gone?" I asked.

"Two weeks."

"Two weeks?" I said, suddenly relieved. If they could do fourteen days, then we could do seven. It was going to feel like a long seven days, probably more so for me (and for my poor husband, who would be watching them) than for the girls, but they would be OK.

"So, what did you do?"

"I pumped," she said.

AS IT TURNS OUT, TSENG HAD A WORK TRIP TO TAIWAN THE SAME week I would be there, and she promised to meet up with me in Taipei for support. And so one night later that month, I found myself putting my girls to bed, kissing Izzy completely as I laid her drowsy little head on her pillow and whispering into Mika's soft curls once she latched off, asleep in my arms, to please hang in there until I got back. I smooched my sweet husband and wished him good luck, and then headed to the airport with one small suitcase and a portable pump packed at the top of my carry-on.

As I walked to my gate, alone, I couldn't stop thinking about something I've left out of the story so far, and that's my relationship with my own mother. All this research about attachment—and even before that, the experience of having my own children—had made me question the bond my mom and I had had, and I started seeing holes appear in my childhood. Yes, she had made the tough choice between her career and her children and had chosen to stay at home with us, chosen to be there for us in those pivotal early years. But still, she had also *chosen* not to breastfeed, both me and later my brother, Noah, for reasons that were still unclear. How had she denied us that closeness, that kind of indescribable love I had witnessed firsthand while nursing my daughters? How had she shrugged away such a profound biological and emotional need that no matter how long I lived and no matter what else on earth I experienced, would never, ever, *ever* be filled? I know she will read this, and I don't want to hurt her, but I was angry. She had moved away just weeks after Mika was born, and now—exhausted with two tiny children, a husband who worked insanely long hours, and no other family nearby—I felt unlatched and alone, like a leaf blowing in the breeze.

But when the plane began to taxi, I remembered what Sears had told me about his own childhood. He had grown up poor and underprivileged, abandoned by his father at a month old and raised by a single mother. She hadn't breastfed, but from early infancy she had surrounded him with loving, caring people. He was held a lot. Growing up in his grandparents' home, he was encircled by scoutmasters, religious leaders, and coaches, and he hung out at the local firehouse. "On the one hand, I didn't have the ideal nurturing, two-parent attachment childhood, but my mother did the best she could in a less than ideal situation," he said. "So despite the fact that [I] didn't have all this attachment parenting, [I] kind of did."

I heard the engines kick in, and as the plane started accelerating down the runway, I grasped for the locket around my neck that Matthew had given me for my birthday after Izzy was born. Inside was a picture of his handsome face smiling next to the impossibly tiny face of our wide-eyed seven-week-old daughter. And then I heard my mother's voice walking me through her own good luck routine that she still runs through, to this day, every time she gets on a flight to go anywhere. *I close my eyes,* I could hear her say. *And I focus on the image of you and Noah in my head until I can see every detail of your faces.*

Whether she breastfed me or not, she had sung me silly songs and sewn my Halloween costumes from scratch. She had dressed me up for my first school dance and then driven me back home to change without hesitation when I showed up and realized that my outfit looked silly. She had hugged me close, wiped my tears, saved us from destitution, and raised us on her own when my father took off after their divorce. She had fought back cockroaches with me in my revolting two-hundred-square-foot New York City apartment, walked me down the aisle, coached me through twenty-six hours of labor with my first daughter, and given me painstaking, loving notes on every chapter I had written of this book. The reason I was the woman I was today, the reason I cared so much about my connection with my own daughters, was that she had always, *always* been there for her children. She had loved us unequivocally, held fast to us all these years.

I fought back my tears and held tight to my girls with my heart. We would be a world away, but like my own mother, I would never let go.

seven

Latch Off, Latch On

From the side, a whole range; from the end, a single peak:
Far, near, high, low, no two parts alike.
Why can't I tell the true shape of Lu-shan?
Because I myself am in the mountain.
—SU SHIH

As I waited for my trusty blue suitcase to make its way around the luggage belt, I was stung by the silence that was five a.m. in Taipei, where people quietly straggled through the haze of their Monday morning. No friendly face nodded to acknowledge the wearisome journeys our group of journalists had completed. I didn't feel tired, though, for time had seemed amorphous on the fifteen-hour flight, without my girls to tend to.

I had drifted in and out of sleep for hours, waking once at what would have been Sunday morning in Los Angeles, just around the time Mika normally bounced into our bed like a panting puppy dog for her Mommy milk. I dutifully shuffled to the lavatory in my flimsy airline slippers, programmed to pump my swollen left breast. Izzy had come down with strep earlier that week, and as I watched the droplets of milk plink into the little collection bottle, I thought of the old wives' tale about gargling with breast milk to fight off a sore throat. But I shook my head at myself in the awful fluorescent-lit mirror, yanked the sink stopper, and dumped the contents of the bottle down the drain. Then I grabbed a couple of Advil from my toiletry kit.

Now, I was calculating, it was early Sunday afternoon in Los Angeles. My sweet little ladies would be distracted from my absence as they waited at the airport for their grandmother, who was flying in from Chicago to help Matthew for the week. I could almost *feel* the unfathomable miles those fifteen hours had put between us. But this was the first time in four years I had had more than four hours truly to myself, without either Matthew by my side or a kid asleep in the other room. My husband's voice was echoing in my head: "Buck up and appreciate the adventure!"

I grabbed my suitcase off the belt and strode toward the arrival hall, my long-forgotten freedom sending just a wee bit of spring into my step.

On the forty-five minute ride to Taipei, I chatted with one of the other journalists from my press tour, a newly married reporter from a local paper in Maine, and gazed out the car window at dense clouds cloaking lush green hills. With the mist rising in the distance, the view would have been primordial were it not for industrial ugliness poking in here and there as we moved closer to the city—first, sprawling power plants; then, shanties flanking dilapidated apartment towers. I could almost hear the cranking of the antiquated air-conditioning units crammed into windows.

By the time we arrived at the hotel, rain had broken through the swelter. Up in my room, I peeled off my sticky jean jacket and lay down on the bed's crisp white comforter, hoping to catch a few winks before my first meeting. My eyelids just started to drop when I realized it was time to pump again. *No wonder why so many of the working moms I know have used a business trip to wean*, I thought. And here I only had to pump one boob a few times a day, since my milk supply was well established after nursing my girls for a number of years. Still, it was going to be a long week. I headed to the bathroom to find an electrical outlet, pumped, and hit the sack once more.

It was some time later when my alarm went off. I leaped off the bed toward my room's teapot and then gulped down a mug of oolong. After a quick shower where I couldn't figure out how to work the multiple handles and accidentally flooded the entire bathroom (don't even ask me about the electronic toilet), I headed down to the lobby to meet my translator, Emily. (The Taiwanese take on English names alongside their Chinese ones, with the names of Hollywood movie stars especially popular. I chose a common name for her here, since "Emily" requested that I protect her privacy.) We headed to our first meeting.

Only a couple of years my junior, Emily grew up in Taipei but had spent time in Australia in her twenties. She seemed curious about the assignment to accompany me on my research excursion into breastfeeding in Taiwan and was clearly mystified by my description of the breast-versus-bottle controversy in America. "I don't understand," she exclaimed.

"Everyone know breastfeeding so good for you, right?" Although she didn't have children yet, she told me that some of her friends had babies, and all of them were breastfed. Some of the moms didn't particularly enjoy nursing, she admitted, but since they knew it was the best choice, they breastfed without question.

After all, anyone who's ever read *Battle Hymn of the Tiger Mother* knows that the Chinese are hard-core about success. The Taiwanese are, too. While Taiwan was briefly colonized by the Japanese and now maintains a democracy autonomous from China, over 95 percent of its population is ethnically Han Chinese. (China still claims sovereignty over the island; only twenty-one UN member states, excluding the United States, officially recognize Taiwan's statehood.) Anything that affords their children a head start in life or an edge in academics, the Taiwanese commit to wholeheartedly. The week I was there, a study had just been released linking extended breastfeeding to both higher IQ and income in adulthood. It was mentioned to me more than a few times.

Yet Taiwanese mothers didn't always adhere to the mantra "breast is best." Not too long ago, the island had one of the lowest breastfeeding rates in the world. Emily was born in 1981, so she didn't remember that in 1986, a barely recordable 5.4 percent of one-month-old babies were fed exclusively by the breast. Now, just a few decades later, 72 percent of Taiwanese infants under the age of one month are exclusively nursed.

Taiwan is also just a few points shy of meeting WHO's worldwide 2025 goal that at least half of all babies under the age of six months be exclusively breastfed. (Taiwan, like WHO, uses the "under six month" designation, which calculates the percentage of babies zero to five months old exclusively breastfeeding at a particular point in time and can conflate percentages. But any way you slice it, the figures are still markedly higher than the 1986 percentage, which was virtually zero.) How an island of twenty-three million people has latched on a new generation of babies and mothers is literally a case study for the United States, and other countries struggling to increase breastfeeding rates, to learn what can be achieved when a government and citizenry step up with full force.

Still, before we can determine just how Taiwan got its babies to latch on again, we have to look first at how Taiwan became *un*latched. The island, in fact, has been on quite the breastfeeding roller coaster ride within the last century. Whereas in 1986, almost no one was breastfeeding, just a generation before, nearly everyone *was*. In 1960, nearly 95 percent of Taiwanese babies were breastfed simply because there wasn't another option. Even if formula had been readily available, the majority of Taiwanese, who were still living in a preindustrial agrarian society, would not have been able to afford it.

Yet a sea change was set in motion when Chinese military leader Chiang Kai-shek came to Taiwan in 1949 to rule in exile, followed by millions of new immigrants who fled Communist mainland China at the end of what had been a brutal civil war. As the new influx of laborers settled in and Taiwan began industrializing, many of its women were compelled to head to the factories to work, leaving their babies behind, just as American mothers had been obliged to do in our Industrial Age a century prior. Not surprisingly, Big Formula made inroads. When Taiwan's economy exploded, the very generation that had breastfed its babies out of necessity suddenly saw the ability to afford pricey formula as a sign of prosperity and encouraged their own children to use it.

Back in Los Angeles, To-wen Tseng had told me of her grandmother, who had come to Taiwan on a refugee boat from China in 1949 with Tseng's father and uncle, then ages three and one. The little boys were crying, and the other refugees on the boat feared their cries would alert the Chinese Communist ships close by. They began panicking and threatened to throw the boys overboard, so Tseng's grandmother tore off her blouse, put one boy to each breast, and calmed them by nursing them continually until the boat made it safely to Taiwan, two days later.

Tseng, who had been formula-fed, said that when her grandmother first told her this story, Tseng was so little she didn't know what breastfeeding was. Yet even then, she could see that her grandmother told the story with great remorse. "My grandma did such a brave thing, but she was not proud of it," she said. "She told me: 'We did this because we could not afford formula. Look how lucky your son is! You now live in America.'"

And without a doubt, the way that the Taiwanese revered American culture influenced their move toward formula. Adopting the names of Hollywood movie stars alongside their traditional Chinese ones was only one demonstration of that veneration; even Taiwanese formula ads and containers featured Caucasian babies, plump and smiling. By the 1980s and '90s, Taiwan's hospitals looked like American hospitals of the 1950s and '60s. Infants were parked in uniform rows behind glass in nurseries, away from their mothers; doctors and nurses diligently schooled in formula feeding dispensed neatly mixed bottles to their charges at regularly scheduled intervals.

In fact, if you want a more complete picture of what Taiwan looked like during those decades, you wouldn't need a time machine but a telescope to peer across the Taiwan Strait at today's mainland China. Since Big Formula's foray there in the early 1970s, China has become the world's largest market for infant formula, dubbed a "white gold" rush by investors who are pouring hundreds of millions of dollars into dairy ventures around the world to satisfy the country's near unquenchable thirst for the stuff—a thirst projected to reach some $30 billion annually by the year 2017.

This may be partially because more women have to balance work with motherhood than ever before. China's 73 percent female employment rate is now one of the highest in the world. "A working mom will put her baby on formula or mix-feed after maternity leave ends [at fourteen weeks]," said Helena Ran, a thirty-something Shanghai-based Nike executive who managed to breastfeed along with formula-feed her son until he was a year old. "It's very hard to keep pumping on time after going back to work." Then there's the reality of China's upwardly mobile and expanding middle class, now willing to shell out one hundred dollars for a twenty-five-dollar container of coveted foreign-made formula. Amazingly, the Chinese melamine-contaminated formula scandal—contamination that killed six babies and sickened three hundred thousand others back in 2008—resulted not in more mothers turning to the safer alternative of breast milk, but to hoarding pricier brands from Australia and even traveling all the way to the United States to illegally smuggle back cases of formula.

But the most obvious reason the infant-formula market is so monstrous in China is because formula advertising there runs rampant and unregulated. Tales abound of doctors being bribed by formula representatives eager to ensure that a newborn's first sip of formula is their brand, or of salespeople calling or texting mothers within minutes of their child's birth to pitch their brand as superior. (Mobile marketing such as this is illegal in the United States; in China, now home to one billion cell phone users, it is ubiquitous.)

In fact, a recent study found that an astonishing 40 percent of Chinese women are contacted *directly* by baby-food company reps. The same proportion of mothers received free formula samples, with one-third of the samples coming not from the formula companies but from health care workers. "In some hospitals they have the Mead Johnson floor, the Gerber floor," said Tseng, whose cousin gave birth in China last year. (Remember Larry Gartner's description of Ross Laboratories' nursery design program in the 1960s?) Factor in that China now also has one of the highest C-section rates in the world, estimated at 50 percent, and it's not difficult to see how the formula companies' aggressive sales tactics have proved persuasive for mothers recovering from the painful abdominal surgery.

Helena Ran told me that because she wasn't able to breastfeed initially in the hospital after her emergency C-section, her son was given formula. While she wasn't contacted directly by formula-company representatives, she did continue feeding her son Similac, the hospital's brand of choice, until her son was a year old. (Her recovery from the C-section was difficult, she said, so her husband bottle-fed their son at night while she got some rest.) Luckily, she was also able to breastfeed simultaneously for the same length of time, thanks to encouragement from her mother. "She told me that breastfeeding is the best gift a mom can give to her baby."

Ran's story, along with the news that Beijing has recently taken some small steps to restrict infant-formula advertising, is encouraging evidence that attitudes are changing. Still, at last check, only 16 percent of urban Chinese mothers and less than a third of rural mothers—who have also come to view formula as a sign of prosperity—have been able to avoid the lure of infant formula altogether. "I think formula is kind of unavoidable in China," Ran said.

One night in Taipei, while having dinner with Dr. Shu-Ti Chiou, Director-General of Taiwan's Health Promotion Administration in the Ministry of Health and Welfare, I relayed what To-wen Tseng and Helena Ran had told me about the apparent "wild west" of formula a mere 110 miles away on the mainland. Chiou declared, "That's thirty years ago in Taiwan."

What I soon discovered, though, was that Chiou's assessment was off the mark. The story of breastfeeding in modern-day China isn't a looking glass into Taiwan's past. It's a cautionary tale—a Bradburian glimpse at what might have been Taiwan's *future* had the Taiwanese government not stepped in.

TODAY, AT THE CORE OF TAIWAN'S PRO-BREASTFEEDING EFFORTS is its widespread adoption of the Baby-Friendly Hospital Initiative (BFHI), which it began implementing for its hospitals in 2001. The BFHI is not exclusive to Taiwan; it's a global program that was created by WHO and UNICEF in 1991, largely to loosen the formula companies' viselike grip on hospitals. It's not surprising that for some time now, breastfed infants have been liberally supplemented with formula before they even leave the hospital. After all, infant-formula manufacturers have long provided American hospitals unlimited supplies of formula free of charge, said Trish MacEnroe, executive director of Baby-Friendly USA. One of the tenets of the BFHI is that medical institutions can no longer serve as shills for the formula companies. "Part of my job is to convince [hospital administrators] that are trying to keep their costs down that you now have to pay for a product that you used to be able to get for free. I make the moral case to these guys."

To date, more than twenty thousand maternity facilities in 150 countries worldwide, including the Kaiser Permanente hospital in Los Angeles where I gave birth to Izzy, have received the BFHI certification. Accredited facilities not only have to abide by the International Code of Marketing of Breast-Milk Substitutes (which means not accepting free formula, as well as abolishing the formula marketing and giveaways once ubiquitous in Taiwan's maternity wards and now pervasive in China), but they also have to implement the BFHI's Ten Steps to Successful Breastfeeding, which includes placing the naked newborn on its mother's bare breast within an hour of birth, encouraging nursing on demand instead of on a predetermined schedule, eliminating pacifiers, and providing instruction on lactation. Formula is offered only when deemed medically necessary.

Perhaps most important, to encourage bonding and frequent breastfeeding, babies room-in with their mothers instead of being monitored communally in the hospital nursery. The biologically unnatural separation of mothers and infants in the hospital has been protocol not just in Taiwan but in the United States and elsewhere around the world for decades. (It was only in America around 1900 that birth first moved out of the home, where labor had been unmedicated, to the hospital, where women were given general anesthesia. In point of fact, the nursery was originally created as a way for women, groggy from the drugs they had received, to recover before holding their babies. Later, regardless of the method of delivery, the nursery was perceived as a necessary "vacation" for weary new mothers in search of a little sleep.)

But studies have shown that the separation of mothers and babies is detrimental to the physical and emotional health of both. Babies kept apart from their mothers cry more and are slower to gain weight. Meanwhile, new mothers not permitted to bond freely with their infants suffer higher rates of postpartum depression and take longer to establish their milk supply. And they don't get any more sleep, as it turns out.

Essentially, the comprehensive Baby-Friendly initiative is a structured, spelled-out version of precisely the way infants coexisted with their new mothers for most of human history: breastfeed a baby when she's hungry; keep an infant close to his mother so he isn't devoured by a wolverine—you know, all that commonsense stuff we seem to have forgotten in the couple generations since we came to see bottle-feeding and separating mothers and babies at birth as the norm. Yet the Baby-Friendly movement has been slow to take off in the

United States, often deemed too extreme by generations of Americans who have come to view breast-versus-bottle as a matter of preference.

Some of that resistance has to do with a need for improved communication with women during pregnancy, to help them understand the evidence behind Baby-Friendly practices and why mothers benefit, admitted MacEnroe, particularly noting the issue of rooming-in. "The most important thing a hospital can do for you is not give you 'the night off' but really teach you how to soothe your baby," she said. "A mother's only got one or two nights to learn from skilled nursing staff until she's on her own at home."

Yet a friend of mine who was confident in her own ability to choose whether her baby should be breastfed or bottle-fed confided to me that she felt patronized by the new formula restrictions at Cedars-Sinai Medical Center in Los Angeles, where she gave birth. The hospital now requires a doctor's prescription for the formula feeding of any baby postpartum. (A year and a half prior, I had given birth to Mika at Cedars-Sinai. But as an established breastfeeding mom, I hadn't picked up on the new policy.) She even took issue with the Baby-Friendly designation itself, although Cedars-Sinai is not on the official path yet toward BFHI certification and thus legally cannot use the term. But when her second daughter was born premature and was determined to have lost too much weight after three days of exclusive breastfeeding, my friend asked the hospital pediatrician why she—an experienced mother who had breastfed her first child—wasn't given the option to supplement with formula sooner. He replied that it was "a pro-baby hospital." "It felt very anti-woman to me," she declared. "Whether or not I was breastfeeding shouldn't be the hospital's choice."

When I visited Cedars-Sinai right before my trip to Taiwan, however, both the nurse and lactation consultant who oversee the hospital's lactation program said the majority of new mothers they saw did not feel that way. According to Anna Greif, nurse manager for Women's Health and Patient Care Services in Cedars-Sinai Labor and Delivery, "When our moms are admitted into Labor and Delivery, one of the things we ask is, 'Is there a feeding preference?'" And she added, "We find *most* mothers come in wanting to breastfeed."

The results of matching policy to the mother's wishes are hard to deny. Before Cedars-Sinai started to adopt some Baby-Friendly practices about ten years ago, it had an exclusive-breastfeeding rate of 46 percent. Now, 75 percent of healthy babies leave the hospital exclusively breastfed. As of this writing, though, only 274 out of the more than 5,000 hospitals in the United States today have achieved BFHI certification, although an additional 700 are now working toward that designation. "There's been a huge cultural shift in the US in the last five years," said MacEnroe, who told me that this, plus a new push of pro-breastfeeding government policy and some long-awaited funding dollars, have at last given the Baby-Friendly movement momentum in the United States.

In Taiwan, where the Baby-Friendly initiative was launched in 2001 with thirty-eight accredited medical institutions, 177 hospitals have been certified to date, covering more than 76 percent of babies born in the country. The goal is to reach 80 percent coverage by next year. And Taiwan has taken other dramatic steps to promote breastfeeding. It banned formula ads on TV and made it illegal to prevent any woman from breastfeeding in public, imposing a hefty fine for violators. The island also created hundreds of public breastfeeding rooms everywhere, from malls to the metro. Each one, marked by a bright pink decal of a stick-figure woman cradling a baby, has at least one comfortable chair in which to nurse, plus a changing table and an outlet to plug in a breast pump. (One I saw even had an espresso machine and was decorated with cutesy panda wallpaper.) And with the help of newly created advocacy organizations such as the Breastfeeding Association of Taiwan, led by volunteer mothers, and the Taiwan Academy of Breastfeeding, which educates medical professionals, Taiwan has raised awareness about the crucial connection between breastfeeding and public health.

Still, more than any other action the government has taken, it is the Baby-Friendly initiative that is directly connected to the marked rise in breastfeeding rates. When I looked at the two lines plotted on a chart—one for the growing number of Taiwanese babies born at Baby-Friendly hospitals since 2004, the other for the percentage of exclusively breastfed babies during the same time period—I could see that the two are nearly parallel.

Given the success story, I was expecting to see something remarkable when my translator Emily and I arrived at our tour of the 118-year-old (and now Baby-Friendly) National Taiwan University Hospital. Yet what was most striking wasn't the majestic Renaissance-style complex itself. It was the sheer volume of humanity coursing through its doors. Even having lived in New York City and now Los Angeles, with their massive city hospitals, I've never encountered anything like it.

As Emily and I zigzagged through waves of people heading to appointments or awaiting treatment, many wearing surgical masks to reduce the spread of germs, an onslaught of orderlies darted to and fro with their ailing patients in wheelchairs. I nearly jumped to avoid smacking into one hospital bed whizzing past. Once in the elevator and packed in like a sardine—along with a mass of hospital patients and our guides, Head Nurse Yi-Hua Lee from the Department of Nursing and a cadre from the Ministry of Health and Welfare—on the painfully slow ride up to Labor and Delivery, I said a silent prayer that this wouldn't be the moment Taiwan got hit by one of its famously strong earthquakes.

Clearly, one of the reasons Taiwan has been able to promote breastfeeding to so many is that *so many* of its people have health care coverage. Nearly 99 percent of Taiwanese, in fact, are covered by the government's universal single-payer system. Taipei's National Taiwan University Hospital is like a city unto itself, treating a staggering eight thousand outpatients a day and employing more than six thousand workers to do it.

As it turns out, in a country where the government has to keep health care costs in check to keep its system running smoothly, promoting breastfeeding just makes good economic sense. The country doesn't have any hard figures yet, but the lowered rates of serious respiratory and gastrointestinal infections in breastfed babies, coupled with reduced longer-term risk for obesity and chronic illnesses such as diabetes, will undoubtedly reduce health care costs. In the United States, one recent study out of Harvard found that if 90 percent of families followed the medical recommendation to breastfeed each child exclusively for six months, the country would save an astounding $13 billion a year.

Safely removed from the throngs and upstairs in Labor and Delivery, I wondered if I would see swank new setups designed to support the mother-baby bonding process, replete with birthing tubs and New Agey music. But as the soft-spoken Yi-Hua Lee led me around upstairs, I didn't notice anything markedly different from the hospitals in Los Angeles where I had given birth to my babies. Lee pointed out an empty room where mothers could labor on a standard-looking birthing bed with bar and stirrups, and she showed me the kit the hospital used to help mothers with pain relief—the familiar birthing ball, massage tools, heating pad, and ice packs. As in America, Lee explained, most Taiwanese women rely on medication (either an epidural or morphine, now not as commonly used in the United States) to help them through labor. Interestingly, Taiwan's C-section rate, too, is even higher than it is in the United States: just over 33 percent, at last check.

Still, the expectation is that mothers can and will successfully breastfeed their babies, and given the absence of formula in the hospital unless deemed medically necessary, they do. Even after a C-section delivery, an infant is immediately laid on its mother's naked chest to initiate breastfeeding, Lee explained. My expression must have looked doubtful. "It's OK!" Director of Obstetrics Dr. Ming-Kwang Shyu asserted merrily, when he joined us after (surprise!) just completing a C-section. In light of the average hospital stay of three days for a vaginal delivery and five days for a C-section (during which time newborns room exclusively with their mothers), the vast majority of babies are successfully latched on when mother and baby leave the hospital.

The jovial fifty-something proudly showed me his International Board Certified Lactation Consultant card, and told me that as a doctor and lactation consultant, and as secretary-general of the Taiwan Academy of Breastfeeding, he spent a good deal of time simply reassuring mothers not to worry, that their milk would come in. This encouragement is essential. Taiwanese elders have considerable influence over a young couple, and the pressure to formula-feed from a generation of nonbreastfeeding parents can sometimes be intense.

To-wen Tseng had shared that even though she was still nursing her son, then two, she let both her mom and mother-in-law believe that she had already weaned him; they had insisted that breastfeeding for more than six months was bad for Tseng's health. And Anne, a Taiwanese breastfeeding advocate and mother of five who nursed all her children for a minimum of two and a half years, said that after she gave birth to her first child, her mother-in-law would just keep staring at her breasts to see if there was enough milk. In the countryside, she added, it was worse. There, when a mother with a newborn baby goes back to her family, everyone actually pokes at her breasts to *feel* how much milk is inside. (And you thought your own family was annoying!)

Then there's the Chinese cultural tradition of *zuo yue zi*, in which new mothers "lie-in" for a month to rest after birth—historically, a means for mom and baby to successfully establish breastfeeding. Nowadays, the tradition is more likely to be used as a justification for grandparents and the newer *zuo yue zi* facilities to "give a break" to weary breastfeeding mothers by bottle-feeding their babies, especially at night. Yet these cultural aberrations are changing, Shyu insisted. "Because of me!" he joked, but mostly as the result of a government unified around a national breastfeeding policy.

I wondered aloud how such sweeping changes would fare in the United States, given how ultrafocused we Americans are on the rights of each individual, not to mention how everyone seems to flip out each time the word *breastfeeding* is mentioned. "Taiwan is small country," Shyu reminded me, "easy to control." Perhaps, but the Taiwanese willingness to embrace change on behalf of the greater good has played an important role. After all, Shyu had bottle-fed his own first two children. Yet apparently, even as a medical professional, he had no ego problems acknowledging his prior lack of knowledge. He switched sides to become an outspoken breastfeeding advocate and added lactation consultant to his credentials.

It was hard not to love Shyu's enthusiasm. It was emblematic of Taiwan's ability not only to achieve a near reversal of its breastfeeding initiation rate but also to encourage an entire generation of Taiwanese mothers to latch on again.

Still, there looms Taiwan's inordinately high C-section rate. And while the rest of the world has moved away from the once-routine but often unnecessarily brutal practice of slicing open a woman's perineum just before childbirth (also known as an episiotomy), Taiwan's episiotomy rate is estimated to remain an unfathomably high 90 percent. The recovery from either procedure can be excruciating and, frequently, painful enough to make the demands of breastfeeding just too challenging. My own recovery from an episiotomy during Izzy's delivery, coupled with the pain of engorgement in the first weeks after her birth, did not make my initial route to successful breastfeeding an easy one by any means.

My sister-in-law Sam, who underwent a C-section after two exhausting days of unproductive labor with my niece, still recalls her own experience too well. "I puked three times during surgery, I'm literally convulsing from all the medication, and then they take her out of me as I'm on the verge of collapse, lay her on my chest and say, 'OK, start breastfeeding!' I mean, if there could be a hell . . ."

Surprisingly, according to Laurie Nommsen-Rivers, the lactation scientist at Cincinnati Children's Hospital Medical Center, a recent analysis of her research revealed that Cesarean delivery by itself does not affect a mother's initial milk supply. The lactation consultant at Cedars-Sinai, too, maintained that method of delivery does not appear to impact that hospital's initial exclusive-breastfeeding rate. But I couldn't help but wonder how Taiwanese women, undergoing such procedures and then being cheered into exclusive breastfeeding, fared when they returned home. Were they able to nurse their babies long-term? Moreover, was it fair to insist (as in the case of my sister-in-law) that women in pain forge ahead with Baby-Friendly without question? Somewhere down the line, I decided, birth interventions and the natural process of latching on would have to be reconciled.

As I would soon discover, though, the full story of breastfeeding in Taiwan was more complicated than merely measuring the influence of C-section and episiotomy rates.

The real mystery was why, in my week traveling throughout Taiwan, the last time I spied a breastfeeding baby was the morning I left the hospital.

THE TRUTH WAS, DURING MY TIME IN TAIWAN, I KEPT MY EYES peeled for nurslings in action. This was for research, yes, but also because I was desperately missing my own babies and kissing them each morning via iPhone was only making it worse. So I searched everywhere. I rode the metro and strolled through a glitzy shopping center flanked by a giant neon Ferris wheel. I breathed in incense at ancient temples and wolfed down giant pan-fried buns at the night markets. I mugged for photos with my journalist pals at Chiang Kai-shek Memorial Hall and scanned the crowds at the changing of the guards. I shuffled through the lines at the National Palace Museum (notoriously fined a few years back for expelling a breastfeeding mom) to gaze at the minuscule Jadeite Cabbage. I took a high-speed train to historic Tainan, where I tried to steer clear of a five-hundred-pound sow on the loose in a small fishing village and thought *surely* I would find mothers hiding away in the pavilion with nursing babes. But no such luck, even though everywhere I went, I saw the pink logo pointing me toward the government's much-touted breastfeeding rooms. (I looked inside those, too: empty.) Where were all the breastfeeding babies? Come to think of it, where were *any* of the babies?

My eyes didn't lie. As it turns out, Taiwan has one of the lowest birth rates in the world. And while more Taiwanese mothers are nursing than they have in half a century, the average mother breastfeeds for only two and a half months. At National Taiwan University Hospital, I had met mothers who nursed for considerably longer. But I discovered that those women are such a tiny segment that the government doesn't even collect breastfeeding statistics for women who breastfeed past six months.

Just as in mainland China, both the current birth and long-term breastfeeding rates are affected by the mandate to work. In China, where Big Formula holds sway, fully paid maternity leave is a generous three and a half months and *still* breastfeeding rates are abysmal. But even in Taiwan, where breastfeeding attitudes are progressive and the government provides eight weeks of paid leave to new mothers and permits up to two years of unpaid leave for both parents (including six months of reduced pay), mothers I interviewed claimed they returned to work after two months for fear their jobs would be passed on to others. And more Taiwanese women are delaying motherhood due to job insecurity and falling starting salaries. The age of a first-time mom climbed from 27.4 in 2004 to 30.5 in 2014, and one in six first-time moms are now between the ages of 35 and 39. Needless to say, many of these older mothers don't have the energy they used to have. Breastfeeding Association of Taiwan Secretary-General Yi-Ling Gao put it bluntly: "Some of the women's-rights activist groups have voiced that breastfeeding is too much effort—that they're so tired."

One afternoon at my hotel restaurant, To-wen Tseng and her two-year-old son Jade met me for fried rice (for Jade) and tea (for me, still jet-lagged). I was homesick and just happy to see their familiar faces. But I perked up when Tseng shared her theory about why moms weren't making it past two months of nursing. The public breastfeeding rooms, she said, were driving the mothers underground. Though certainly helpful for *pumping* women (raise your hands, ladies—who likes pumping in public?), the rooms were, in fact, making breastfeeding women feel as though they were consigned to isolation in order to breastfeed. Tseng explained, "The breastfeeding rate in Taiwan has moved up so much compared with thirty years ago, so people think breastfeeding is being protected. The truth is it is being protected; but it's not being *normalized*."

We sat and chatted for more than an hour, and understandably Jade started to get a bit cranky. I asked Tseng what would happen if she nursed him while sitting at our table. Wasn't there now a fine for evicting a breastfeeding woman from a restaurant? She told me, "They'll just say, 'Um, we have a breastfeeding room. You can go there, where you're more comfortable,'" To which Tseng said she would have absolutely no trouble declaring, "I'm more comfortable *here*."

I flashed to my own recollection of the physician who had once draped me with a sheet of changing-table paper as I was nursing Izzy in her office. The message then was loud and clear: what I was doing was wrong. According to Tseng, that is exactly how so many Taiwanese women still feel about breastfeeding, despite their higher initial breastfeeding rates. Even her friend, who had breastfed her son until he was three years old, confessed to Tseng that she felt seeing another woman's breasts being used to feed a child, just as she herself was doing, was disgusting. That revulsion was apparently shared by Tseng's former employer *World Journal*, the Taiwanese-owned newspaper that had published the article maintaining that breastfeeding in public was "gross."

I recalled that when I had asked Gao, of the Breastfeeding Association of Taiwan, if she had nursed her baby openly, Emily had translated (through their peals of laughter) that yes, she had, but her friends had called her a "grandmother" for doing it. Gao explained that breastfeeding in public was something a rural, old-fashioned woman—like Tseng's grandmother on the refugee boat from China—would have done. "Young people don't really do that," Emily added.

Ironically, Gao was instrumental in designing the public breastfeeding rooms to meet the needs of nursing mothers. It was her idea to add an outlet for a breast pump near the nursing chair as well as to include obvious peripheral needs such as a changing table. Yet there seemed to be a real conundrum: Were these spaces making breastfeeding possible for modest Taiwanese women who would have otherwise resorted to bottle-feeding, or as Tseng suggested, were they setting nursing mothers back even more?

Near the end of my trip, at my dinner with Health Promotion Administration Director-General Dr. Shu-Ti Chiou, Chiou insisted that the breastfeeding rooms were only an option and that the government's promotional efforts emphasized that women were encouraged to breastfeed "anywhere, anytime." Chiou, elegant and dignified in a turquoise Chinese collar jacket and jade flower lapel pin, said this without the slightest hint of political gloss over, and I believe she was sincere. After all, the soon-to-be-grandmother was not only the political powerhouse behind Taiwan's pro-breastfeeding campaign, but she was the one who had achieved a landmark victory against the formula companies, ushering through the Taiwanese Legislative Yuan a law that banned the advertising of the ultrapopular toddler formula, or follow-on milk. (The formula added unnecessary calories to a populace already struggling with obesity, said Chiou. Some might even point out that the sale of it is paradoxical. After all, if—as some people believe—babies over the age of one shouldn't still be breastfeeding, then why would toddlers need breast-milk components such as DHA and probiotics added to their cow's milk?)

Yet over a dish of sea cucumber, Chiou confessed that, in the beginning, there had been much debate over whether to provide for breastfeeding rooms in the legislation since some members of Congress believed that people should recognize there was nothing wrong with breastfeeding openly in public—a position Chiou didn't oppose. I asked her if she thought they should have named the rooms something else, so as to avoid the more than subliminal message: *Breastfeeding [go to a] Room*. Chiou said that this issue had been debated as well; she had originally proposed that the name be Family Room. In the end, they decided that the only way to make the public rooms safe was to limit them to breastfeeding mothers. Whether the rooms would ultimately help or hurt was something only time would tell.

WAS I MAKING TOO MUCH OF THIS BREASTFEEDING-IN-PUBLIC thing? After all, I had nursed for nearly five years running without ever posting a breastfeeding selfie and had only become truly unselfconscious about nursing around family and in public fairly recently in the scheme of things. (And I still nurse so discreetly that most people don't even realize I'm feeding a baby, let alone a preschooler.)

Those places around the globe where mothers flap their breasts at their toddlers without batting an eye (like Mongolia) have been rapidly disappearing. Likewise on this tour, I quizzed fellow journalists from European countries, like the Netherlands and Hungary, that boasted much higher breastfeeding rates than both Taiwan and the United States. On the surface, they seemed to have such relaxed attitudes about breastfeeding, although when I asked specifically about breastfeeding in public, they demurred. My German and Portuguese colleagues admitted that mothers in their countries almost always nursed discreetly. Moreover, those colleagues said, it was uncommon to spot a child breastfeeding past the age of one and would be quite strange to see one past the age of two. (Later, my German friend e-mailed me to share the news that there had just been a controversy in Hamburg about a woman chucked off a bus for breastfeeding her baby.)

On the plane ride back to Los Angeles, something To-wen Tseng had said still haunted me. It was about trying to rekindle humanity's relationship with breastfeeding for the next generation: "If our children grow up never seeing anyone breastfeed in public, if they grow up surrounded by the Hollywood message of sexualized breasts, then how can they have a healthy idea about women's bodies?"

Back in Los Angeles, reunited with Matthew and my girls, Mika latched on as though I had never been gone (how was she to know I held my breath each day, thinking about her, and fearing I had irreparably broken our bond?). I wondered if either of my daughters would one day dash back from a business trip to bundle their own babies to their breasts. Would they treasure the closeness we had when they were small, and would they want to replicate it? Or would they decide—in the even faster, more mechanized and complicated world to come—that the hassle involved wouldn't be worth it? Worse, would they be ashamed of their female bodies; those very things that my own body had created, and that my own breasts had nurtured?

I decided breastfeeding rooms and Baby-Friendly hospitals were a big step forward, but they wouldn't be enough for women to one day reclaim their breasts as truly their own.

eight

Breasts Are for Men

So what is it about this small gland of postnatal nourishment that puts a great nation in a dither? . . . Perhaps the problem has to do with generations of men who didn't get enough nipple when it really counted.

—GLENN O'BRIEN

"I don't know if you want me to go into the personal details," my mom hedged. Truth be told, I really, *really* didn't. But I was now thirty-five years old, with two children of my own, and still, I had never heard the full story about why I hadn't been breastfed as a baby. Of course, I knew it had something to do with the fact that I was born at a time when the overwhelming majority of mothers formula-fed. In 1979, the year I was born in New York City, only 29 percent of new moms breastfed their babies after birth in the hospital (versus 89 percent today), even though some public attention had shifted to the issue that same year and, in an across-the-board effort to increase rates, the New York City Department of Health had begun to gather hospital data on breastfeeding. But I had long suspected that there was another reason for my milk-deprived childhood, one having to do with a subject that few daughters of any age want to talk about with their mothers: sex.

During the years since I had started breastfeeding my own children, my mother had tossed off remarks here and there about why she hadn't used her own breasts to feed me, as well as my younger brother. She had mumbled something about how my father (her long-estranged ex-husband) had been the *real* baby in the family. "He was rather, um, possessive about my breasts," I think she had said, but I wasn't sure.

Now here I was on the phone, ready to officially interview her and already starting to cringe. I felt just as I had as a preteen, packing my bag for sleep-away camp, when my mother pounced on me with a pile of sanitary napkins "just in case" and then promptly launched into "the talk."

I decided to put on my serious journalist persona and thus block whatever awkwardness the conversation might evoke. And I would use the same tactic, I decided, when I contacted my father—whom I hadn't spoken with in years—for the necessary follow-up for my "unbiased" story. *Ugh,* I thought, *is eleven a.m. on a Wednesday too early to start drinking?*

"Are you still there, sweetheart?" my mom asked, on the other end of the line.

"Uh, yeah. Sorry. I really don't want the personal details, but I kind of need them," I said. "Can you give them to me as gently as possible?"

Before she could speak, I heard my stepfather's voice near her as he evidently passed through the room. We both burst into giggles at the comic relief.

"I'm doing my breastfeeding interview now, sweetheart," she told him. I could hear her trying to shoo him away.

"Anything I should be worried about, Jen?" he called to me and laughed.

"Just the loss of my appetite," I groaned.

"And the loss of my dignity," my mom added.

"Oh, well," said my stepfather, and left the room. My mom dove in.

When she was pregnant with me, she explained, she thought she would probably breastfeed me after I was born. She was the first of her friends to give birth, and breastfeeding and La Leche League had already started to become a topic of conversation among young wannabe parents in Manhattan. A few years before I was born, her sister (my aunt) had nursed my cousin for a period of time. And my grandmother had breastfed both my mom and aunt from birth, although apparently for too brief a time for her to advise my mom on the matter. The short story was: When my mother was expecting, no one told her about the health advantages of breastfeeding. Even her obstetrician didn't raise the subject other than to ask about her feeding preference. "But nursing seemed like such a nice thing to do," she said wistfully.

My father, on the other hand, was focused on what kind of formula I should be fed. He had suffered from serious allergies as a child (he had not been breastfed, I should note), and his sister's firstborn had not reacted well to cow's milk formula. The pediatrician switched the infant to a new soy formula, and my cousin seemed to improve after the change. My father thus decided I, too, should be put on soy formula to keep adverse reactions at bay. My mother still had longings, though.

"I remember telling your father, 'Well, I thought I would breastfeed for a while,'" she recalled. "But I think he thought it was kind of a weird suggestion." Save for one couple, the two had no Manhattan friends who were nursing their children, and my father was armed with a whole list of reasons why breastfeeding would be impractical: they'd be tied down and wouldn't be able to go out in the evenings or away on trips, and I would have to be given a bottle, anyway, whenever they left me with a babysitter. "Socially, he felt [breastfeeding] was going to be very restrictive," my mom sighed.

There wasn't a long discussion about the matter. It was a different world then, she explained, and in those years, she was fairly deferential to her husband's wishes. Graduating high school in 1971 and married less than four years later, my mother was wedged between 1960s suburban repression and the freewheeling post-Woodstock generation. Since she was never much for free love and drugs, she clung to the former. "Most of the men I knew in those days still gave their wives allowances!" she admitted. (The fearless woman I knew, who had single-handedly raised me and my brother and saved us from bankruptcy and near-homelessness, wouldn't emerge for more than a decade later.)

So my mother didn't fight my father on the breastfeeding decision, but she didn't completely buy his explanation, either. "I do remember thinking at the time that it was also a sexual issue," she offered.

"Um, did you ask him that?" I asked.

She laughed. "He never said, 'I don't want you to breastfeed *because they're for me*,' but I knew that was one of the reasons."

Then she ventured further, explaining that when she was pregnant again with Noah, and she and my father had rehashed the same conversation and decided again to formula-feed, her new obstetrician didn't really buy my father's "social" excuse for not breastfeeding. The doctor was an Orthodox Jew with a large family, and all his children had been breastfed. He cleverly warned my mom not to engage in any "activities" during her pregnancy that might inadvertently trigger labor. (When breasts are stimulated in a lactating woman, the hormone oxytocin triggers the milk-ejection reflex, but when the breasts are stimulated in a *pregnant* woman, the release of oxytocin can trigger contractions.) My mom tried to elaborate, but I got it: my father had been a breast man.

Later, when I phoned my sixty-five-year-old father in Florida to ask him about this, I was anticipating a pretty awkward conversation: *Hey Dad! Haven't spoken to you in nearly three years or for most of my adolescent or adult life. Oh, by the way, did you used to enjoy sucking Mom's boobs when you guys were married?* But as it turns out, he didn't recall there ever having been a conversation about breastfeeding. "Everyone bottle-fed their kids back then, Jen. The only women I knew who breastfed were radicals," he said, referring to his hippie friends from his Woodstock days. What's more, he had the misperception that breast milk, like cow's milk, was a form of dairy. In order to avoid my inheriting his milk allergies, he said, the only option would have been soy formula. Not surprisingly, there was no recollection of nixing breastfeeding because of any erotic attachment to my mother's knockers. After all, what father would admit to this? I have to give my mom some serious credit, too: How many mothers (other than my own, evidently) would concede that sex had clouded her decision as to how to nurture her children?

Yet the truth is that in the United States, more so than any other place on earth, there is an exceptional bias lurking beneath the debate of breast versus bottle, and it affects what rights mothers have in the workplace, whether it's "acceptable" to breastfeed in public, and how long it's "appropriate" to nurse a child. And that is, on some gut level, Americans believe that the primary function of breasts is for sex rather than for feeding babies. In America, to some degree or another, we are all "breast men," and I can't say I'm exempt from that category. After all, the first time I saw someone use a breast to feed a child was after my cousin had given birth to her first daughter; I was already in my *twenties*.

At the tender age of six, however, I was fully entrenched in the American breast bias: playing with my naked and buxom Barbies, taking full note of my mom's cleavage as she headed out for the evening in a low-cut top, and watching way more 1980s "jiggle TV" than I should have. By the time I was twelve, I was reading teen magazines that showed me how to get "bikini ready," and I had mastered my best Victoria's Secret catalog pose. And at twenty, the only thing that separated me from millions of images of implant-enhanced pornographic nudity was the click of a mouse.

My mother's childhood memories are a lot tamer, but growing up in the era of Jayne Mansfield and Marilyn Monroe, the cultural messages she absorbed were no less titillating (which, by the way, comes from the Latin *titillare*, "to tickle." *Teat*, interestingly, is of later Germanic origin and the slang *tits* surfaced only in the 1920s). Both her father and her best friend Marilyn's father (yes, her little friend was of course named after Marilyn Monroe) had collected *Playboy* magazines from the very first issue, and the prepubescent ten-year-old girls enthusiastically scoured piles of issues when their parents weren't around.

"Every little girl I knew wanted to grow up and be a Playboy Bunny," my mom told me. It had been a glamorous choice in a time when girls' career options were still mostly restricted to teacher, secretary, or another exciting alternative: "airline stewardess." But, she said, even those who didn't make the Playboy Bunny cut still seemed to be auditioning for the role of Marilyn, assisted by concentrically stitched bras and body-hugging fashions. At her parents' glittering cocktail parties, women poured themselves into skin-tight strapless fishtail gowns that left little to the imagination. And it wasn't solely actresses on TV who were blonde and busty, she recalled. "Even when I was in grammar school, my teachers wore tight sweaters with waist-cinching belts, and pencil skirts and high heels. In retrospect, that era was a very sexualized time."

My mom added *in retrospect* because she had only been a young, unknowing girl in those years but also because she now views the Marilyn era in the context of the radically altered female silhouette that followed it: first, the flat-chested Twiggy phenomenon of the late 1960s, followed by the braless abandon of the Woodstock-era counterculture. That these looks accompanied the second wave of American feminism is no coincidence; as feminists and female hippies tried to reclaim breasts as their own, the debate was sparked about what breasts were really *for*. It's no irony that women began to "rediscover" breastfeeding in the early 1970s, while the first sexual harassment case was brought before a US district court in 1976.

But just as in the 1920s—in the wake of the women's suffrage movement, when women bound their breasts and the boyish flapper look came into vogue—the reprieve from breast obsession was only temporary. The mid-1930s saw the introduction of the padded bra and actress Jean Harlow routinely icing her nipples before filming a scene. And the 1980s and '90s saw implants of silicone breast enhancements skyrocket. In fact, the augmentation infatuation shows no sign of a slowdown. Breast implantation rates climbed 40 percent in the last decade, and the procedure is now the most prevalent cosmetic surgery in the United States, with nearly three hundred thousand operations performed last year alone.

That breasts equal sex is something most Americans take for granted. So you might be surprised to hear that the breast is *not* a sexual organ; that is to say, it is not a part of the anatomy directly involved in reproduction, such as sperm or eggs. Scientifically speaking, the breast isn't even considered a secondary sexual organ like the penis or the vagina, which aid in the transport of sperm and eggs, respectively. Instead, the mammary glands are classified as a *secondary sex characteristic*, the biological purpose of which is to differentiate males from females and to signal to a potential reproductive partner that an age of sexual maturity has been reached. Visible secondary sex characteristics in humans do include enlarged breasts in females but also encompass facial hair, a deeper voice, and the Adam's apple in males, and the appearance of pubic hair for both genders. So why, in America, did it first become sexy for a woman to prop up her breasts like twin torpedoes (à la Marilyn, in the 1950s) and, later, like two overinflated balloons (à la Kim Kardashian)? Why hasn't there been an epidemic of Adam's apple augmentations? And why don't we use visible tufts of pubic hair to sell cars and beer?

One could argue that unlike pubic hair, which has no nerve endings, breasts are sexy because they are responsive to touch and can result in feelings of arousal. Yes, when a baby suckles at its mother's breast, oxytocin triggers milk letdown and generates intense feelings of love between mother and baby. And the hormone is released during orgasm, too. But oxytocin is an expansive hormone that reaches every organ and is present during other enjoyable activities, such as eating and giving someone a hug or friendly handshake. Oxytocin is even now being studied for its important role in muscle regeneration and is thought to be a crucial factor in the biology of autism.

So is the pleasure ascribed to nipple stimulation during foreplay real, or is it something we've learned from our breast-obsessed culture? Anthropologist Katherine Dettwyler believes it's the latter and, in her writings, has pointed out a number of activities our culture has learned to associate with sexual arousal that are also not focused on the sexual organs themselves, including earlobe nibbling and bondage. "Of course, when the baby suckles [at the breast], messages are sent to the brain to release oxytocin, which gives a warm sort of overall feeling of love and affection," added the professor, who I knew now just as "Kathy" when I tracked her down yet again. "So it's perhaps easier for a person to learn to associate pleasure with breast stimulation than, say, elbow stimulation."

One definitive analysis of human breast tissue, though, found no evidence that breasts are particularly sensitive. Other research Dettwyler cites has shown breasts to be insensitive overall to pain, pressure, and changes in temperature. This, despite a recent study from the University of California, Davis, that found nearly *half* of new mothers experience problems with breastfeeding pain in the weeks after birth. But it's important to know that while some temporary discomfort during the engorgement stage is normal, ongoing agony isn't, whether the source of pain is a breast infection, a poor latch due to an undiagnosed case of infant tongue-tie, or more commonly, the result of improper positioning. (I didn't realize that improper positioning was at the root of my excruciating pain until after a third and thorough session with a very persistent lactation consultant.) That breastfeeding pain is pervasive in our culture speaks volumes to the lack of early breastfeeding support that mothers so desperately need.

Now that I know that nursing isn't supposed to hurt and, in fact, usually feels pretty nice or is barely noticeable at all, Dettwyler's explanation of mammary toughness makes sense, especially considering what my own breasts have endured throughout years of breastfeeding: nursing outside during a Chicago winter, not to mention hour-plus suckling sessions when my girls were teething and needed endless comfort. And as a toddler, Mika thought it was hilarious to vault into a headstand with my nipple still in her mouth.

Recent studies, though, may add some validity to the breast-as-erogenous-zone argument. Using functional magnetic resonance imaging (fMRI), researchers found that touching a woman's nipples lit up the same part of her brain as touching her genitals. The finding was surprising, said the study's lead author Barry Komisaruk, a neuroscientist and distinguished professor of psychology at Rutgers University, since the nipple had actually been designated as the control in the study. He had expected stimulation in that area to light up only the corresponding chest area on the body-part "map" of the brain's sensory cortex known as the homunculus ("little person"). Still, that study looked at the responses of just eleven women, and at the time, Komisaruk emphasized that the findings didn't necessarily mean that nipples were directly linked with sexual arousal. Because nipple stimulation is also nature's way of triggering uterine contractions to help prevent postpartum hemorrhage and to efficiently shrink the uterus back to pre-baby size after birth, he hypothesized that the signal may have been pointing to the uterus, rather than signaling some other independently experienced pleasure.

But when I called Komisaruk last July to hear more about that 2011 study, he excitedly told me that, just two days before, he and his team had completed a follow-up study, this time using twelve *men* as the subjects. And once again, nipple stimulation made the genital region of the subjects' brains "light up." Only this time, with obviously no uteruses to point to for explanation, there are stronger implications for his research. "This could be a basis for why women and many men claim that nipple stimulation is erotic," contended Komisaruk. What's more, he added, the signals were crossed, with the left and right nipples each activating their opposite sides of the genital sensory cortex, as is the case for all sensory systems in the human body (think of how lefties are "right-brained" and vice versa). This, he said, is further biological evidence that the nipple-genital connection is a direct neural pathway.

But before you think *Aha! Maybe breasts are a sexual organ after all*, here's the tricky part: From an evolutionary standpoint, Komisaruk theorized that the purpose of the "erotic" nipple sensation was likely not to enhance sex but to help perpetuate *breastfeeding*. Just as genital gratification ensured that we would continue to reproduce, breastfeeding enjoyment ensured that our babies would continue to be fed. (This "wiring" in men could be vestigial, he said, although I would add that male lactation, though rare, has been observed in many species, including humans.) "Maybe that's an iconoclastic idea that nursing shouldn't be erotically pleasurable," he said. "But what's pleasurable is propagated and maintained in the species. I mean, if it were aversive, then maybe women wouldn't want to nurse."

So does this mean that breasts are inherently erotic? Or did we in the Western world just take a naturally pleasurable experience and exploit it to the extreme? Perhaps a better gauge would be to compare our views to the rest of the world's. In 1951, Yale University anthropologists Clellan Ford and Frank Beach did just that, conducting a sweeping survey of the sexual habits of 190 different cultures from the Arctic Circle to New Zealand, along with comparisons to different animal species including our closest animal relatives, the primates. Their resulting book, *Patterns of Sexual Behavior*, is still the definitive work on the subject, and their findings, even today, are eye-opening. Out of 190 cultures, a mere *thirteen* (other than our own) commonly employed breast touching either before or during intercourse. And of the same

190, only thirteen indicated the size and shape of a woman's breasts as important to her sexual attractiveness. (Only three societies considered breasts erotic *and* integrated them into foreplay.) Other cultures seemed to show as much preference for things like fleshy calves, a particular mouth shape, or wide hips.

"Thinking of breasts sexually is a recent phenomenon," noted Kathy Dettwyler. Back in the 1980s when she conducted research in the west African country of Mali, people either laughed or looked horrified when they heard that American sexual foreplay often involved mouth-to-breast contact. ("You mean men act like babies?" they exclaimed.) She reminded me that present-day hunting and gathering societies may be our best glimpse at how humans viewed the female form for thousands of years. In these cultures, breasts are regarded for the function they were designed to meet: feeding babies. "We can reasonably assume that [early man] didn't have any of that layer of weird cultural beliefs about breasts being sex objects," Dettwyler said.

A lot has changed since prehistory, though, and even since Ford and Beach conducted their survey in 1951. As America exported Marilyn Monroe and Hollywood to the rest of the world (along with consumerism, industrial agriculture, and fast food), our notion of breasts as sex organs proved especially pervasive. Breast implants are now the second most popular plastic surgery worldwide, and the prevalence of the practice continues to rise dramatically, with countries like Brazil and even austerity-stricken Greece now topping the list for most surgeries. Yet as Brazil, the United States, and other countries conduct national public awareness campaigns in the effort to normalize breastfeeding, it seems that very few people are willing to acknowledge that an implant/infant-feeding paradox exists.

Instead, plastic surgeons reassure women that they'll still be able to nurse their babies provided their implant surgery is done correctly—this, despite evidence from a few small studies that women who have had periareolar breast incisions (one of the most common implant incisions) are five times more likely to suffer lactation insufficiency. Additionally, breast augmentation overall is associated with a 40 percent decrease in the likelihood of exclusive breastfeeding among those women who are even able to breastfeed after surgery. (Despite the ubiquity of implants, I could find no extensive study on this issue, which shows you how truly backward our priorities are.) Importantly, as many as one in five women with implants chooses not to breastfeed at all because of the ongoing controversy around the health impacts of silicone and the concern that implant materials could cause their babies harm.

How did it come to this? Dettwyler has no problem being blunt: Breast augmentation surgery, or "female mammary mutilation," as she labels it, is no different than the female foot binding in China that persisted for a millennium beginning in the tenth century. To achieve a woman's desirable "lotus foot" length of four inches, a little girl's toes would be broken and her feet progressively bound, stunting their growth and crippling her for life. "The fascination with women's breasts is something [Western countries] learned, just like the Chinese men learned to like little bound feet," Dettwyler asserted. In both cases, a healthy organ tasked with an essential function for life (for the feet, walking; for the breasts, nursing) is surgically disfigured to attract males or make females feel more alluring. And in both circumstances, the resulting effects on health can be debilitating and can include scarring, infection, pain, and (in the case of breast augmentation) possibly no life-giving breast milk for a child. As it happens, there's a term for a sexual desire so obsessive that gratification is fixated on a singular part of the body at the exclusion and expense of all others: a fetish.

MY HUSBAND, NOT SURPRISINGLY, WAS PRETTY KEEN ON READING this chapter about breasts as sexual organs and the object of fetishes. But it was here that Matthew stopped me cold. It was one thing, he said, to try to use the lens of history to point out just how truly crazy is our cultural practice of putting a woman under general anesthesia to slice her open and stick plastic pillows in her breasts, all in the name of turning someone on. But was it fair to demonize his admiration for my female form in its natural state? Was it realistic to think that millions of googly-eyed men were suddenly going to stop finding curves entrancing? After all, I had managed to successfully nurse our two girls without declaring my breasts off-limits to him. Why couldn't we have it both ways—give the kids what they need and save a little something on the side for our partners?

Evidently, I'm not the only breastfeeding researcher whose spouse feels this way. In her book, Dettwyler penned an acknowledgment to her husband, "who has a hard time accepting that breasts may not naturally be erotic, but who is, at least, willing to consider the notion." Yet here's the crux of the problem: in a culture where both men and women automatically think *sex* when they see a naked breast, it is a real challenge for a mother to whip out one of those sexually loaded things every time she needs to feed her kid.

In fact, breastfeeding in public remains one of the toughest obstacles a nursing mom faces. In his zeal to convince me of his side of the argument, Matthew had conveniently forgotten that breastfeeding in front of others was something we fought about constantly after Izzy was born. Did he not recall giving me "the glance" anytime our friends or, especially, his brother came over (the glance indicating that I was to quietly disappear into the other room to breastfeed)? Did he not recall tossing a sweatshirt over me like a possessive lover, horrified that a nipple might suddenly be exposed, virtually anywhere I tried to nurse Izzy? (He admitted that the sweatshirt tossing and my annoyed response of "Stop it!" probably attracted more attention than a nip slip would have.) "Well, I didn't want weird guys checking out your breasts," he said, adding that I wasn't as good at nursing inconspicuously in public back then.

That's true. In those early days, I had no clue what I was doing and spent most of my time nursing at home, fully exposed with Izzy propped up on two Boppy pillows. When I was out and about, there was a fair amount of fumbling before I could get a good latch. Nowadays, I could be on a float in a parade and discreetly feed Mika by simply nudging my top up a bit from the bottom in such a way that it looks as though I'm merely carrying her. But it took me years to develop this sleight of hand, and frankly, the onus should not be on the mother to become a professional-level public breastfeeder.

The unfortunate truth is that in a breast-obsessed culture where both men and women *are* staring, not every mom is willing to fight through the glares, the sweatshirt-tossing, or the humiliation of being kicked out of a restaurant or off an airplane simply for feeding a child who is hungry. (Nor should she be obliged to sport one of those giant floral bibs. My kids hated nursing with their heads shrouded.) And yet, despite the fact that breastfeeding in *any* public or private location is currently legal in forty-nine states (ahem, Idaho), I know breastfeeding women still get kicked out of places every week in the United States because I get the Google Alerts. Many women, including me not too long ago, don't feel comfortable openly nursing even at home among friends and family. One mom Matthew and I know got so fed up being locked away in her bedroom with her newborn that she decided to pump and feed her baby breast milk exclusively by bottle.

I felt bad dredging up the past with Matthew because we were having this "remember when" conversation on a relaxing Saturday morning when, miraculously, the kids weren't fighting, but also because after seeing me nurse for so many years, he had agreed that the only way to make breastfeeding more "normal" was to be unashamed of doing it openly. (This was what To-wen Tseng had insisted as she described the problem with the secluded public breastfeeding rooms in Taiwan.) But I couldn't help bringing up another issue we had so often locked horns over in those early days: How long it was "appropriate" to nurse Izzy.

I hadn't made the connection before, but Matthew's qualms about breastfeeding a child beyond toddlerhood were undoubtedly tied to our cultural belief that breasts are for men. An infant's needs are clear: he needs to be fed, and comforted when distressed. But an older child who wants to breastfeed—one who can both verbally and physically express not only need but *want* of her mother's breasts, just as a mate can—is off-putting in a world where breasts are seen as sexual.

Matthew hadn't been conscious of that bias. He had just felt it wasn't "normal" to nurse Izzy past the age of two, although he couldn't verbalize why. But others have no problem expressing their squeamishness. Some have even compared nursing an older child to a sexual act. "[*Time* magazine] got attention because it put a topless chick, Jamie Lynn Grumet, getting her breast . . . sucked by a far-too-old boy," wrote one conservative commentator. "At this rate, *Time* is going to have to put a man (or woman) getting oral sex on the cover."

Extended breastfeeding mothers have even had to fend off charges of sexual abuse, prompting La Leche League to publish an in-depth article addressing mothers' fears about having their nursing toddlers taken away. Thankfully, this has rarely happened as awareness of the prevalence of extended breastfeeding has grown, although God help the mother who may admit to the "pleasure" of nursing revealed in that recent nipple-genital pathway study. In our American culture, such a confession would be perceived as weird and sexual and would no doubt impede any campaign for breastfeeding normalcy.

Yet in America, Matthew rightly insisted, we don't just have strange hang-ups about breasts; we have totally messed up views about sex in general, and that's where our real problems lie. He reminded me that the statue of Lady Justice in Washington, DC, didn't even depict breastfeeding, but that didn't stop then–Attorney General John Ashcroft when, in 2002, he reportedly ordered her covered up with a giant blue drape so that he wouldn't be photographed speaking in front of an exposed breast. And modern online pornography, with its endless shocking images, doesn't just fetishize breasts, Matthew pointed out; it fetishizes the normal biological function of sex itself. Contrast this with the hippie communes of the late 1960s and early 1970s, where sex was unencumbered and natural and women moved about with their babies slung on a hip, breastfeeding openly as in tribal cultures where people live in very close quarters and sex is not something to be hidden away.

In such cultures, a woman's breasts are just there, whether to feed her babies or as an ordinary part of her naked body to be enjoyed during sex. A woman in such a culture transitions instinctively between the two functions, and no one questions the appropriateness of her feelings in either instance. More important, in both situations, her breasts are inarguably her own, with no man, woman, or public outcry dictating when she may use them, reveal them, or tuck them away.

IT'S SAFE TO SAY THAT IN FRANCE NO ONE WOULD EVER TELL A woman to cover up her breasts, nor would they direct the cloaking of a naked female statue. The national symbol of France, Marianne, is often depicted bare-breasted and triumphant, and as anyone who has ever seen a French film (or a French commercial, or even photos taken at a topless beach in France) can testify, the French are far cooler about nudity and sex than are their American counterparts. In fact, when I contacted Rachel Lamb, a lactation consultant based in Paris, one of the first things she told me was that even at her local swimming pool, topless sunbathing was common. "Children and men don't seem to bat an eyelid," she said.

Indeed, the French are blasé about naked breasts. So it was quite a surprise to discover that France has one of the lowest breastfeeding rates in the Western world, far below that of even the United States. Whereas 40 percent of American babies are exclusively breastfed at the age of three months, a scant 10 percent of French three-month-olds are. Even if you factor in mixed feeding (the practice of both breastfeeding and giving formula), just 23 percent of French moms are nursing their babies at six months versus 49 percent of their American counterparts. (You can forget about breastfeeding French toddlers. A practically nonexistent 9 percent of *bébés* are nursing at the one-year mark.) And here's the real shocker: of women worldwide, French women have some of the most negative views about public breastfeeding, with 41 percent of those recently polled labeling it "embarrassing," compared with 18 percent of American women who would shrink at the sight.

How could this be? A mom who had no problem whipping off her top at the public pool to reveal her breasts in front of someone else's kids is mortified at the sight of another woman's breasts being used to feed her own child? I thought then about the time I went to see the Charlotte Rampling thriller *Swimming Pool* on a second date, my cheeks burning crimson through the darkness, and I just didn't get the hypocrisy: We Americans are prudish about everything. Why are the French alternately brazen and grossed out about the same body part?

Rachel Lamb, who grew up in Scotland but moved to France thirteen years ago after the birth of her first child, had an interesting insider-yet-outsider perspective on the French paradox. The French are squeamish about breastfeeding, she said, because while they don't view breasts "in a Victoria's Secret way" (you would never see a pair of overinflated mammaries making their way down the streets of Paris like I do here every day in Los Angeles), culturally breasts are seen as sexual objects nonetheless.

Ameena Gorton, another expat mom living in France who writes the blog *Mummy in Provence*, pointed to the ubiquity of pricey lingerie shops in France (and, oddly, the utter lack of nursing bras). She chose to breastfeed her daughter for an unheard of twenty-eight months and along the way endured a litany of "advice," including "The only reason you breastfeed is for selfish reasons," and "It's abnormal to be still breastfeeding a baby of her age. Give her a bottle like normal babies." (Those comments were both from her French doctor when her daughter was seven months old.)

Speaking with Lamb via Skype while she was on holiday in Scotland, I learned that for the French woman, getting bedroom-ready again after birth is nearly a full-time job. And indeed, despite the fact that French mothers receive sixteen weeks of fully paid maternity leave, a recent study found that nearly half of them had given up breastfeeding within three weeks. "There is pressure for women to return to their sexual prowess and for the 'couple' to enjoy their sex life not long after baby arrives," Lamb explained and then went on to tell me that, working as a lactation consultant in the hospital's *maternité*, she had even once accidentally walked in on a couple doing the deed only one day after their baby's birth. (Oh, the horror!)

Lamb is also a leader for La Leche League Paris and has heard her share of shockers from the new mothers in the group. One breastfeeding mom was told by her mother-in-law that it was her duty to keep her husband in the bedroom and that if she focused too much on the baby and her husband strayed, it would be her fault. This attitude is common in France, Lamb maintained, adding that the pressure was customary not just from nosy in-laws but also, as Gorton revealed, from doctors. In the hospital directly following the birth of a baby, at a time when most new moms can't even hear the word *sex* without shuddering, French mothers are asked to choose their method of birth control (primarily the pill, which can be harmful to milk supply) and are given their prescription before they head home.

Then there's the singular French tradition of *la rééducation périnéale*, which a woman also receives a prescription for immediately postpartum. The form of physical therapy, which has been provided gratis by the French government since 1985, employs a physiotherapist and an electronic dildo to retrain the pelvic floor muscles, which are weakened by pregnancy and childbirth. Basically, it's biofeedback for the vagina, and while the purported reason is to reduce incontinence and pelvic pain in new mothers (there are studies that support this), Lamb thinks it's pretty obvious who's really benefiting from all the muscle tightening. "I can't understand it, and I personally didn't do it," she sighed.

But many women, including a friend of mine here in the United States who paid to have the therapy, attest that it has real benefits. Personally, if the US government wanted to foot the bill to ensure that I will never again have to cross my legs when I sneeze, I probably wouldn't balk. But when you place *la rééducation* in the context of the utter lack of breastfeeding support for new moms in France (French doctors receive one *optional* hour of breastfeeding training in medical school; lactation consultants are scarce), it's easy to come away convinced that it smacks of sexism. Yet it's positively fascinating to me that for many women in France, *la rééducation* (along with the notion that a new mother should return to an intimate relationship with her husband as quickly as possible post-baby) isn't sexism; it's *freedom*.

That's because birth control, medicalized birth, and baby formula are all things that have liberated women in the twentieth century and freed them from becoming slaves to their biology, say French feminists like the philosopher Elisabeth Badinter, author of the book *The Conflict: How Overzealous Motherhood Undermines the Status of Women*. Her thin tome elaborates her point, but the subtitle of the work pretty much says it all. In *The Conflict*, she argues that the "new" naturalistic brand of motherhood is dangerous and threatens to turn a generation of empowered working women into on-demand-breastfeeding, natural-childbirth-bearing, and (why not throw it in there?) cloth-diaper-washing drudges. She points to breastfeeding, in particular, as a misogynistic practice liable to send women back to the Dark Ages, confining them at home with "despotic, gluttonous babies who devour their mothers."

It would seem that in the Badinter world, the choice between woman and mother is either-or, and in fact, the book's original title in France was *Le conflit: La femme et la mère* (the woman and the mother). Yet Badinter seems willing to ignore the fact that there is a broad middle ground of intelligent working women who don't want to give up the bonding and health advantages that millions of years of breastfeeding evolution have brought to children and mothers. And she doesn't take into account that there are countless intelligent (often working) women based at home, just like me, who treasure their time with their little ones and would never describe their situation as shackled. If I could convey a single image of the truly liberated modern woman to Badinter, it would be that of Victoria Donda Pérez, a member of Argentina's legislature, who recently tweeted a photo of herself openly breastfeeding her eight-month-old daughter during a parliamentary session. Perhaps American mothers, especially, wouldn't feel thwarted in their careers by the constraints of breastfeeding if nursing at work, maternity/paternity leave, and universally provided lactation rooms and pumping breaks became the indisputable norm.

Yet Badinter's "feministic" thinking about women and breastfeeding—that babies are going to tie them to the kitchen sink—is something that persists, said Lamb. Indeed, the word *fusionnel*, the French version of *attachment*, she said, has become a sort of swear word in France, and new moms often receive advice that they shouldn't let their babies manipulate them with their cries. "Your baby isn't trying to *control* you; your baby is trying to *communicate* with you!" Lamb insisted.

But she believes there's another swear word making its way down the pike, and this one may be more universal: sacrifice. Yes, there are the women who believe they're giving up their womanhood by becoming a breastfeeding mom, but there is also a generation of both men and women raised in the self-serving yuppie culture of the 1980s who believe they're giving up everything by becoming parents. I've witnessed this cultural shift among my own friends who have delayed having children until their midthirties. Never mind the fact that first-time mothers over the age of thirty-five encounter more problems with milk insufficiency. Many of these moms now find nearly every aspect of parenting, even apart from breastfeeding (soothing a crying baby at night, cooking dinner, looking up from their iPhone to talk to their child), to be too demanding.

The question is, does France's renunciation of breastfeeding eliminate the burden of "sacrifice" in that one area of parenting? Or does the "reeducation" of a woman's vagina, along with a boudoir brimming with fancy lingerie, simply shift the recipient of the breast from the baby to the man?

My mother is definitely not French, but she made the choice in America in 1979 not to breastfeed my brother and me for largely the same reasons that many French women would stand by today. She succumbed to the pressure to return to life as usual with her husband and deferred to his reluctance to be "tied down" to their children. Today, she freely expresses her regret about those decisions and claims she is only lucky that she and her two children are as bonded as they are. "Probably a happy byproduct of having been a single mother and having you both all to myself," she offered.

"But emotionally, health-wise, psychologically, and otherwise, I still wonder what we all missed out on because of my decision," said my mom. "Nursing may have seemed restricting to my husband, but for me, choosing not to breastfeed was never a matter of freedom—sexual or otherwise. It was just ignorance and, I suppose, the times. For me, freedom would have been to make the decision my body and my heart were telling me to make, with my partner and the world supporting me all the way."

SO, JUST HOW DID THE BREAST OBSESSIONS IN FRANCE AND AMERica spin so far away from evolutionary origins, albeit each in its own completely bizarre way? Certainly, women's breasts have moved in and out of focus throughout the course of history. Among the goddess-worshipping ancient Minoans, women wore bell-shaped dresses that were completely open in front, leaving both breasts proudly exposed. However, Christians in the Middle Ages believed that all flesh was sinful; their women were cloaked from floor to throat.

Yet there are only two notable periods in the history of the world in which the breasts have been truly fetishized: modern-day America, the engine behind the now globally pervasive billions-of-dollars-a-year drive to surgically embed plastic sacs in women's mammaries; and eighteenth-century (and to a lesser extent, early modern) France, which spawned a craze of Marie Antoinette–style plunging bodices that practically assured a teasing nip slip in lascivious company. Between the two periods of breast fetish, there's a correlation that now seems obvious: these exceptional instances in the history of humankind were times in which, on a massive scale, breasts were not required to perform their primary biological function of feeding babies.

Not so surprisingly, it was only after the age of formula became entrenched in 1950s America that Marilyn and her epic proportions rose to prominence. Did men ogle—first rouged nipples, then later, double Ds—out of some deep-seated Freudian longing for the fulfillment they never received at their mother's breast? Or was the explanation so much simpler: That *because* breasts were no longer a visible fact of life—*because* they were no longer openly feeding the young and instead were hidden from view—they evolved into a corrupted new form? Many a fetish has been created as a result of a body part becoming concealed (think *feet*).

But perhaps we should be talking about what actually enabled this shift in priorities: wealth. After all, it was not only the upper classes in France, but since antiquity, members of the aristocracy in other cultures, too, who have entertained the luxury of ascribing their breasts to purposes more erotic than feeding. And it was the parents in my mother's upwardly mobile Manhattan social circle who could afford to pack their closets with cases of formula and leave the kids at home so they could go off to enjoy the world. The underprivileged never had the choice to avoid breastfeeding.

For the first time in history, that scenario has flip-flopped.

nine

Big Brother and the Breast

For goodness, growing to a pleurisy, dies in
his own too-much.
—WILLIAM SHAKESPEARE

Los Angeles is a city of unfathomable wealth and unimaginable poverty. And perhaps more so than any other place in America, the line between the haves and the have-nots is not only clearly demarcated, it can shift within a matter of blocks. Ten-million-dollar estates in Hancock Park jut up against apartments teeming with the largest Korean population outside of Seoul. Impeccable midcentury spreads perched in the Pacific Palisades loom over homeless camps on the beaches below. Celebrities and privileged parents shuttle their kids in Mercedes and BMWs to walled-off private schools just around the corner from public schools in the Los Angeles Unified School District, one of the most segregated and underperforming school districts in the country. And no matter where you live, tireless Mexican immigrants hold Angelenos' lives together with their sweat and care: mowing their lawns, building their houses, cooking their food, and caring for their children.

When the blazing California sun illuminates the city and the palm trees, it's easy to misread LA's underlying inequity as its edgy aesthetic. But on one overcast August morning, as I drove through the iconic Westlake neighborhood just west of Downtown and scanned the Payday Advance signs dotting the landscape between the faded storefronts and the shopping carts of the homeless, the scene looked like something out of a third world country.

Don't get me wrong. This is a neighborhood I love. As a young couple and then as young parents who lived paycheck to paycheck for most of the decade we've called Los Angeles home, Matthew and I have long cherished the delicious and affordable food lovingly doled out by the area's largely Mexican and Central American community. But as I turned off Alvarado onto Eighth Street searching for the address of my meeting that morning, I realized that just because I enjoyed *pupusas* didn't mean I understood a single real truth about the lives of the people who lived in the area. Having lived hand-to-mouth until very recently in a more privileged part of town, I had always considered myself a have-not, but I was about to get a very abrupt awakening.

First, I saw the news trucks. And then, as I approached the building that was my destination, I spied the dark water stain creeping up the entire first floor of the building's brick facade. The sign stacked among the others in Spanish and Korean spelled out my destination, WIC, in bright blue-and-white lettering, with an arrow pointing me to the back of the building. I parked, grabbed my notepad, and darted across the street, not sure what I would find.

I had come that morning for a tour of the Eighth Street WIC office, a meeting that had been granted with a twenty-minute time limit and my assurances that I would arrive without tape recorder or camera and would not interact with participants. I understood the need for discretion. The US government's Special Supplemental Nutrition Program for Women, Infants, and Children, more commonly known as WIC, is a federal assistance program under the Food and Nutrition Service of the US Department of Agriculture (USDA) that provides nutrition and health assistance to low-income pregnant women, new mothers, infants, and children under the age of five. Enrollees must earn no more than 185 percent of the poverty level, currently just under $45,000 for a family of four, although some higher-earning participants may automatically qualify if they're enrolled in Medicaid or other public assistance programs.

As a mother so protective of her children's privacy that I will not post identifiable pictures of them on Facebook, I could imagine that most WIC enrollees wouldn't be too keen about details of their children's assistance becoming public. But there were other things worth shielding from journalistic scrutiny, I had discovered, and they had to do with WIC's recently ramped up breastfeeding promotion program. Faced with the growing epidemic of cancer, obesity, and other chronic diseases, the US government has issued aggressive calls to action for our country to increase breastfeeding rates in the name of public health. WIC's breastfeeding promotion has been a much-touted part of that effort, offering no-cost lactation support, along with the incentive of larger food packages to mothers who continue breastfeeding. The program has been far-reaching, since all by itself WIC serves an astonishing 53 percent of US infants.

There is, however, a glaring paradox that cannot be ignored. Since WIC became permanent in 1975, the program has also provided free infant formula. WIC is now the largest supplier of infant formula in the United States, purchasing anywhere from 57 to 68 percent of all formula sold in the country every year. In other words, the US government is the formula companies' biggest customer.

This would seem to fly in the face of simple common sense. If you're trying to encourage someone to do something (especially something like breastfeeding which, in the beginning, can easily take six weeks to get the hang of), why would you offer, up front, the very thing you advise to avoid? Little did I know that my journey to answer that seemingly straightforward question would not only send me combing through the bureaucratic tangles of the WIC program for the better part of this book but, ultimately, to the government "absorption" of an ocean of milk surplus most of us had never heard about.

In the event that my gut assessment of the WIC breastfeeding/free-formula paradox was an oversimplification, I contacted the USDA for feedback. No one was available to speak with me. Then I phoned the CDC and the US Department of Health and Human Services. They refused my requests and directed me back to the USDA. I moved on to the California Department of Public Health (CDPH), which administers the largest WIC program in the United States. (The federal government provides the funds, but the states individually manage each program.) Interview declined. Finally, I contacted CDPH's breastfeeding coordinator, who manages breastfeeding education and support services for the hundreds of local WIC sites around the state of California. No response. A lower-level director at one local WIC agency, the largest in the county, could only tell me, "WIC is being really funny these days about what kind of information we're putting out there."

Dozens of phone calls later, I managed to score an interview with Danielle Arce, a lactation educator and the supervisor of the Eighth Street WIC office, one of the busiest WIC locations in Los Angeles. I was hoping to see a good deal during the twenty-minute visit I had been allotted. Only now, as I followed the news trucks to the back parking lot of the building, it looked like the meeting wasn't going to happen at all. There had been a flood, I was told at the front door. A pipe in an upstairs office had burst in the middle of the night, and staff and cleaning crews had been there since the wee hours, trying to mitigate the damage.

The entire office on the ground floor had been cleared out, save for one desk set up like a triage station just inside the propped-open front doors. Blowers had been placed strategically across the bare linoleum floor, and men were wheeling dollies in and out. Scanning the scene, I couldn't help inwardly scowling; I knew I'd be heading home shortly to type up a few lines of notes if anything. There would be zero chance of jumping through the same hoops again for a visit to a different WIC site. Then I quickly checked myself. *Forget about the interview*, I told myself. A stream of hungry mothers and children would soon be at the door, looking for their grocery and formula vouchers or breastfeeding assistance. Everyone would be turned away, and then where would they go?

Just then, a surprisingly cheerful thirty-something woman with a wide smile and curly strawberry-blonde hair walked up to the group of workers gathered at the front entrance. I grabbed my opportunity. "Hi, I'm looking for Danielle Arce," I said. "I was supposed to meet with her this morning."

"Jennifer, that's right!" said Arce, reaching out to shake my hand. "You were supposed to do the tour today. Well, I've got nothing else to do now but talk," she sighed, gazing at her vacant office. "Come on, let's chat." I was astonished by her openness, given not only the situation but all the government pushback I had encountered up until this point. I nodded and followed her outside.

Arce was wearing slim dark jeans and low heels. She looked camera-ready for the interviews she had just given the KABC and NBC LA news crews, although she had learned about the flood only when she showed up for work. There was to have been a breastfeeding clinic for new mothers that morning, she told me, so we stationed ourselves by the front door so she could share the unfortunate news with those mothers and any other WIC clients, as she referred to them.

"Who are the moms you're going to have to turn away today?" I asked.

"A lot of working moms," she said. "They want the formula because it's free." She explained that many of the mothers she sees are Spanish-speaking immigrants from Guatemala and Mexico. They often work long hours doing janitorial work, pushing fruit or *pupusa* carts on the street, or laboring at manufacturing jobs downtown. Their bosses are often Korean, she said, and though legally, the mothers are supposed to get breaks to express breast milk (Arce's WIC office even provides hospital-grade breast pumps to any mother who wants one), the women can't speak Korean or English to communicate their rights. Even if they could take breaks, Arce said, many would choose not to, since workers are often paid by the piece in the garment industry. Recently, she sent her coworker to the factories to observe some of the moms' working conditions. "The women wouldn't even talk to her, because that would have slowed down their work," she said.

I learned that many of the moms go back to work less than a month after a new baby is born. Typically, their babies are watched by a family member or sometimes a babysitter who isn't as concerned about how the child is fed, only that the child *is* fed. Other mothers may not work, Arce explained, but often have multiple back-to-back pregnancies. "It's oftentimes easier to prop up the baby with a bottle and tend to the other kids," she told me.

Deterring breastfeeding even further were the families' source of medical care—the innumerable *clínicas* scattered throughout the city offering low-cost and sometimes questionable advice. "They don't know *anything* about breastfeeding," Arce confessed. If a baby is jaundiced, for instance, they'll just say "bottle-feed," giving moms no indication of how long—even though AAP protocol is to give formula for only twenty-four hours to bring bilirubin levels down before resuming breastfeeding.

"And they're using the wrong growth charts!" she added, explaining that the clinics have yet to adopt the newer government-endorsed WHO charts that are based on the breastfed child as the standard for normal development. (Breastfed children gain weight more slowly than their formula-fed counterparts. Using these new charts has proved critical in identifying overfeeding and preventing childhood obesity in its early stages.) "I've got moms that will come in from the clinics asking for PediaSure because they think their child is underweight," she said. "And then we'll weigh the child, he'll be in the fiftieth percentile, and I'm like, 'OK, this kid definitely does not need to be on PediaSure!' "

But the elephant in the room, it appeared, was the formula itself. Most of the mothers Arce and her team saw had babies under four weeks old, and the moms were running into breastfeeding problems even before they went back to work. Not prepared for how frequently newborns need to feed (at least ten to twelve times in a twenty-four-hour period and often more) and how many times they wake in the middle of the night to nurse, a mom would assume her baby was hungry because she wasn't producing enough breast milk. So the mom would top off each breastfeeding session with the WIC formula she got for free via the US government.

"Not only does it affect their supply, but then you've got babies who are getting way more food than they need and who are crying because they're hungry, because they've come to expect more at every feeding," said Arce, stepping over a rush of water as she excused herself to take a phone call. "Sometimes, as a nutritionist, I feel like what I'm doing is unethical, watching moms overfeed their children with formula," she sighed.

Arce's coworker Jessica Lopez stepped up to helm the entrance. She was a curvaceous beacon in a bright orange peasant shirt, sporting a strategically placed lip piercing and an astounding amount of skillfully applied eye makeup. Shortly after we were introduced, a petite Latina mom in jean shorts and flip-flops shuffled into the parking lot, balancing a toddler boy nearly half her size on her hip. Lopez, a young Latina herself, greeted the mom in Spanish and held up a sheet of paper highlighting the other WIC locations nearby. The closest one, Pico Union, was a twenty-minute walk away. "She was coming to get her check," she told me, once the mother had left the parking lot.

Lopez, like Arce, had worked with WIC for seven years and was now a nutrition program assistant and lactation educator training to become an International Board Certified Lactation Consultant (the lactation consultant credential required by WIC). Like Arce, she was warm and easy to talk to, and I asked her to walk me through the WIC voucher system. She explained that the food packages and formula weren't kept at their office. Moms would come in and pick up their monthly checks, which they could then redeem for specifically approved items at most of the big supermarkets in the area. There were also WIC-only stores where mothers could shop for supplies.

Depending on whether they were exclusively breastfeeding, mixed feeding, or fully formula feeding, moms received different benefits, with fully breastfeeding moms receiving the largest amount and greatest variety of food.

This recent incentive conjured at the federal level was supposed to encourage more moms to breastfeed, but the perceived high value of the formula made many moms feel as though they should choose a formula-feeding package regardless, even if they were breastfeeding successfully and even if they didn't have to go back to work, Lopez explained. "They'll say, 'I deserve the formula,' " she confided, as Arce rejoined us. Even if breastfeeding is normal in their home countries, the two women told me, a lot of moms would see how expensive formula is on store shelves here and then covet it—especially since it was free through the government's WIC program.

Arce leaned in and whispered, "And some of them sell it."

Lopez concurred, and said she had once been approached on the street by one of the formula resellers. "Talking to the wrong person!" she laughed.

Conversing with them felt a lot like chatting with sisters or mom friends. Both are working mothers who have breastfed; Lopez has a three-year-old boy she nursed well into toddlerhood, and Arce has three boys and was nursing her one-year-old ("Yeah, I'm going crazy!" she admitted about trying to balance it all). And both women have personal motivations for encouraging WIC moms to give their children the nutritional and immunological advantages of breast milk. Looking at Arce's slim figure, I found it hard to believe that she had once been a bored three-hundred-pound eleven-year-old before a teacher gifted her a hefty nutrition textbook. She devoured all thirty-eight chapters, lost a hundred pounds in a year hoisting peach can weights during workouts, and then set out on a path to help others with her newfound passion for human nutrition. As for Lopez, her baby had been in a neonatal intensive-care unit after birth but had fully recovered largely because Lopez had persisted in breastfeeding. I could see how both Arce and her coworker were unflagging sources of support for their WIC clients.

Through WIC, they also had a great number of tools at their disposal to help their clients—far more than anything I had personally encountered even after I had been fortunate enough to obtain private health insurance. There were trimester visits wherein WIC moms received breastfeeding counseling and newborn education; the Eighth Street office offered free breast pumps to any mom who needed one; there was a breastfeeding support group offered once a month; there was a free lactation consultant available in the office every Friday; and every single staff member received lactation education from Public Health Foundation Enterprises, the nonprofit that manages their WIC program. When it came to breastfeeding support, Eighth Street WIC was the "crème de la crème" of the fifty-two WIC clinics in Los Angeles, Arce declared with pride.

Even so, the numbers don't lie. Seventy percent of the moms at Eighth Street WIC start out breastfeeding, she revealed, but soon after the one-month mark, even moms who are successful become adamant about wanting formula. And when the moms supplement with formula this early on, by the second or third month their breast-milk supply can't be maintained. Then they stop nursing altogether.

Over the course of our conversation, Arce and her coworker repeatedly alluded to the obstacles they were up against. Finally, I had to ask outright: Was the real obstacle the government-sponsored availability of free infant formula? "Undeniably," said Lopez. "If you have it there, what are you going to do: Seek help or grab a can of formula? As humans, we want the easy way out."

BACK AT HOME AFTER MY MORNING AT WIC, I THUMBED OVER ONE of the organization's brochures Arce had handed me upon my departure. *Once you are home, continue to avoid formula*, it spelled out in large type in the highlighted sidebar of a glossy entitled "The Hospital Experience." *Just one bottle of formula: can reduce your breast milk supply; can increase your baby's risk of developing allergies and diabetes as well as intestinal and bacterial disease; [and] lessens the protective effect of your breast milk on your baby.* Precisely how, I wondered, was WIC expecting mothers to avoid formula when according to the government's own statistics, some 88 percent of WIC infants were receiving formula directly through the government's program? How had the program reached such massive proportions?

When WIC was launched in the early 1970s, it served eighty-eight thousand participants, including twenty-six thousand infants. Back then, the poor weren't malnourished and overweight by way of junk food; they were *hungry*. The creation of WIC attempted to rectify these inequities by providing infant formula, primarily, but also vouchers for milk, cheese, eggs, cereal, and fruit juice to supplement the diets of the mothers and babies who needed it the most.

Yet today, WIC serves more than eight *million* people, including two million babies. Certainly, no one would argue that a disadvantaged mother who has to go back to work in a factory should be left with no other option than to let her baby starve. But the colossal scale on which the US government now dispenses infant formula to more than half of American infants is an issue that surely warrants deeper examination, especially in light of the government's own effort to now so emphatically promote breastfeeding.

For George Kent, professor emeritus of political science at the University of Hawaii, the situation is clear: What we have on our hands is an infant-formula promotion program on a scale unlike anywhere else in the world. "There is no government that has an agency pushing formula . . . to the degree that WIC is set up [to do]. The US government now becomes the agent of the formula companies," he stated flatly.

Kent is also the author of the book *Regulating Infant Formula*, and I had contacted him because he is one of the few who have publicly addressed glaring inconsistencies in the government's WIC program—a program beloved by antipoverty and children's health groups alike for the access to health care and "real food" staples it provides. (Contrast this with the federal food stamp program, which gives participants license to buy fast food and soda—but that's another book.) A number of the breastfeeding advocates I contacted for comment could only applaud WIC's breastfeeding promotion efforts, while preferring to term the pervasiveness of formula in the program as a "choice."

Kent didn't deny that a mother had the right to choose how to feed her child. But "giving mothers a free product is not supporting their right to choose," he argued. Instead, he maintained, the WIC program amounted to something of a generous free-sample program that helped get a disadvantaged mother "hooked" on a product—the very kinds of free samples that the WHO International Code of Marketing of Breast-Milk Substitutes forbids. (If you remember, the code is the global driving force behind ridding hospitals of formula "gift" bags and other formula marketing practices known to have a negative impact on breastfeeding. The United States has taken no action yet to implement it.)

Looking at the data, Kent has a point. WIC moms have been breastfeeding at far lower rates than non-WIC moms, even compared with non-WIC moms of a similar income level. This would suggest that it is the lure of free infant formula available through WIC—not solely low-income mothers' life circumstances—that is deterring them from breastfeeding. He went on to point out that since WIC is a supplemental program and doesn't always provide families with a full month's supply of formula, families who have taken the formula and then moved away from breastfeeding actually become "guaranteed" formula customers, left to deal with the cost each month when their free supply runs out. And once their WIC benefits expire (often after six months), these families have to continue to buy formula on their own, which could cost up to $200 each month.

And so it appears that the formula companies are the clear economic winners here, but the US government benefits as well, I discovered when I examined the convoluted process by which WIC obtains the infant formula it dispenses to recipients. Remarkably, it is not US taxpayers who foot the bulk of the bill for formula handed out through the program but the formula manufacturers *themselves*. Via a competitive bidding process for each state WIC contract, the winning formula company discounts its product up to 92 percent below wholesale prices in exchange for becoming the sole WIC formula provider for that state.

That may sound like a steep price for a formula company to pay, but the payoff is massive. It's simple economics: The winner of the WIC contract wins the customers, and the market share for a "winning" brand increases, on average, 74 percentage points in the state in which the contract is obtained. Some of the market ownership is a direct result of WIC participants purchasing the contract brand at the store with their vouchers. But there is also a spillover effect as that brand of formula takes up more eye-catching shelf space in stores, and non-WIC participants become more likely to buy it, too. Not surprisingly, with a mega triopoly dominating the US infant formula market (Mead Johnson, which produces Enfamil; Abbott Laboratories, which makes Similac; and Nestlé, which now owns Gerber Good Start), competition for the state contracts is fierce. In the end, the steep discount the formula companies provide the federal government could be construed as the cost of an advertising campaign—a campaign that has had an exponentially increasing audience in the years since the formula rebate program was instituted in 1989. That's because the government does not use the billions of dollars saved each year to reduce overall WIC costs but in fact to fund more WIC enrollees.

"Basically, what you have here is an addiction program," Kent said, likening it to the days when tobacco companies used to hand out little packs of cigarettes in airports. "You get [WIC participants] hooked into a particular brand [of formula], and then you have them as customers for years and years, beyond infancy—not only for formula, but for other products as well."

OF COURSE, COMPARING INFANT FORMULA WITH TOBACCO ON ANY level may be a tough sell since no one *needs* cigarettes while infants who aren't breastfed do need formula to survive. Yet Kent's mention of the handouts brought to mind another program that had been ushered through the US government: the free cigarettes provided by the tobacco companies to servicemen in GI "care packages" via the US military during World Wars I and II. Those freebies had resulted in generations of smokers hooked on tobacco for life.

So was the WIC free-formula program—now entrenched enough to be bizarrely counterproductive to WIC's breastfeeding initiative—simply a well-meaning concept gone astray, or had it, in truth, begun as something more akin to the great tobacco marketing stratagems of the twentieth century? Something Larry Gartner, the eighty-two-year-old neonatology and breastfeeding medicine pioneer, had said months earlier popped into my head. I had no memory of his comment until that very moment, but our entire conversation now reverberated as though I had pressed *play* on a tape recorder.

Gartner had been telling me about the formula industry back in the 1960s and about the cost of manufacturing formula. It was cheap, he had said, nothing more than powdered milk, some vitamins, and some fat added to it in one form or another. The business model turned out to be a lucrative one, for while the production cost was low, the purchase price for formula-feeding families was high. That is, until the WIC program came into being in the 1970s, he pointed out, which provided formula to low-income families for free. He told me that handing out government-sponsored formula probably wasn't what we should be doing, but "WIC was started to use surplus food products," he said casually. "That's why it's in the Department of Agriculture."

I went back to Gartner for more details, but the topic was outside his area of expertise, he said. So it was hours later that I found myself on the phone with an unlikely interview subject for a book on breastfeeding: Chris Edwards, director of tax policy studies at the Cato Institute, a libertarian think tank funded largely by the billionaire Koch brothers (whose efforts to dismantle current reproductive rights for women are widely acknowledged).

Edwards didn't balk when I asked him where he stood on certain initiatives that might be helpful to breastfeeding mothers, such as a national maternity leave policy. ("I'm a small government guy, so I wouldn't support such things," he said.) But he did have an awful lot to say about how subsidizing formula via the federal WIC program was undercutting the government's own public health message urging women to breastfeed. "It's sort of akin to how the government tells people to eat healthy, but the eighty-billion-dollar food stamp program subsidizes untold billions in junk food spending."

It wasn't always this way, he explained. The case was a classic one of oversupply gone awry. It all started in the aftermath of the Great Depression, when the Hoover and then Roosevelt administrations wanted to ensure that dairy farmers—a vital cog in our economic machine—never went out of business. So the government began artificially pushing up the price of milk by buying up the excess, which meant that farmers never had to worry about the economics of supply and demand. They just pumped out as much milk as they could, and Uncle Sam dealt with the rest. One of the ways the government got rid of the excess milk was by selling it to foreign markets; the other way was to put it to use for charitable purposes here at home, which was how food subsidy programs like food stamps and WIC first got started.

"[WIC] really was founded as a formula giveaway program," echoed National WIC Association President and CEO Rev. Douglas Greenaway when we spoke by phone. (Greenaway is in the unusual position of being both lobbyist and priest. Perhaps he felt a moral obligation to return my call, as well as to speak with me forthrightly.) His advocacy organization was now very much focused on breastfeeding, he emphasized. He confided that they had just passed a resolution dissolving their relationship with the formula manufacturers, who would no longer be allowed to sponsor conferences, events, or other promotional materials.

Still, the government handouts in the early days of WIC had been for good cause, I learned when Greenaway shared the horrific history that had led to the creation of the program as a two-year pilot back in 1972. In the 1960s, impoverished American babies and children were emaciated and dying.

The US infant mortality rate, even today one of the highest in the developed world, was remarkably higher. Ironically, one of the reasons babies in poor families were suffering was because huge numbers of American women had turned away from breastfeeding in the decades prior, feeding their babies with evaporated or condensed milk formulas instead. Poverty-stricken families would water down these homemade concoctions to stretch supplies.

In the beginning, distributing free iron-fortified infant formula made a huge difference in the lives of babies who had been malnourished and whose growth had been stunted by inadequate feeding practices. Needy older children and pregnant mothers benefited tremendously from the additional nutritious food. And, at first glance, the program has appeared to help over time. Low-income mothers who participate in WIC while pregnant have babies with higher birth weights who are more likely to survive infancy. At age two, those children score higher on cognitive assessments than children of mothers who don't participate.

But while using commodity surplus for charity may have been all well and good back in the days when those calories actually alleviated hunger for poor women and children, the situation of lower-income families had dramatically changed over the years, Cato's Chris Edwards had pointed out. Obesity was now not only epidemic among adults and children alike, but poorer health outcomes linked to formula feeding—including higher rates of SIDS, asthma, diabetes, and obesity itself—were being well publicized by the government. And yet, Edwards has asserted in his writings, "if you subsidize something, you get more of it," evidenced by the fact that infant formula is now the single largest food cost in the nearly $7-*billion*-a-year WIC program. "And presumably, more formula means less [health-promoting] breast milk."

Yet the strange thing was, there *wasn't* less breast milk. Looking at the data, which reflected the national trend toward "breast is best" awareness, there was now more breast milk being produced in America than at any other time in the last seventy-five years. And thanks to WIC's breastfeeding promotion efforts, there was more breast milk being produced by WIC mothers than at any other time since the program's inception.

Given the statistics, I expected the opposite of what Edwards had said to be true. *More* women breastfeeding in recent years should translate into markedly *less* formula being consumed. So I wanted to know: Just how much formula had American babies consumed each year since the WIC program began in the 1970s? Amazingly, I was told by a USDA spokesperson that the department does not track infant-formula consumption.

In search of enlightenment, I decided to call Elizabeth Frazão, an economist with USDA's Economic Research Service. She had coauthored the scores of WIC reports I had been parsing on the department's website, so I hoped she would be willing to speak with me. I had noticed a small sampling of infant-formula consumption statistics in two of her reports, and I wanted to ask if she had access to more data.

She took my call and asked me to call her Betsy, but disclosed that, as a government economist, she could talk only about the facts and could not express any opinion about the WIC program. But there wasn't much to talk about, she said. Those few years of stats were all she had; they had actually been projections based on shopper scanner data, and the Economic Research Service had had to contract Nielsen and Information Resources Inc. to obtain even those numbers. "Some of this information is just really hard to get," Frazão told me.

That turned out to be quite an understatement. While the government carefully tracks breastfeeding data within WIC and fastidiously tracks overall US breastfeeding statistics by month, by state, by whether the mother is a college graduate, and even by whether she is a firstborn child, the research regarding how much formula American babies consume? Nonexistent. We're doling it out for free to half of all the infants in our country; heck, we've been giving it away for more than four decades. Yet the answer to *how much* our babies consume remains the proprietary knowledge of the formula companies. *Beyond* proprietary. I tried to enlist the services of a top information scientist I know, a woman who regularly uncovers elusive business intelligence for the Fortune 500. After doing some preliminary digging for me gratis, she informed me it wasn't worth hiring her to take on the job. Evidently, infant-formula data wasn't reported to any government agency, she explained—neither its sale, nor consumption, nor production. In fact, she continued, there was an extremely strong likelihood the data didn't even exist.

Perhaps there's a reason certain entities don't want this information readily available. Despite the huge gains in breastfeeding since the 1970s, it appeared from the limited obtainable data that the amount of formula consumed by

American babies had decreased only gradually between 1994 and 2007—not dropped off sharply, as one would have expected. And what about the twenty years prior, when breastfeeding rates had truly skyrocketed? We simply had no way of knowing how much formula those babies had consumed.

True, breastfeeding statistics could be murky. (Overall breastfeeding rates, for instance, could include a mother who tried breastfeeding once in the hospital and then switched over to formula.) Even so, the implication for our children's health was impossible to ignore. Childhood obesity had tripled in the 1980s and '90s, and here was a previously unidentified piece of the puzzle: a period in which women were giving their babies healthful breast-milk calories at ever increasing rates, but also a time in which the government's WIC program—with its distribution of free formula—was expanding year by year.

The data were limited but the undeniable probability was there. Formula calories weren't being *replaced* by breast-milk calories; formula calories were being dumped *on top* of breast-milk calories, just as Danielle Arce had attested. US dairy farmers kept pumping out surplus milk; WIC handed out more and more formula; and American babies, evidently breastfed ones, too, just kept gobbling it up.

I called Chris Edwards again. What about high-fructose corn syrup? I asked. Was the sudden pervasiveness of the cheap sweetener in the wake of subsidized corn-crop surpluses a story comparable to what had happened with milk surpluses and the expansion of infant formula? There was a long pause. "Uh, yeah. I think you're right," he conceded. "It's just another classic example of how government subsidy programs are arguably harmful to human health."

I went back to George Kent, who also found the corn syrup analogy apt. "We have had subsidized dairy and excessive milk production, and infant formula helps absorb a whole lot of that excess milk." Larry Gartner had it right, Kent said, about why the USDA had originally been tasked with overseeing WIC. "It comes out of the government's interest in responding to the urgings of farm states. Of which is commodity production."

"But the implications for that are pretty shocking," I countered. "It would seem that—I don't even know how to phrase it—" I paused, as I connected the dots. "It would seem like the US government was pushing its leftover commodities onto the nation's poorest people. Onto *babies*."

"I think that's exactly what happened," Kent said calmly. "Without paying attention to the health impact."

WAS THE PUSH INTENTIONAL? IF YOU LOOK AT ANOTHER SURPLUS product of the dairy industry, cheese, which was foisted on Americans with the goal of getting them to eat more, the answer is an unequivocal *yes*. As Pulitzer Prize–winning investigative reporter Michael Moss uncovered in his bestselling exposé of the processed food industry, *Salt, Sugar, Fat*, US dairy producers started tackling the factory-farm-fueled oversupply of milk and milk fat in the early 1980s by converting both into cheese and then tasking the government with the stockpiling of the stuff inside caverns and empty mines—all to the tune of four billion taxpayer dollars each year.

The foodstuffs were stockpiled until 1983, when the US

government ingeniously began to resolve the oversupply predicament by nudging us into overconsumption. Through an act of Congress (the National Dairy and Tobacco Adjustment Act, which also came to the aid of the tobacco industry), US dairy-farmer funds were directed into advertising designed to expand markets for dairy, and the National Dairy Promotion and Research Board was created. Now helmed by Dairy Management Inc., the organization has worked since its founding to increase sales and demand for US dairy products.

I knew firsthand about the power of the agricultural lobby to whet Americans' appetites. My father-in-law, a renowned jingle composer of the 1970s and '80s, scored the classic commercial "Cheese, Glorious Cheese," which, to the tune of "Food, Glorious Food" from the musical *Oliver!* waxes poetic about the deliciousness of cheese. The spot, built around cuts of Velveeta-drenched broccoli and a man crunching into a cheddar-exploding taco, was paid for by the National Dairy Board. Thanks to enticing commercials like this one along with exhaustive cheese marketing efforts from the processed food industry (think stuffed-crust pizza), the boost-consumption model worked: cheese consumption tripled between 1970 and 2007. And as Moss revealed, our waistlines have never been the same.

But cheese wasn't the only thing that had been stockpiled in those government-owned caverns before the National Dairy Board helped create a market around our expanding stomachs. Nonfat dry milk powder, the main ingredient in many infant formulas at the time, had been hoarded there, too. (Nonfat milk is still an ingredient in formula, but a larger proportion is now whey.) And while no government agency may have tracked how much infant formula had been consumed over the years, what the USDA did track was per capita dairy consumption. I had, in fact, located a USDA chart broken down by food or commodity, including nonfat milk powder and whey, going all the way back to 1975.

The chart revealed that the rise in nonfat milk powder and whey consumption was subtle, not nearly as eye-popping as I could see it had been for cheese. The data also weren't as straightforward to interpret, since while infant formula eats up a sizable portion of the nonfat milk and whey sold every year, the two are also incorporated into a host of other food products, including ice cream and meat filler. Even so, average consumption had climbed steadily in the twenty years since 1983, the year the National Dairy Board was tasked with expanding the markets for cheese and other dairy products. What's more, the increase appeared to parallel the rapid expansion of congressional spending on the WIC program (the other chart I was staring at on my computer), which had grown swiftly under presidents Clinton and George W. Bush but remained flat during the Obama administration.

WHETHER OR NOT ANY RISE IN INFANT-FORMULA CONSUMPTION can ever be directly correlated to the National Dairy Board and dairy industry efforts to increase our babies' appetites for the stuff, the fact of the matter is that America is now struggling with childhood and adult obesity and other insidious diet-related health issues the magnitude of which we have not seen before.

While the government, researchers, the media, and parents examine the nuances of how formula feeding in and of itself may or may not be directly tied to obesity, maybe someone—anyone but the formula companies themselves—should take a hard look at precisely how much formula American babies are consuming. Too many calories are too many calories, whether they come in the form of high-fructose corn syrup, cheddar cheese, or infant formula. And consuming too many calories leads to obesity.

The problem of overfeeding with formula may not be confined only to WIC. As I scrutinized our national breastfeeding statistics, it seemed as though the question of *how much* is equally vague for the general population. At six months, nearly 50 percent of American babies are mixed-fed (that's breastfeeding plus formula or other foods) versus less than 19 percent who are fed breast milk only for that recommended duration.

It is true that even before coming to WIC, individuals with lower incomes are more likely to be obese. And lower-income populations overall are less likely to breastfeed. One economist cautioned that the breastfeeding rates in WIC could be low because these mothers were just heading into WIC to get the free formula. And the program's immense scale, USDA economist Betsy Frazão said, could be explained by the harsh reality that the problem of poverty in this country is equally as vast.

To further complicate the picture, I discovered that a factor termed "nutritional risk" is a qualification for entrance to WIC—even though "nutritional risk" for a newborn could include a mother already suffering from an "inadequate dietary pattern" such as obesity! So theoretically, a new mother could qualify for WIC benefits for her newborn *because* she is obese and then be given free formula for her baby, despite the fact that the government has linked that very formula to a higher likelihood of obesity in her child. There seemed no end to the contradictions, with underprivileged mothers in search of assistance and their babies ultimately paying the price.

Which only led me to wonder: Was the government labeling half our country have-nots and then handing them free cans of formula the answer? If anything, the practice seemed to perpetuate the cycle of poverty, providing those mothers a fast and cheap way to feed their babies while they toiled at their low-wage jobs, and permitting the rest of us to turn a blind eye to reforms that could give their children a much better start, such as enacting a living minimum wage or paid maternity leave. Do we really want to live in a world where breast milk—the very connection between a mother and her child—is a luxury for the wealthy, while the poor are blithely handed a subsidized, industrialized substitute?

Within the WIC program, there has been enough concern about obesity that, in 2007, WIC revised its food packages in an attempt to encourage breastfeeding. The new packages provided nursing mothers with a larger and more varied food offering. But this measure hasn't been sufficient. "The research I've seen suggests that, overall, it doesn't appear to have swayed women toward breastfeeding," Frazão said. More recently, a one-can rule designed to help new mothers establish their milk supply without interference was issued at the federal level. The rule dictates that breastfeeding mothers be issued only one can of formula in their baby's first month, versus the four or five they were formerly eligible to receive. That change hadn't yet trickled down to Danielle Arce at the local level, but she was hopeful that it would support her agency's effort to help more mothers to breastfeed.

One thing at least is clear: the government can promote breastfeeding all it wants, but as long as it continues to hand out free formula, mothers will assume that formula is endorsed by the government. The day I was at the Eighth Street WIC office, I asked Jessica Lopez what would happen, hypothetically, if WIC suddenly stopped providing free formula and instead provided breastfeeding counseling and more nutritious food. "There would be a lot less moms," she said. "They see WIC equals formula." Over time though, she hoped, things would change. "They would have to," she said. "In the real world, formula costs money but breastfeeding is free."

ten

“We Complete, Not Compete”

As soon as you get a mother insecure, it’s a recipe for stopping breastfeeding. And the formula companies play on this.

—PETER HARTMANN

It was morning in Hanoi and, through our connection, I could hear Nemat Hajeebhoy sniffling over the din of honking horns and whizzing scooters. More than seven thousand miles away from each other, we evidently both had colds, and I was glad we had the video portion of Skype turned off so she couldn’t see me bundled up in bed with a pile of Kleenex next to my notepad. “Give me a second, Jennifer, I’m just going to shut the window so we don’t have to compete with this traffic noise,” she said.

Hajeebhoy, who is originally from India, had just returned from a two-week trip back home, and I could imagine the pace of her work was finally catching up with her. She had spent part of her visit spending time with her family in Bombay. But the real purpose of her trip was to check in on a new infant and young-child feeding project she was overseeing in the northern state of Uttar Pradesh for Alive & Thrive, the Bill & Melinda Gates Foundation–funded global health initiative she had helmed in Vietnam. Hanoi had been Hajeebhoy's home for the past six and a half years, but the Vietnam portion of the project would soon be coming to an end, although in many ways this was only the beginning. Alive & Thrive has set out to reverse the worldwide erosion of breastfeeding on a sweeping scale once afforded by only the formula companies.

The effort couldn't come soon enough. While American infant formula and "toddler milk" sales have slowed, worldwide thirst for the stuff has gone viral. And our dairy surplus here at home only continues to swell, except now—along with overproducers like New Zealand and Ireland—we're simply off-loading our excess onto the rest of the world. Soaking up the glut is, of course, China, which, thanks to unchecked formula-company advertising and an exploding middle class, has now far surpassed the United States as the world's largest formula market. But there are also underdeveloped countries like Mongolia, where the march to modernization has made its mark and so many mothers—driven far from their rural homes into the cities to find work—have been left with little choice but to arrange for their babies to be given food, water, and formula (if they can afford it) in their absence.

In the United States, where water is clean, food is overabundant, and people have access to routine health care and immunizations, many believe the question of whether to breastfeed or formula-feed is just fodder for the mommy wars rather than an urgent health matter. But in the developing world, where diarrheal diseases and pneumonia are the leading causes of infant death, the fallout from the move away from the immunological power of breast milk is clear. More than eight hundred thousand children's lives worldwide could be saved each year if all mothers (instead of the current 38 percent) optimally breastfed.

Over the years, there have been many small pilot efforts to reverse abysmal breastfeeding rates, some with positive results. Hajeebhoy, who has worked for more than fifteen years on the front lines of public health on three continents (and can speak the seven languages to show for it), has many of these infant and young-child feeding projects to her credit. Now forty-five, she has worked it all since her first job in Maharashtra, India, where she assisted with the training of government *anganwadi* health workers and conducted group breastfeeding education sessions for rural mothers. Efforts like this were impressive, but headway was slow nonetheless. By 2008, the Bill & Melinda Gates Foundation, which had set its sights on funding a breastfeeding-based initiative, had seen enough baby steps, Hajeebhoy recalled.

"They said, 'We don't want to see small pilots anymore, because we *know* people do good work.' They asked, 'Can you show that change is possible and at scale? What would it take to achieve that?' "

One answer was money, which the Gates Foundation was ready to provide. So when one of Hajeebhoy's previous employers (the nonprofit AED, now FHI 360) bid for the project and Alive & Thrive was formed that same year, her old colleagues called her up and asked her to get on board. Hajeebhoy said yes; they won the bid, and she was suddenly thrust to the forefront of an unprecedentedly ambitious challenge: Take three countries with immense populations. Develop breastfeeding and complementary feeding programs that could reach millions of mothers, babies, and children. Then document the results. Alive & Thrive chose Bangladesh, Ethiopia, and Vietnam.

Breastfeeding practices in the first two countries were poor primarily because of long-held cultural misperceptions. In Bangladesh, for instance, before a mother's mature milk came in, newborns would often be given honey, which can interfere with a baby learning how to suckle as well as cause infant botulism (hence the warning labels on honey jars in our own part of the world). In Ethiopia, where in the south average daily temperatures hover around 95 degrees Fahrenheit, parents mistakenly believed that a breastfed baby also needed to be given water, which actually exposed the child to deadly water-borne bacteria and parasites. Infant formula had yet to make its inroad into these countries because, even in 2008, these were areas of the world where very few parents could afford it. Formula-company advertising dollars simply weren't spent there then, although today this is rapidly changing.

But in Vietnam, where Hajeebhoy was to be stationed, "there was a whole different set of issues around infant feeding," said Alive & Thrive Project Director Jean Baker, who spoke with me from her office in Washington, DC. "It was a blooming economy, it was Southeast Asia, it has high literacy rates, it has a lot of women in the workforce." In other words, Vietnam represented so many countries (including our own more developed one) that are struggling to hold on to their humanity in the face of a rapidly developing and technologically exploding world.

Yet Vietnam offered a singular advantage for Hajeebhoy and her appointed mission: the country was then, and continues to be, an incredibly pro-breastfeeding society. Even before Alive & Thrive arrived there, more than 90 percent of mothers nursed their babies.

"[In Vietnam] there are no taboos like you have in the US or Europe," said Hajeebhoy, who lived in the States when she received her master's in public health from Johns Hopkins University. "You can breastfeed in public and nobody will say anything." In that regard, she added, Vietnam was like her home country of India, where a woman in a rural area would hide her face from a man but not hesitate to pop out a breast to feed her child.

But despite Vietnam's breastfeeding-friendly environment, the infant feeding situation there was far from optimal, Hajeebhoy disclosed. "I always tell people you need to remember the one, six, twenty-four: you need to start breastfeeding within an hour of birth, exclusively breastfeed up to six months, and then continue to breastfeed for up to twenty-four months, or beyond." Yet mothers weren't even coming close to those marks, with only half of Vietnamese infants being put to the breast within an hour after birth. By three months, babies were overwhelmingly supplemented with infant formula or rice gruel. And by twelve to fifteen months, women had given up breastfeeding, way before the recommended minimum two years of nursing.

If you're American and reading this, I know you might

be thinking, *Twelve to fifteen months?! That's pretty long!* Except that it's not, when you consider, first, that two and a half to seven years is the biological norm for nursing and, second, that Vietnam may have a booming economy, but even today malnutrition continues to be a very serious issue there. (And that's malnutrition as in genuine hunger. The obesity rate there is under 5 percent, although it's becoming increasingly higher in the cities.) By missing out on months of breast-feeding, Vietnamese babies were missing out on months of essential nutrition, and the consequence was so severe that every mother and father in Vietnam could see it with their own eyes: nearly one out of three Vietnamese children under the age of five was a victim of permanently stunted growth. The children, Hajeebhoy told me, will never reach their full potential.

If the problem was so visible, I asked, why weren't Vietnamese mothers continuing to nurse their babies? According to Hajeebhoy, before the Alive & Thrive initiative, many parents just hadn't put two and two together. Not only were they unaware that incomplete breastfeeding was tied to stunted growth, they had come to believe—with the help of pervasive formula advertising—that a *combination* of breastfeeding and formula was actually the best source of nutrition for their babies.

Hajeebhoy also ran down a list of other obstacles that were impeding breastfeeding in Vietnam. By this point in my research, the culprits sounded all too familiar. Hospital staff routinely offered infant formula or water to crying babies, to soothe them. A high C-section rate (as high as 80 percent in private hospitals) yielded mothers who were too tired to nurse after surgery. Meddling family members insisted that breastfed infants also needed water during the hot summer months. Maternity leave was fixed at four months, so moms started introducing food and formula before they had to head back to work. (At the time, very few Vietnamese women had ever used or even seen a breast pump.) Finally, even if a mother was able to express breast milk, there was no clean place at work in which to do it.

Still, underlying all these impediments, said Hajeebhoy, was one common theme—a premise so universal it was prevalent in nearly every country worldwide, concurred Baker, who had racked up more than thirty years in international public health: overwhelmingly, women believe they are inherently incapable of producing enough breast milk.

I had heard this concern expressed over and over again not just by mothers but by historians, doctors, researchers, educators, and government officials alike. It was time to tackle it head-on.

"IF YOU'VE GOT SOMETHING WRONG WITH YOUR LIVER, WHAT would you expect to happen?" asked Professor Peter Hartmann in a soft-spoken Aussie accent.

I was video chatting with Hartmann, founder of the Human Lactation Research Group at the University of Western Australia, and inarguably one of the world's leading authorities on human lactation. He likewise could be called a pioneer in that space. Now in his seventies, he is also professor emeritus and senior honorary research fellow at the university's School of Chemistry and Biochemistry (read: retired but not *really* retired). When he arrived at the school in 1972, after beginning his career in bovine lactation, and began to apply for research grants to study breastfeeding women (the birth of his daughter in 1971 turned his interest toward humans), less than 50 percent of Australian women were breastfeeding. "They wanted to know why I wanted to study these 'unusual women,'" he said with a smirk.

As the neatly bearded Hartmann smiled at me from behind his desk, I had an inkling that he was setting me up for a professorial explanation. I ventured, "What would happen if there was something wrong with my liver? Um, I would be in danger of possibly dying or my whole body shutting down."

Hartmann stared at me patiently. "Yes, but what preventive measures would you take?"

I scanned my brain for any knowledge I had about ways to prevent liver failure (*not mixing alcohol and Tylenol?*) and then guessed that this probably wasn't what he was driving at. "What do you mean?" I asked.

He tried again. "If something was wrong with your liver, would you go to the doctor?"

"Yeah, of course," I replied.

"OK, stop right there," he said. "If you've got a breastfeeding problem and you go to the doctor, what's going to happen?"

"Well, yes, I know," I started. "If you're lucky enough to have access to one of the few breastfeeding medicine doctors in the US, maybe they'll order a couple of diagnostic tests. Otherwise, hopefully, you'll be referred to a lactation consultant."

"There are no tests," he said. I spied a twinkle behind his glasses. "No tests for normality."

Translation: If a mother was having a hard time getting her infant to latch on, or she thought that her body wasn't producing enough milk, a lactation consultant could help her only with the mechanics and would doubtless suggest she put her baby to the breast more frequently. A breastfeeding medicine specialist (essentially a doctor with lactation consultant qualifications) could also check for overall hormonal imbalances, such as a thyroid condition, that could impede milk production. But Hartmann pointed out that there was no specific test that targeted the *breasts*—the organs themselves—to see if their function was "normal." In fact, he added, the reference range for what is normal doesn't even exist. He offered the analogy of being screened for diabetes with a glucose tolerance test. If results fall outside the expected range, the patient is likely to be diagnosed with the disease.

Yet no one had definitively determined the same kind of expected range (known as a reference value) for lactation, even though Hartmann and his colleagues knew from their own research that a woman's daily milk production could fluctuate from about 500 mL to as much as 1,200 mL a day. They had also pinpointed other biochemical indicators such as progesterone, which dropped off precipitously after a baby was born and before the onset of lactation.

"Every hospital around can measure progesterone," he stated. "Why wouldn't you measure progesterone in a mother who seems like she's having a bit of a hard time with initiation?"

Hartmann thinks the utter void of knowledge about the breast is downright astonishing, especially given its role as one of humankind's most essential organs. "The energy output in lactating breasts is about 30 percent of a mother's resting energy in total. That's more than the brain. That's more than the *heart*!" he exclaimed. "Anything in the body that consumes 30 percent of its energy has, evolutionary-wise, got to be incredibly important for survival."

Of course, if prehistoric mothers had been facing problems of milk insufficiency with the global pervasiveness that exists today, it is pretty conceivable that mankind would have died out a long time ago. True, it's been estimated that anywhere from 1 to 5 percent of women are physically unable to produce breast milk, which is known medically as "failed lactation." (Yup, we've got a term for it, but we don't have any idea how to definitively diagnose or possibly treat it.) But looking at what was happening in Vietnam, it was clear that the problem had become more widespread. And in the Unites States, an astounding 50 percent of mothers cited insufficient milk, or low supply, as their reason for stopping breastfeeding, in one recent study.

This isn't normal, said Hartmann, and neither are the unbelievably high incidences of pain and mastitis that women all over the modern world suffer through. "Why is mastitis in women running at 20 percent?" he asked, adding that no other mammal had a rate that high. "Try looking up mastitis in pigs or any suckling animal in a textbook and you'll find that there isn't even half a paragraph." In the undeveloped world, mastitis is practically nonexistent, he said, pointing to the Aboriginal Australians as an example.

Hartmann expressed his moral concerns about the situation we had created—that we were promoting "breast is best" while simultaneously allowing women to breastfeed through horrific pain and without the medical knowledge to reassure them that they were actually making enough milk to feed their children. "If we're telling all these mothers to breastfeed, then we should be able to give them the same medical care we do for any other organ in the body," he insisted. "Until then, we shouldn't have them go through purgatory trying to breastfeed their babies."

Hartmann believed that something had gone terribly wrong in our modern world, and he had devoted much of his life and research to uncovering the cause—and the solutions. He and his team had been responsible for discovering how suckling actually works (by strong suction to the nipple via the baby's lips), disproving the prior misconception that an infant's tongue squeezes the nipple. This is why a good latch is so important. Not surprisingly, this is also why the pump manufacturer Medela has funded Hartmann's research for the past decade. It was also Hartmann's own work that revealed an infant's demand regulates milk supply, which is why scheduling breastfeeding, or even the introduction of just one bottle of formula, can seriously hinder production.

Yet this latter discovery—with its implications for the seemingly benign act of "supplementing" a mother's breastfeeding efforts with a bottle of formula—more than anything else, may pinpoint a leading cause of our worldwide breastmilk insufficiency epidemic. Hartmann had witnessed too many modern-day mothers blaming themselves for not making enough milk for their babies. Already apprehensive about their fundamental ability to provide nourishment, any negative feedback from well-meaning family members or doctors (*You sure you've got enough? Your baby looks a bit thin.*) tended to tip them right over the edge to formula feeding.

This, in spite of the evidence that the onus isn't actually on *any* mother to create the "right" amount of breast milk. It is a *baby's appetite*, not his mother's production capability, said Hartmann, that determines milk supply. I knew this to be true. I had reviewed studies revealing that even when a mother ramped up her milk supply with increased pumping sessions or with the intake of substances called galactagogues, a baby would still consume the same amount of breast milk. Researchers suspect this is due to the presence of appetite hormones in breast milk that we are only just beginning to understand. Breastfed babies regulate their natural food intake very well, Hartmann concurred. So well, in fact, that when formula is introduced into the equation, babies adjust to take in less breast milk.

But babies have no such self-regulating mechanism when it comes to formula, which doesn't contain those natural satiety hormones. With formula, they just keep sucking away. "The formula companies, they've had the slogan of '*We complete, not compete*,'" said Hartmann, his eyes boring through my computer screen. "How about that? They've turned that information on its head to their own advantage."

IN VIETNAM, THE $13 MILLION THE FORMULA COMPANIES SPEND on advertising each year is but a drop in the $35-*billion*-a-year global baby-food and formula market. But when Hajeebhoy and her team first arrived, they saw that the modest investment had clearly paid off: There was a widespread belief among Vietnamese mothers and even health care workers that the women weren't capable of producing enough high-quality breast milk to feed their babies for the first six months. What's more—buying in to the advertising without question—they were convinced that breast milk *plus* infant formula offered the best nutrition for a child.

Fortunately, with a generous endowment of $24 million over five years from the Gates Foundation, the Alive & Thrive Vietnam team was given unprecedented resources with which to tackle the formula company–planted misperception. The team knew how quickly the misperception became reality, as mothers supplemented their breast milk with formula and then saw their milk supply dwindle, just as Hartmann had described to me. The team decided to fight fire with fire.

"The infant-formula industry, they do fantastic ads," said Hajeebhoy. "I haven't seen a bad infant-formula ad in my life. They're so cute. The babies are cute. The mom is cute. The dad is cute. [The ads] really build on emotion. You watch them and you are convinced: *If I can afford to buy this can of formula, my child will be more intelligent*."

With things left as they were, however, parents—not just in Vietnam but around the world—were hearing only one side of the story, Hajeebhoy explained. While Abbott, Nestlé, and Mead Johnson (the second two of which declined and refused to comment for this book, respectively) were spending untold hundreds of millions on advertising, governments and ministries of health were not advertising breast milk.

"If this was a Coke-Pepsi war, you would have Coca-Cola advertising and Pepsi advertising," Hajeebhoy pointed out. "But in this case, you only have Coca-Cola advertising."

So to compete with the formula companies on their own playing field, she hired advertising powerhouse Ogilvy &

Mather to produce TV commercials that would rival the formula ads, addressing Vietnamese mothers' concerns about insufficient breast milk, as well as the other dangerous practice of giving infants water. Of course the spots featured cute babies, but in these ads the tiny stars "told" each other (via the magic of digitally enhanced baby mouth movement) that they needed only breast milk, not water, or they reassured their moms that they didn't need to supplement with formula. *Mom, don't be afraid that you will run out of breast milk! You just need to keep breastfeeding me.*

Another commercial opened on soft-focus images of an expectant mom dancing baby booties on her belly, followed by an ultrasound photo, then a shot of the woman caressing her tiny infant's hand for the first time. *Dear future mom*, the voice-over intoned, *when your baby is born, so are you—as a mother!* The screen then revealed moms tenderly breastfeeding their babies while music swelled in the background. A closing voice-over added words of encouragement to mothers about the bond that would grow along with the child if mothers stuck with it even on days that were tough. My eyes teared up in the first twenty seconds.

The poignant commercials aired all over Vietnam. And in nearly a quarter of the country's provinces, an accompanying mass media campaign encouraged mothers to move forward through their fears about insufficient milk and warned them not to give formula or water. The ads ran on LCD screens in supermarkets, hospitals, and health centers. There were posters in those health centers, too, along with print ads on buses and billboards. Audio messages played on outdoor loudspeakers. And a website was created to share breastfeeding information with mothers, along with a Facebook fan page and a mobile app that allowed moms to connect with one another and share baby milestones.

Despite being outspent on advertising thirteen to one, competing head-to-head with the formula companies worked. The organization's campaign reached 2.3 million mothers of children under the age of two, and the number of women who exclusively breastfed for six months skyrocketed—from 26 to 48 percent, just one year after the mass media campaign was launched.

By itself, this would have been an impressive victory. But when Hajeebhoy and her team (initially only five people but later thirty-five) were in the planning stages for the Vietnam project, they were all too aware that the Gates Foundation grant, however generous, had an end date of five years. Whatever changes they effected would have to have real staying power. So, simultaneously, the group set its sights on sweeping policy change that would support the mothers' efforts to believe in their own breast milk–producing abilities.

Being at work, away from their babies, prevented Vietnamese women from breastfeeding frequently enough to maintain their milk supply, so Hajeebhoy and her team worked with Vietnam's labor confederation to convince more than a hundred companies as well as government ministries to create clean lactation spaces in which working-mother employees could take breaks to express breast milk. (Breaks for working mothers already existed in the labor law.) This solution was particularly needed in factories that produced big-brand goods and employed young childbearing women by the thousands.

And before a Vietnamese mother headed back to work after having a baby, it was pivotal to give her unhampered time to exclusively breastfeed for the recommended six months, without feeling pressure to supplement with formula. So the team partnered with a coalition already well established in the country (it included the Vietnam Women's Union, UNICEF, WHO, and others) to push for increased maternity protection. They won a landmark victory when the National Assembly extended paid maternity leave from four to six months (with 90 percent of the vote in a largely male legislature, no less).

Alive & Thrive also pushed for an expansion of the existing ban on formula-company advertising in order to eradicate the formula companies' message that formula was a necessary complement to the nourishment produced by a woman's body. The ban in place already prohibited advertising of formula meant for infants under the age of twelve months, but clearly it hadn't been effective enough, since "cute baby" formula ads were pervasive in the country when Hajeebhoy first arrived. So, three days after the National Assembly voted for expanded maternity leave, the legislators upped the restrictions on infant-formula advertising to include all children up to twenty-four months.

However, none of these efforts would have made a difference if Vietnamese mothers had continued to be misinformed by health workers who believed (via formula-company advertising) in formula supplementation. So Alive & Thrive moved to correct the dearth of lactation support in the health care system. The organization worked with the National Institute of Nutrition to nest 781 "social franchises" within already existing health care facilities, training midwives to provide breastfeeding support and counseling, so they could serve as quasi lactation consultants (think WIC, but without the infant formula). These services reassured the mothers and encouraged them to exclusively breastfeed for the first six months, then to keep up the breastfeeding for two years or more. Alive & Thrive then created an additional 675 support groups in rural villages across the country, to help mothers encourage one another and to bring nay-saying fathers and grandmothers on board.

All in all, Hajeebhoy and her staff trained close to twenty-five thousand community workers who would be self-sufficient once the Vietnam project came to an end. That would happen this year, Hajeebhoy told me from a conference in Stockholm, when I checked in with her again close to midnight her time. In the interim, she said, they were tracking their efforts to make sure all the hard work wouldn't be undone once the project was over. I asked what she was planning to do next. "Take a vacation," she laughed.

All kidding aside, Hajeebhoy must be proud of what she and her team have been able to bring about in a mere five years. In the areas where her team's work on the ground was coupled with the mass media campaign, an incredible 62 percent of Vietnamese mothers are now fully breastfeeding their babies; this, compared with a slim 19 percent just three years earlier. The stunting rates for children are already starting to decline.

Even now, the biggest turnabout may be the one yet to come. The increase in Vietnam's breastfeeding rates and the accompanying policy change proved so dramatic, said Hajeebhoy, that other countries in the region have taken notice. "Laos, Cambodia, Thailand—they all started inquiring: 'How did you guys do this?' "

So after her much-needed respite, Hajeebhoy will be returning to Hanoi to direct Alive & Thrive's effort in six more countries in Southeast Asia and some regions in India. With additional Gates Foundation funding, Hajeebhoy and her team hope to replicate Vietnam's success.

Half-joking, I asked Hajeebhoy what would happen if the Gates Foundation gave Alive & Thrive millions of dollars to work its magic on the United States. She responded in all seriousness and said that such an effort *could* work—if it were done the right way. "You have some of the best creative agencies. They could look at how to market breast milk well, and create a new normal."

But there are deeper problems in the United States, she told me, that first have to be confronted. Unlike in Vietnam, the bigger issue is that, in America, public acceptance of breastfeeding just isn't there. "Nobody [in Vietnam] is saying, 'Sorry, I don't believe in this,' " she explained. After all, in Vietnam, no one would kick a woman out of Starbucks for nursing her child.

And not only is public support lacking, *personal* support is, too. "In Asia, families are around to help take care of a child," she said, completely unaware of the irony unfolding on my side of the computer screen. Mika had woken up unexpectedly from her nap, and as I tried to keep her preschool chatter from overtaking my Skype call by shoving my boob in her mouth, she suddenly leaped off my lap and lunged for a dark-chocolate bar I had absentmindedly left next to me on my bedroom nightstand. As Hajeebhoy went on with her point, I flapped my arms wildly at Mika to stop, but she just laughed maniacally at my pantomime, shoved half the bar in her mouth, and then—chocolate smeared from chin to eyebrow—made a run for our white comforter. I put the call on hold, parked Mika in front of an episode of *Daniel Tiger's Neighborhood* in the other room, and then scurried back to my call.

"You were saying?" I asked breathlessly.

For a moment, Hajeebhoy mused about how much more isolated parents are in Western and other developed countries. Then she declared simply, "Women need support!"

SO WHILE WE WAIT FOR THE GATES FOUNDATION OR ANOTHER forward-thinking organization to set its sights on the United States, an endlessly innovative machine—Big Formula—is free to fill the void left by the glaring lack of support for American mothers. Over the course of writing this book, I heard time and time again from breastfeeding advocates that the formula companies effectively set up mothers to fail by implying through clever marketing techniques—as they had in Vietnam—that mothers will be unable to feed a child for six months by breast milk alone. "Breast is best, but . . ." went the oft-repeated phrase.

Yet if you look at the messages overwhelmingly conveyed by formula-company advertising in the United States today, they are no longer "concerned" with suggestions of potential breastfeeding failure. Now those messages are more likely to be *We are here for you; you are safe. You can feel comfortable that there's an alternative that will work for you and that we've done all the research.* In a world where breastfeeding moms have to tough it out on their own through mastitis, pumping at work, ejection from Starbucks, and hyperactive toddlers with chocolate smeared all over their faces, the formula companies are the warm-and-fuzzy antidote to the blame-and-guilt we mothers face.

This "We're here for you" marketing tactic isn't unique to the formula companies, of course. Every company wants its customers to have a positive attitude toward its brand and to feel that the company cares about them and truly understands the difficulties they face. Tide wants people to feel that they can do their laundry successfully. Coca-Cola wants people to think it actually cares about obesity, which is why it announced four global commitments to help "fight" the epidemic. And legions of brands spend millions of dollars figuring out how to make that caring relevant not only to their users but today's world, which is why Nestlé recently announced it will provide fourteen weeks of paid maternity leave for its workers (now gender-neutrally termed "primary caretaker leave"; *see, we're really relevant!*). And Abbott has created its instantly viral "Sisterhood of Motherhood" campaign for Similac, urging parents to move past the mommy wars and just All Get Along. "The sisterhood has only one rule," declares the website that sends you to a Facebook page where moms can connect and share ideas. "Nourish each other the same way we nourish our children."

This is the *we complete, not compete* approach Peter Hartmann was talking about, and it is inarguably a shrewd one in a "breast is best" world. Of course, there will always be families who must exclusively formula-feed from the get-go (including mothers on certain medications, adoptive parents, and gay male parents), but the overwhelming majority of mothers today do start out breastfeeding. The better the job a formula company does to support a woman in those efforts, the more likely she is to turn to that company when she starts worrying about insufficient milk, or when she goes back to work and the only place to pump is in a disgusting bathroom stall, or when she, like one exhausted new mom I know with a barely out-of-the-womb two-week-old, starts introducing formula at night on the advice of her *pediatrician*, who said it might help this mom get some more sleep. (Studies have shown it won't. Infants are *supposed* to be up at night, and supplemental formula feeding at night can be detrimental to a baby's development.)

The formula companies know all of this, of course, and I'm sure somewhere alongside that classified WIC formula-consumption chart there's a graph showing exactly where all the breastfeeding mothers fall off and for which specific reasons. Then, like a suitor lying in wait for a woman to break up with her boyfriend, the formula companies can swoop in at just the right time to help pick up the pieces.

But what the formula manufacturers also know, just like everyone else who has access to the research, is that one bottle of formula can start inhibiting a mother's ability to produce breast milk the way nature intended. So even if the very reason for that first bottle of supplemental formula is because of a mother's *imagined* fears about insufficient milk, it won't be long before her milk supply issues are very real, indeed. Some mothers I know have been able to successfully supplement and continue breastfeeding, but they inevitably stopped nursing a couple of months after that first bottle. (One friend said that once she saw how quickly her husband could put her daughter to bed with a bottle, sitting there nursing for thirty minutes every night started to feel like a *really* long time.) This is why formula companies have worked so hard to get those free samples into hospitals and the federal WIC program. "Sampling helps build awareness to trial and then to repurchase," said one consultant I know who has worked with formula manufacturers. "And repurchase is what *every* company wants."

This source had to speak to me in vague terms, as any consultant would. But what I really wanted to know from her was, why are we so willing to trust the "we are here for you" line the formula companies are trying to sell us? The product isn't laundry detergent, after all. And at stake are not our socks, but our children's health.

Her answer: We believe the formula companies because in a world where "breast is best" but where there's an utter lack of support for mothers to meet that ideal, we have to. The formula companies know this, too, she stated plainly. "If the chord of 'breast is best' now makes sense, but you also have to sell formula, do you want mothers looking at it as a horrible product, that they're buying garbage, that they're pouring gasoline into their babies? No. You want them to feel safe and secure that you're the go-to brand to love and take care of their special offspring in the most scientific, caring manner possible."

What the science really says, however, is a different matter altogether.

eleven

The Human Experiment

Remember: you're not looking for answers,
you're looking for questions.
—MARGARET NEVILLE

The sunlight glinted through the trees as I followed the winding path of the campus's main thoroughfare and turned toward my destination. A lone college kid wearing checkered shorts and Vans pedaled in front of me on a bicycle. It was August, and the campus appeared empty; I hadn't seen another car or person yet. But as I approached the formidable seven-story glass, concrete, and aluminum building marked Biomedical Research in clinical silver caps and watched the young man coast to the front, it appeared not everyone was on hiatus for the summer. The half dozen bike racks at the building's entrance were packed full, and I watched him artfully maneuver his into the bunch before walking up to the glass door and disappearing inside.

If you wanted to design a laboratory for the research of

the future, the Health Sciences Biomedical Research Facility at the University of California, San Diego (UCSD), would be it. Completed in 2014 to the tune of $113 million, the 196,000-square-foot LEED Platinum–certified facility not only houses some of the greatest research minds in the world, it groups their lab space together in an unprecedented way: across disciplines, so that an infectious-disease researcher can swap cells with, say, a pediatric scientist; and a glycobiologist (a scientist who studies sugar molecules) can share data with a microbiologist. (You'll see the importance of this kind of collaboration in a moment.) Rob Knight, the star microbial ecologist unlocking the microscopic wonders of the human microbiome, was a recent score for UCSD and the new facility. His lab is housed on the building's first floor.

"So for us [scientists], this is heaven, right?" said Lars Bode as I stepped off the majestic open concrete staircase on the fourth floor and he walked forward to greet me with a firm handshake.

Bode, director of the Bode Lab and associate professor of pediatrics in UCSD's Division of Neonatology and Division of Pediatric Gastroenterology, Hepatology, and Nutrition, is one of the world's foremost microbiologists studying one of science's least understood (and very challenging to pronounce) molecules: human milk oligosaccharides. To save time over the course of a conversation, Bode sometimes uses the abbreviation *HMO*, but for me that removed some of the mystery and made me feel as though I were talking about a health plan. Thankfully, during our conversation, I discovered that the more I just went for it and said it, *oligosaccharide*, the more it started to roll off the tongue. *Oligosaccharide* sounds particularly elegant coming from Bode, since he's originally from Germany and pronounces the word with a short *o* that made me think he was going to launch into "A la peanut butter sandwiches!" the first few times he said it.

Human milk *oligo* (little, or few) *saccharides* (sugars) are, as the etymology describes, complex sugar molecules. That prefix may be deceptive, however. Though tiny, there is nothing "few" about them. Remarkably, oligosaccharides are the third most abundant component in human breast milk. First, there's lactose (sugar); then there are lipids (fat); and right after that come the oligosaccharides, even more abundant than protein. To date, more than 150 different types have been identified. And it's also worth noting, of course, that these numerous, intricate, and still largely mysterious compounds are not present in infant formula.

Given the prevalence of human milk oligosaccharides in breast milk and the fact that they're glaringly missing from formula, you would think that more people had heard of them, especially since these compounds were discovered more than fifty years ago. But what may be most remarkable of all is that very few of us have, which includes those individuals who should be uniquely interested in how they affect our health: doctors.

On my two-and-a-half-hour drive down to San Diego from Los Angeles, I listened to a podcast of a talk Bode had given to a group of neonatologists, and he had launched the presentation by asking who in the audience had heard about oligosaccharides. There was mumbling throughout the crowd, and I could guess that only a few hands hesitantly went up. That was an opening he really liked to use, Bode told me sometime later as he parked his athletic frame in his desk chair while I sat across from him in his office. And he used it a lot, since he now was invited all around the world to share what he had learned about the wonders of human milk.

"Usually you have about twenty, twenty-five hands that go up in a room of eight hundred people," he said. "Then you ask the same question when you're done with your talk and of course *all* the hands go up. That's [eight hundred] people that you just educated about compounds in milk they didn't know of before. They're like, 'Oh wow. I didn't know this. This is cool!' "

Sometimes, on these trips, he learns something surprising himself. Like when one Christmas, he traveled back to his hometown of Hamelin, Germany, famed village of the Pied Piper, to give a lecture in German. ("It's not very easy," he said. His German has gotten a bit rusty after living in the United States for more than a decade.) As his mom drove him to the lecture, she casually remarked that Bode, born in 1974, had actually been formula-fed as a baby. Bode had already received his PhD from University College of London, studying oligosaccharides, and had begun a postdoc in molecular biology at the Sanford Burnham Prebys Medical Discovery Institute (then called The Burnham Institute) in La Jolla. At the time of her confession, he had been studying human milk for *years*.

"I said, 'What?! That can't be! I've been talking about breastfeeding this whole time and you're just telling me *now*?' She said, 'Yeah, that was just the way we did it in the seventies. They would come to the hospital and give you the bottles and show you how it worked.' "

Times are very different today, said Bode, pointing to the

hospital breastfeeding rate in San Diego, now over 95 percent. He himself is the father of a six-year-old daughter who, not surprisingly, had been breastfed. Bode likes to include her picture in presentations and publications, which sometimes come with fun titles, like his article "Human Milk Oligosaccharides: Every Baby Needs a Sugar Mama." (Evidently the editors of the journal *Glycobiology* also have a sense of humor.)

Still, just what is in breast milk that makes it so special remains largely a mystery. What we do know, he said, is that breast milk is not a liquid or a food but an extremely powerful *tissue*. And the overwhelming presence of the complex sugar molecules, oligosaccharides, remains a mystery, too. Yet Bode insisted that, in all likelihood, their abundance indicates that they have had a very important role to play. He told me to think in the context of a woman giving birth hundreds of years ago. "You're already drained from the pregnancy. [Food] is not unlimited like it is today. Then you have to put all this energy into making milk. Why would you make oligosaccharides that are the third most abundant component? Why would evolution allow that, if there is not a benefit for the infant or the mother or both, right? It must be a huge advantage, otherwise you wouldn't do it."

But just what was that advantage? We know what purpose the other primary components in breast milk—lactose and lipids—serve. They are the essential energy sources a baby needs in order to grow. But babies can't even digest oligosaccharides, which are completely resistant to stomach acid, pancreatic enzymes, and even the brush border of the small intestine. As it turns out, inside a baby those oligosaccharides may be feeding someone or *something* else entirely: the intricately fine-tuned universe of trillions of microbial cells in our gut that compose the human microbiome.

THE MICROBIOME IS A WORLD WE ARE ONLY BEGINNING TO UNDERstand, and yet the simple knowledge of its existence is as mind-blowing as staring up at the ever-expanding glitter of a star-lit night sky. While we have been exploring outer space and combing the depths of the ocean to unlock the mysteries of life, it turns out that there is an entire unexplored world inside every one of us. Our bodies are made up of human cells, of course—some forty trillion, along with their twenty-two thousand corresponding genes. But the tiny organisms living in our guts, on our skin, in every crevice and every fluid of our bodies, far outnumber that. It is estimated that each of us is host to one hundred *trillion* microbes, along with their two million microbial genes.

Simply put, microbes are the oldest form of life on earth. We have fossils of these organisms from 2.7 billion years ago, back when the atmosphere had almost no oxygen and methane droplets shrouded the skies in a hydrocarbon haze. And the home they have inhabited in our bodies, the microbiome, may be as old as human beings themselves. Ancient bacterial DNA was uncovered in the body of Ötzi, the fifty-three-hundred-year-old ice mummy of a man discovered in the Ötztal Alps. Some of that very same ancient microbial history may even be living inside of us today, since the microbiome is handed down from generation to generation, from mother to child, during birth (via the birth canal) and breastfeeding. It may—or may not—still be there, however. While one recent study looking at the microbiota in the fossilized stool of humans who lived a thousand years ago found that they closely resembled those of modern-day hunter-gatherers, what's going on in our guts today, in the modern industrialized world, is a very different story.

"In the middle of the twentieth century, people finally understood germ theory in a meaningful way," said the evolutionary biologist Katie Hinde, who had recently left Harvard to become associate professor at Arizona State University's School of Human Evolution and Social Change and the new Center for Evolution and Medicine when I caught up with her again. Unfortunately, she explained, their takeaway was that all bacteria and such were the enemy. "All of a sudden, [everyone was saying] 'Germs are bad! Everybody sterilize your house!' And women were douching with Lysol—*douching with Lysol!*" she exclaimed. In addition to dousing our crops with pesticides, and processing and packaging our foods to make them more sanitary, she said, "there was a transition across the board as to what was perceived to be safer, healthier living. And a feature of that was formula."

It is just now that we are beginning to understand that the ancient microbial colonies in our breast milk, our vaginas, our *guts*—the fellow citizens in our bodies, so to speak—may not only be imperative to our health; they may turn out to be the very things that save us from our ever-expanding epidemic of chronic disease. Currently, one of the hottest areas in medical research is the examination of the connection between the microbiome and the skyrocketing incidence of autoimmune disease, allergies, autism, cancer (you name it, someone is studying it) in the Western world.

According to UCSD microbiome pioneer Rob Knight, speaking to more than a million viewers who have tuned in to his TED talk last year, "the three pounds of microbes that you carry around with you might be more important than every single gene you carry around in your genome."

Yet for decades now, we've been fighting back the microbes as if they were an invisible army, wiping them out with our antibiotics and disinfectants, with our processed-and-packaged-in-plastic Western diet, and in fact, with nearly every facet of our germaphobic modern world. But more profoundly, we may have broken this unseeable chain in our human evolution before we've even begun to understand it, by abandoning the two ways we inherited it from our ancestors: birth and breastfeeding. Take, as an example, a baby in the industrialized world—born by C-section, fed infant formula, doused with multiple doses of antibiotics in early life. All of a sudden, that baby and untold millions of our children start to look a lot like the germ-free rats researchers like Bode employ in their studies. Now imagine an even worse scenario. The aforementioned practices don't just wipe out vast quantities of microbial life in a baby's gut; they actually introduce pathogens that were never designed to be in there in the first place—deadly microorganisms like the *Staphylococcus aureus* that lurked in the hospital where the baby was delivered via C-section, or the *Enterobacter sakazakii* that can turn up in infant formula. (Powdered infant formula is not sterile.)

Translation? "In our antibiotic-infused world, we may have severed our ties with all the gut flora we've acquired over the last ten thousand years or more," said Simon Murch, a clinical pediatric gastroenterologist at the UK's University

Hospitals Coventry and Warwickshire and emeritus professor of pediatrics at the University of Warwick.

Murch's area of research is pediatric gastroenterology with a special interest in gut immunology, and I spoke with him in anticipation of his contribution to a series of papers in the *Lancet*. Since published, the papers spurred a great deal of buzz: one revealed that improving breastfeeding practices could save the lives of more than 800,000 children each year. Another less publicized but equally astounding finding: breastfeeding is connected to the priming of a baby's microbiome in a way that has never before been understood.

"What happens in early life is critical," he told me and then went on to explain that the transfer of the microbiome via a mother's breast milk could have a lasting effect on a baby's immune system later in life. "There is now evidence that a mother may transfer the organisms from her gut community into her breast milk, contained in immune cells, and thence to the intestine of the baby," he said, adding that the breastfeeding mother is also transferring elements of her own specific immune cells as well. "She's supplying matched immune inputs to the baby."

According to Murch, science is only just starting to reveal how these inputs are directly linked to our health. It is too early to tell, for instance, whether formula feeding might even result in a too-twitchy immune system—one more likely to develop cancer, for instance. But what we do now scientifically understand, he said, is that the interaction of mother, baby, and microbiome is complex and long lasting in a way we are only beginning to comprehend.

"It's breast milk as personalized medicine," he declared. "[A mother's breast milk is] specific for the genetic needs of the baby. The mother is genetically, exquisitely attuned with her baby."

AS IT HAPPENS, EVERY MOTHER PRODUCES A PATTERN OF OLIGOsaccharides that is unique to her breast milk and her child. Back at the lab, Lars Bode explained to me that this is partially determined by genetics, although the pattern changes over the course of lactation.

As we toured his unbelievably expansive, multimillion-dollar laboratory space, I remarked with some embarrassment that I hadn't actually stepped foot in a lab since AP Biology in my senior year of high school. This looked radically different. As we passed row upon row of shelves piled high with glass jars capped in myriad colors, I spied Post-it notes slapped above webs of wires that ran to boxy gray machines resembling giant copiers and printers.

"I just love it," he said, watching me take it all in. "I'm like a little kid on the playground." For Bode, all of it—a super-lab that stretched as far as my eyes could see—was about figuring out one tiny piece of the puzzle. That puzzle piece of oligosaccharides is where everything begins.

"In the early days of life, [oligosaccharides] drive who moves into your intestine and who doesn't," said Bode. "It's the priming of your gut microbiome." He explained that in this one way in which oligosaccharides function, they are known as *pre*biotic. This differs from the endless rows of *pro-*

biotics that line the shelves of health food stores as the public has become more aware of the influence of the gut on overall health. Probiotics, Bode pointed out, are the beneficial bacteria themselves. Prebiotics are what the bacteria and other microorganisms consume; they are what make it possible for a community of microflora to take shape.

As complex sugars that only specific bacteria or communities of bacteria can break down, some of the oligosaccharides work in precisely this way, feeding the good microbes and allowing them to proliferate so that they crowd out the bad guys. (To help get the point across in his talks, Bode puts up a slide of Pac-Man eating up all the pac-dots and kicking out the ghosts.) One of the good guys is *B. infantis*, a powerful bacterium that can overwhelm pathogens and has shown particular promise in the treatment of irritable bowel syndrome.

But human milk oligosaccharides aren't simply lunch for the good guys. They can also act like a decoy transport on a suicide mission, fooling the pathogens into thinking the oligosaccharides are the same sugars that line the baby's intestinal wall, luring the pathogens to bind, and then flushing them out of a baby's body before illness can ever take hold. (The fancy term for molecules acting in this fashion is *anti-adhesive antimicrobial*.) This may explain the protective effect of breast milk against diarrheal diseases that frequently prove fatal in developing countries, said Bode, since different oligosaccharides have been shown to act precisely this way against cholera toxin, *E. coli*, rotavirus, campylobacter (which leads to more than two million cases of food poisoning in the United States alone each year), and the devastating protozoa

E. histolytica (warning: do not Google amebiasis, the disease this parasite causes).

And the untold powers of oligosaccharides don't stop there. Bode and his team discovered that HIV-infected mothers with high levels of oligosaccharides in their breast milk were less likely to transmit the disease to their babies via breastfeeding, which may explain the low incidence of HIV transmission via breastfeeding to begin with. Oligosaccharides also provide the baby with sialic acid, he added, which may be an essential nutrient for brain development and cognition. Bode's research with neonatal rats also found that oligosaccharides had a powerful effect on the prevention of necrotizing enterocolitis, the often fatal intestinal disorder afflicting preterm infants. This may prove to be the reason there is a six- to ten-fold higher risk of death in preterm infants who are formula-fed versus breastfed.

Astoundingly, Bode also may have uncovered a link in the epidemic of obesity, as he and his team recently pinpointed oligosaccharides that correlated to lower body mass in breastfed infants at the age of six and twelve months. Obesity isn't merely a case of bad bacteria lingering in the body of an overweight person who ate junk food, Bode explained. While certain oligosaccharides correlate to lower body mass, it could be that other oligosaccharides feed specific bacteria that actually cause obesity. (Other researchers have recently discovered that when you take bacteria from mice that are obese and put them in the mice that are lean, the lean mice become obese, too.)

It's important to clarify here that taking a whole group of oligosaccharides and infusing them into an individual would not necessarily produce desired effects. "Structure determines function," Bode maintained. With 150 to 200 different oligosaccharides, all with completely unique and increasingly complex structures, every single oligosaccharide quite possibly has a different role (or roles) to play. And pinpointing which do what, let alone isolating the oligosaccharides from human milk, has been a time-consuming process.

Bode pointed to a meter-long white cylinder that looked like a skinny bong held upright by a metal clamp. He explained that three of his PhD students were in the process of using it to isolate the molecules from the milk. Inside the tube were little porous tunnels that channeled the oligosaccharides. The big molecules filtered through more quickly; the smaller ones took their time. The process for that single sample of milk took two hours.

Thankfully, most milk samples no longer have to be analyzed one by one as this one was. With the use of a new robotic platform, Bode's team can now analyze ninety-six samples at a time, receiving all the data in twenty-four hours. At this rate, they can analyze several hundred milk samples a week. (I asked if his wife provided any samples, but he laughed and said that they had plenty from the breastfeeding moms in his unit. And other moms sometimes mailed theirs to the lab after coming across his scientific articles.)

Oligosaccharide research is progressing at a faster pace all across the board. Currently on the shelf in Bode's lab is about half a kilogram of 2'-fucosyllactose, the most abundant type of oligosaccharide in human milk. His team did some calculations and discovered that if they had bought that half kilo at the going rate when Bode was a PhD student just over a decade ago, when the process of isolating oligosaccharides was still painstakingly slow, it would have cost $50 million. "It would not be sitting on the shelf, for sure!" he chuckled.

Yet even with the research now advancing more rapidly, he cautioned that there still remain far more unknowns than knowns. For instance, why have these mysterious structures evolved in humans to begin with? How are they made in the mammary gland? Why are we so different, compared with any other mammal out there? (Other primates and animals produce oligosaccharides in much smaller amounts, and the structures are far simpler.) How does each one function differently in the body? What benefits do they really have for the infant? We just don't have these answers yet, he conceded.

And in fact, Bode's research has revealed that not all oligosaccharides are necessarily beneficial. In the case of that HIV study, higher total levels of oligosaccharides in an HIV-positive mother's milk were associated with a lower risk of infecting her baby, but one particular sugar molecule, 3'-sialyllactose, actually doubled the risk of a baby acquiring the virus from its mother.

Of course, this cautionary revelation has not stopped companies from trying to cash in on the early studies. Bode had just returned from a research conference he had organized in Montana (where formula-industry members were in attendance), and he told me to grab a small white package that was sitting on a shelf right next to me. "I just got that at the conference," he said. "You could take one if you like." Inside the box were little, individual white packets that looked just like creamer you could stir into your coffee. But they contained just one specific oligosaccharide, he said—the

2'-fucosyllactose that would have cost a couple hundred thousand dollars for a packet's worth of the molecule a decade ago. This packet of 2'-fucosyllactose was meant to be added to an infant's formula, even though no one yet has any idea what effect that "enrichment" would have. Bode was surprised that the company had chosen to market 2'-fucosyllactose, since only 70 percent of mothers produce it. To him, the implications were huge.

"There are about 30 percent of infants that should not receive this because mom could not provide it. Is this good? Is this bad?" We just don't know, he warned, and by taking a single sugar out of the more than 150 and then adding it into the formula mix, we could be knocking everything out of balance.

I had a hard time imagining that any mother or father would knowingly opt to make their baby into a guinea pig. Yet apparently, the formula companies have been making that decision for parents everywhere for quite some time, Bode revealed. He said that while *human* milk oligosaccharides are not yet in infant formula, two *non*human versions have been quietly added for years: fructooligosaccharides (FOS), isolated from plants, and galacato-oligosaccharides (GOS), synthesized from bovine lactose. For a while now, he and other researchers have cautioned that such supplementation—with little real understanding behind it—could be harmful, and, in fact, one recent study has indeed linked a rare form of anaphylaxis to the GOS in cow's milk formula.

The anaphylactic reaction was highly unusual, he explained, since it's usually proteins that trigger such reactions, not carbohydrates. In light of this new evidence, he pointed out, there is the very real possibility that all the infants who have reactions to cow's milk formula are not actually allergic to cow's milk as previously assumed but are allergic to the added nonhuman oligosaccharides. And the long-term effects of this experimentation can be equally scary, said Bode. "What if these kids, when they're thirty, are all of a sudden at a higher risk of being obese, type 2 diabetic, or you name it? We wouldn't know [that] right now. We'll know in thirty years, *if* someone does the research."

NO ONE BUT THE FORMULA MANUFACTURERS THEMSELVES HAD done the research when, thirty-five years ago, on the advice of my pediatrician, my parents chose to feed me Isomil, a soy formula produced by Abbott Laboratories beginning in 1966. That's because, to this day, the Food and Drug Administration (FDA) does not actually approve a formula before it can be marketed. Companies need only to provide documentation that the formula meets the federal nutrient requirements for infant formula and that the ingredients in their proprietary products have either already been approved by the FDA or are listed in a category known as GRAS.

GRAS stands for *generally recognized as safe* but boils down to innocent until proven guilty. The manufacturer of the substance tells the FDA it appears safe, or takes a look at the existing research around that additive and then tells the FDA it appears safe. And so FDA adds it to the GRAS list—no further study or testing required. Soy protein isolate, the primary ingredient in soy formula, is one of those GRAS ingredients, as are dozens of other additives in the more widely used cow's milk–based formulas. Both galacto-oligosaccharides and fructooligosaccharides—the two nonhuman oligosaccharides Bode warned about—are GRAS ingredients. The genetically modified soy- and corn-based ingredients in most infant formulas are not technically on the GRAS list, but the FDA clarified in a 1992 policy statement that foods derived from genetically modified organisms, or GMOs, are presumptively GRAS as well. Trans fat was on the GRAS list until the FDA called an *oops* on that one this past year.

Since breastfeeding my own children and then subsequently realizing that the early building blocks of my own life were barely FDA approved, I've often wondered just how safe soy protein isolate and other formula additives really are. The overall evidence on soy, for instance, is inconclusive, but there have been many questions raised about its role as a possible endocrine disruptor. Although maybe someone should consider using me as a case study since I've struggled with health issues for half my life to date: debilitating chronic fatigue in my teens; a hypothyroidism diagnosis in my early twenties; and now, in the wake of hormonal changes from pregnancy, an intermittent asthma-like condition that leaves me coughing for weeks anytime I catch a cold. (Thankfully, I was able to conceive and give birth to two healthy daughters, knock on wood.) All this in spite of the fact that I'm a light drinker, my favorite pastime is hiking, and I've been teased my entire life about a diet so ridiculously pristine that even when I lived in my two-hundred-square-foot New York City apartment, I made three meals a day from scratch.

Some of my health problems were probably just hereditary, doctors said, and when I looked around at my family, that seemed plausible enough. My father suffered severe food allergies as a child; my brother, too, has severe allergies; my mother and aunt and a bunch of cousins have autoimmune thyroid disease; and there have been two family members with another, more severe autoimmune disease: multiple sclerosis. But when I began to dig into all those health histories, I realized that a common thread had been overlooked. Every single one of those family members had been either exclusively or predominantly formula-fed as a baby. This is not to say, of course, that formula feeding had been the cause of my family's collective health issues. Yet, in my attempt to get to the root of my health problems (and in my family members' attempts to get to the root of their health problems), it is remarkable that no doctor ever asked a very simple question: *How were you fed as a baby?*

In light of the astonishing findings that Bode and other researchers are only beginning to uncover about the intricate systems at play in the beginning of our lives, this is a question we should be asking. Because here's the crazy thing: despite the fact that no one but the industry itself is extensively testing infant formula and its additives for safety, despite the fact that we're essentially giving companies the benefit of the doubt when it comes to a substitute that has only been around for a mere century (and is not, as it turns out, a substitute for a food but for a *human tissue*, as Bode explained), we've placed the burden of proof on our bodies and our lives, while breast milk has sustained our species for hundreds of thousands of years. *Breast is best? Prove it!* the media shouts with every study, unraveling a stream of headlines like "Should I Breastfeed My Baby to Make Him or Her Smarter?" Such headlines, unfortunately, trivialize the depth or greater context of the real science, or else misrepresent it altogether. The unthinking substitution of formula for breast milk is virtually as if, during the past century, we had decided to swap out the blood supply in our bodies, to replace it with an artificial blood substitute—and then demanded that the people who support real blood prove that it really worked better than the manufactured alternate.

Let me be clear: I am not claiming that formula is poison. I sincerely hope that it's not, because if it is, I'm in big trouble. But the media and even the scientific studies now urge consideration of the *benefits* of breastfeeding, and that makes it seem as though formula is the norm and the eons-old elixir streaming from our bodies is merely providing a boost the likes of which one would get from a packet of vitamins. Of course, our era isn't the Dublin Foundling Hospital of the 1700s or even America at the turn of the last century, where feeding an infant anything other than breast milk was tantamount to a death sentence. Four generations of human beings have now been reared on infant formula, and millions upon millions of people would attest that they're fine. But maybe we should stop talking about the *benefits* of breastfeeding and instead start considering the *risks* of *not* breastfeeding, since I'm certainly not fine. Are you fine? Are *we*—an overweight nation of chronically ill, medicine-dependent formula feeders—fine?

Here are the facts: Nearly 40 percent of Americans will be diagnosed with cancer at some point in their lifetimes. Obesity and diabetes are epidemic, with childhood and adolescent diagnoses of type 2 and type 1 diabetes (long thought to be genetic) rising more than 20 percent in the past decade alone. Autoimmune diseases and allergies are skyrocketing, including anaphylactic food allergies in children and the mysterious affliction of autism. In my work as an environmental journalist, I have long examined health-damaging pesticides, flame-retardant chemicals, and other pollutants in our air and in our water. These are viable threats to consider. But in the weeks and months after Izzy was born, amid all the joy and the love I felt as I put her to my breast, there also existed an uneasiness; questions suddenly loomed before me, as a mother and a journalist. In the epidemic of our nation's ill health, what if we are overlooking an utterly simple piece of the puzzle—that *what* and *the way* we feed our young, radically altered for the first time in human history, has played a role?

According to Bode, we need to look at this possibility not per person, but as a question of population statistics. "People tend to forget that. They say, well [I was fed formula and] I'm fine. That's not how it works. On a population scale, it might not be that subtle."

He has a point. When you look at the population statistics for pneumonia, or gastroenteritis, or SIDS, or obesity and diabetes, or childhood leukemia, or necrotizing enterocolitis, the risks of not breastfeeding are dramatic. But more diffuse ailments like mine, which fall in the realm of autoimmune disease and allergies and which often appear later in life and are difficult to diagnose, may be truly challenging to tie to mismatched immune inputs in the cultivation of a microbiome.

Still, just because we don't know at present doesn't mean the evidence doesn't exist. And just because some evidence *is* there doesn't mean we fully understand it, either. That's pretty much the stance taken by Margaret "Peggy" Neville, a scientist who has studied the functional biology of the mammary gland since the 1970s. When I contacted her to talk about the link between breastfeeding and the reduced risk of breast cancer, she initially remarked, "Not as clear-cut as the breastfeeding crowd would have you believe." Later, she added, "The breastfeeding advocates describe me as a really terrible person, because I like hard data."

At first, her comments caught me off guard. I hadn't expected a lactation scientist to rip on the La Leche League crowd et al. It was a bit like a climate scientist telling me she wasn't too keen on the work of environmentalists. But as the plucky semiretired grandma (and professor emerita of physiology and biophysics as well as obstetrics and gynecology at the University of Colorado Denver) and I spoke, she explained that she had breastfed her own kids back in the 1960s, when she was living in Africa, simply because it would have made no sense to boil water for bottle-feeding when there was "a lovely source of clean milk readily available." Back then, she thought breastfeeding was great, but that didn't make her blind to her job as a scientist. "You have to realize, I'm a hardcore biologist," she said.

And in the case of the oft-repeated statement that breastfeeding reduces breast cancer risk, the current data were far more nuanced than that, she insisted. Yes, breastfeeding appears breast-cancer protective, she said, but only if you breastfeed a lot of kids for a very long time. "That's not how most people breastfeed in the Western world," she said.

As it turned out, a great deal more research that went far beyond the realm of breast cancer was needed. So, right before Neville retired from CU Denver, she called every lactation researcher whose work she admired, and brought them all together for a conference that spelled out, in one clearly defined document, the myriad unresolved questions surrounding lactation and human milk. From January 18 to 20, 2012, the veritable conclave of superheroes convened at the University of Colorado School of Medicine. Evolutionary biologist Katie Hinde was there, as were many of the researchers featured in this book.

Here, in very simple terms, is the consensus of the greatest minds in lactation science: We don't fully know what's in breast milk. We don't understand how the thousands of components in breast milk affect a baby's development, especially when it comes to a baby's cognitive and emotional development. We have no idea what happens to these thousands of components or to a baby's development when we add infant formula into the jumble (mixed feeding), which is how the overwhelming majority of American women feed their babies. We don't know how human milk establishes the microbiome, and we don't know how that develops an infant's immune system and inflammatory response. We have little information on how a mother's health or even the food she eats influences the mammary gland. We don't even have a fundamental understanding of what affects the ability of a mother to produce sufficient milk for her child. We also don't have a clue as to how environmental pollutants and our epidemic of prescription drug use might affect a baby's development via his mother's breast milk.

I could go on, but I think you get the point.

"The best thing for you to say is 'We need more research,'" said Neville as our conversation drew to a close. "Just keep saying it." Then she added one more thought: in order for our society to make more research a priority, a mind shift has to occur. She recounted how she had recently stumbled across an op-ed in the *New York Times* about a new field called the study of ignorance—or agnotology, as coined by Robert Proctor, the historian of science at Stanford who is pioneering the field. Neville hadn't heard of the study of ignorance before she read the article, but it encapsulated what she had been telling her students for years. "We focus on all the new stuff, and we think we know everything, but in fact, every time we learn something, we have new questions to ask. So what we really need to focus on," she said, "is, what are the questions that we need to ask?"

I told her I would look for the *Times* piece, and she wished me good luck with my book. But she left me with a stern warning: "Remember: you're not looking for answers, you're looking for *questions*."

REGRETTABLY, WHILE PROBING RESEARCHERS LIKE NEVILLE AND Bode search for the right questions to ask to unravel the mystery of human milk, others are all too ready to give us answers—even if they're not the right ones. There is already the unsettling presence of untested nonhuman oligosaccharides in infant formula, yet the determination to "innovate" and artificially match the wonders of human milk will hardly stop there. The formula industry is rapidly expanding the use of what it calls "high value-added ingredients," such as the breast milk–proteins lactoferrin and alpha-lactalbumin (both already used in Asia) and even the building blocks of

DNA known as nucleotides (already added to some US formulas), despite the fact that these human-milk molecules are as barely understood as oligosaccharides. Still other companies, like the microbiotics start-up Evolve Biosystems (founded by Bruce German and other esteemed University of California, Davis, human-milk researchers), are developing bacteria-based probiotics and prebiotics targeted to an infant's microbiome. They plan to bring these products to market themselves.

"They are very obsessed with what's in milk and believe me, [their research is] not to help mothers breastfeed," offered the Cincinnati Children's Hospital Medical Center lactation scientist Laurie Nommsen-Rivers.

But perhaps we can't fault industry for attempting to capitalize on all this breast-milk research since the reality is that the formula companies are the ones funding a lot of it. According to Katie Hinde, federal funding rates for researchers are incredibly low, typically with less than 20 percent of submitted grants being funded. She hasn't yet taken nonfederal funds, but for many researchers, this option is inevitable. "Such grants are usually conditional on the researcher having total independence," she maintained, "but they do require [the researcher] to ethically disclose the source of funding."

"It's impossible to do everything just on the academic level," Bode concurred, adding that a few years ago when he submitted to his granting institution, the NIH, his research was marked as "pseudomedical research" in the review section. "Because what? It's human milk? I mean, seriously," he protested.

Clearly, if our government is going to continue to prioritize breastfeeding as a major public health issue, then our lawmakers must boost funding for Bode and other researchers. At the very least, they need to start taking human-milk research seriously.

But let's say that one day we unlock all the secrets of oligosaccharides and other wondrous milk molecules. Then what? Well, formula would get better, said Bode, and ostensibly there was nothing wrong with this, since there would always be mothers who either didn't want to or couldn't breastfeed. Still, he said, he is often asked, "How would we put one hundred fifty oligosaccharides together to make the ideal formula?" This isn't a question we could ever definitively answer, he explained, since every mother has her own specific blueprint for her individual child, and that blueprint is ever changing.

"You may as well breastfeed," he said. "In the end, let's face it, human milk will always be superior."

I had to ask him, did he foresee a moment in time when the science will catch up? When formula becomes so close to the real thing that the choice—breast or bottle—becomes merely a matter of preference?

"No," he said, looking at me, across his desk. "For the simple reason that human milk is not just molecules and mixing things together. You breastfed your two daughters. You're still doing it. There is a connection between the mom and the infant that you just could not mimic in a bottle, in a powder."

twelve

The Weaning

I'll never forget about you, Milky.

—IZZY

One month before Izzy turned four years old, Matthew and I decided it was time to wean her. By *decided it was time*, I mean that Matthew had set down age four as the limit, we had talked with Izzy for months about what it would mean when she no longer drank Milky and thus became a "big girl," and she had stopped sobbing at the mention of giving up Milky. She even seemed a little proud about making the transition. So I acquiesced and reluctantly agreed that she might, at last, be ready.

Looking back, I wish I had had the confidence to let her stop nursing in her own time, but this book doesn't just encompass my daughter's rite of passage; it represents my own journey, too. The truth is, though Matthew has since come around, *neither* of us understood what I now know: how normal it has been throughout human history to breastfeed a child for many, many years, and how normal it was in America until just over a century ago—a mere blip on the continuum of human existence. In fact, neither of us had grasped how intricately hardwired into our biology human milk is. We had no sense of the utter lack of knowledge existing about how the mysterious transfer between mother and child actually works.

And let's face it; I had finally caved to societal pressure, doubtless like millions of women have over the course of history. Because the fascinating thing about breastfeeding is that while it is as hardwired and essential a biological process as breathing or sleeping or peeing or having sex (let industry try to come up with substitutes for those), it has always been, and probably will always be, largely influenced by cultural practices. After all, the biological and evolutionary norm for nursing, two and a half to seven years, is a very wide range. And while for peoples such as the Mongolians and the !Kung the youngest child in a family has always nursed to the very upper end of that range and even beyond, every culture historically has also had its reasons to wean sooner, such as the birth of a new child or the desire to conceive a sibling—or maybe even because a cave mom was just having a really tough time chasing down woolly mammoths while lugging around her five-year-old.

So Matthew and I did what cave people probably did when it was time to wean a child: we decided to take Izzy to Disneyland. Seriously though, there wasn't a lot of information out there about how to go about weaning a child at the more advanced age of four. But the few blog posts and the like we had read said that it was important to mark the occasion. And interestingly, the "weaning party," as it's often called, has historical precedent. When the ancient Jews weaned a child (anywhere between eighteen months and five years of age, according to Jewish law), it was cause for great celebration, because at a time when infant mortality was undoubtedly high, this meant that a child had survived the dangerous period of babyhood. "And Abraham made a great feast on the day that Isaac was weaned," says the book of Genesis. (It also says that Abraham's other son, Ishmael, the one he had with his Egyptian concubine Hagar, made fun of the celebration. He and his mom were promptly tossed out of the family, which just goes to show you how seriously we Jews take our weaning parties.)

It seemed like the ancient Jews really knew what they were doing. I made Izzy a photo book that took her through the story of her babyhood and all our wonderful "Milky" times over the years, ending with a picture of Izzy in her Snow White costume above the caption that we were going to Disneyland. Happily, she seemed to buy the whole thing and excitedly shared the news with anyone who would listen, including every member of our family, the parents of her friends at preschool, her preschool teachers, and even the baggers in the checkout lane at the grocery store. "Guess what?! In a couple of weeks, because I'm a big gurrl now, I'm going to go to San Diego and have chocolate cupcakes with Grandma and Paw and then leave Mika at home for the day and then go to Disneyland with Mommy and Daddy and I'm going to meet Mickey and Minnie for my weeeening party!" She lingered on the word *weaning* for so long that I didn't know whether to jump in like a newscaster trying to cut off a crazy guest, to stand there mute and mortified, or to just crack up while I waited for her hopefully clueless victim's reaction.

Thankfully, and much to her delight, people usually jumped in right after hearing *Disneyland* with a simple "How exciting!" A few caught her emphasis, however, and knew exactly what it meant. "Oh, wow!" they said, smiling at her, and I just grinned right back and nodded, as though throwing a four-year-old a party to celebrate the cessation of breastfeeding was as customary and wholeheartedly American a rite of passage as one's graduation from high school.

On the July day that Matthew, Izzy, and I went to Disneyland, it was a sweltering ninety degrees, but our visit was as magical as any parent taking their kid to Disneyland for the first time could hope for. Izzy got a hug from Cinderella and toted around one of those swirly lollipops the size of her head, and we went on the Pirates of the Caribbean ride twice (her little arms never once let go of my side in the dark). But somewhere between Peter Pan and the Haunted Mansion, she turned to me. "So is this the last night I'm going to have Milky?" she asked. "Yes, sweetie," I said, and she responded with a cheerful OK, sharing the news with the pickle man at the snack stand, the train conductor, and even the guy who, at the end of the night, at the gate, handed Izzy her "My first visit to Disneyland" pin. On the way out of the park, I cried.

Everything after that, though, was really all right. Izzy fell asleep in the car before I had the chance to nurse her for that one last time, so we moved her official weaning to the following night, once we were back in Los Angeles. Matthew was at work, and I tucked Mika into her crib first, just like any other night, and then Izzy and I got cozy in my bed and read the weaning book together. I don't remember what exactly I told her—something along the lines of that my love for her, and Daddy's love for her would never change. But I do remember her response. "Everyone loves me," she said, leaning in to nuzzle up to my breast one last time. "Everyone in all the cities and even the whole planet."

As I watched her close her eyes, her hand absentmindedly caressing my neck and chest in circles as she latched off for the very last time, I took a deep breath and tried to focus on the moment. But before I knew it, it was over. That was it. Four years—now just the memory of my darling baby girl at my breast. Amazingly, though, in all likelihood this would be her memory, too.

At first, weaning seemed a smooth transition. Izzy had a couple of sad nights, but she was easily distracted and quickly channeled her tears into acting like a goofball, lunging for a boob and screaming "My Milky!" at the top of her lungs while Mika was nursing—then dissolving into a fit of giggles. Later, she played the guilt card to a T, telling her aunt (with a saucy grin) that she needed extra ice cream because it was *really* hard to give up Milky. Then she went through a period when she contented herself before bedtime by taking a good, long sniff of my breast, like a chocoholic who had recently gone on a diet. "Ahhh, delicious!" she'd say and then roll over and snuggle under the covers. And finally, one night, she leaned in extra close after that bedtime inhale, as if to share a secret with her cherished childhood friend. "I'll never forget about you, Milky," she said, holding my hand as she drifted off to sleep.

The year since Izzy's weaning has not been an easy one.

Now that I no longer can offer my breasts as the answer to every complex and often unknowable need of my kindergarten-aged daughter, I have struggled, as all parents do, with the outbursts and the tantrums. I have tried as I might, to help her fall asleep at bedtime amid the endless requests for stories and songs, to quell her fears not only about the fake monsters in her closet but the real ones out in the world, to dry her eyes after a fall from her scooter or a bonk on the head from her sister. Like other mommies everywhere, I try, with words alone, to explain the mysteries of life and death and the universe, of which I know she is becoming all too aware. And now that Izzy is no longer able to turn to Milky to comfort her through all the above, she, too, has struggled to verbalize all the things that are swirling inside her. I know she has fond memories of the old days ("Milky tasted better than vanilla ice cream," she has told me repeatedly), but I also know that there is pain. The other day, when she was in the tub, I asked her what she remembered about Milky, and she looked at me, hair slicked back, like a wet mini Yoda. "Weaning only happens once in your life, Mommy," she said, with a sad little smile.

I often wonder what it means that this tiny person has such a profound understanding of the processes of life, of having loved and lost (Milky, not me, obviously), and of having had the strength to move forward and to feel proud that she could. Some might say that avoiding this kind of heartache is all the more reason to wean a baby while she's young, but the memories Izzy will have of her nursling days and of her weaning are, more likely than not, ones that human beings shared throughout much of our history. Are we supposed to have these memories? Do they make us stronger? Of course, these are questions I cannot answer, but I do know that life has a lot of ups and downs and that it rarely is easy. I wonder what it will mean to Izzy and Mika that they will always have this memory of their early days, of their early *years*, when every essential human longing and human need was utterly and completely filled.

OUR MODERN WORLD IS QUICK TO DISMISS A NEED THAT IS UNquantifiable. When I talk about breastfeeding with people from societies that are closer to the way human beings have always lived, the reaction is usually just a shrug. "Nurse for four, five, six years; for us, that's *normal*. Such a big deal here in America," said one of Mika's preschool teachers, who was born and raised in India. The reaction is also similar from people who *study* the way human beings have always lived (such as biologists and anthropologists). "Four years is getting into the normal sort of range," said the human lactation professor and researcher Peter Hartmann, who added that primates and hunter-gatherer peoples like the Aboriginal Australians often nurse far beyond that. "It's probably four and a half."

But when people from our industrialized world discover that I breastfed Izzy for four years and Mika for three and counting, they often gasp (this happened in Taiwan) or politely continue the conversation while I watch the *She's crazy* alert switch flip on behind their eyes. But there's a third response I encounter quite a bit, where someone waves away nursing at that age as "only for emotional need," as though I were merely acting as some sort of fleshy pacifier for my child.

Modern-day Americans, especially, are quick to demand self-sufficiency from our children at a young age. We view traditional practices like "extended" breastfeeding as emotionally overindulgent while, at the same time, we decree that it's perfectly normal to expect a five-month-old to sleep in a dark room alone at night (and to sleep through the night, to boot). The other day, I was at one of those indoor toddler play places with Mika, sitting next to a mother who was scrolling through different websites on her phone while her twenty-month-old sobbed and sobbed at the other side of the child gate, begging to be picked up. "Ugh, I don't know why he's doing this," she turned to me and sighed, eyes still fixated on her screen. "He just has to learn that he needs to play alone."

Yet the irony is that older American children are increasingly overprotected and their parents become overinvolved. The proliferation of technology has enabled an explosion in helicopter parenting, allowing parents to supervise a child's every move and to intervene at the slightest hint of discomfort. There are now even smartphone apps that allow parents to monitor whether their *college*-aged children are going to class. Strangely, we have become disconnected from children's innate biological need for physical connection and closeness early on in life, and it would seem that we are overcompensating on the flip side. We have become unlatched, yet attached.

The question is, what is really going on here? Are the demands of the modern world—a 24/7 work culture, raising kids with no family nearby, the endless stream of e-mails to answer—too overwhelming for us to give our children the connection they need, to parent the way we did when time was once plentiful? Does our squeamishness about breastfeeding boil down to the fact that it is simply no longer practical for mothers to breastfeed for two years or more? Or is something more insidious at hand: a disconnection from what it means to be human, enabled by our own technologies?

If a group of aliens touched down on our planet right now and took a good look at us, they might conclude that we were trying to scrub away every last reminder that we were ever once animals. We deliver babies by surgery. We open a plastic package and call it dinner. We ignore circadian rhythms ingrained in us by the rising and the setting of our sun, and comfort our isolation in the darkness with little blue screens before our faces. We've even grown to fear every natural scent from our bodies, scrubbing ourselves down with antibacterial soap, piling on deodorant, and spritzing every possibility of bodily emission with air freshener.

The problem is we have made an admirable though misguided attempt to reintroduce breastfeeding back into this sterile twenty-first-century world, believing that we could do it by continuing to substitute the industrial for the human. We turn to iPhone apps to tell us when it's time to nurse. We add on a bottle of formula at night, not trusting that the impossible-to-measure fluid in our breasts could somehow be enough. And more and more, we've come to view breast *pumping* as the same as breast *feeding*, attaching ourselves to machines more than we attach ourselves to our own children.

I'm not saying that breast pumps are bad, per se. Allowing mothers to express milk at work lets them continue breastfeeding longer than they could before the technology existed. (It's worth noting, too, that the largest pump manufacturer in the world, Medela, is a family-owned company that donates profits to a foundation supporting breastfeeding education and human-milk research.) But in the United States, we've championed pumping to the exclusion of giving a new mother the time to bond with her newborn, by packing her off to work with a health care–sponsored breast pump and zero paid maternity leave.

If we continue to view breastfeeding as the transfer of "liquid gold" rather than as the most fundamental human connection between a mother and her child, then we open ourselves to exploitation of what is, in fact, one of our most precious natural resources. Already, human milk is one of the most valuable commodities in the world, worth four hundred times the cost of crude oil. Some of the trade in breast milk serves to feed premature babies in neonatal units and to develop cutting-edge treatments that could one day cure cancer. But some involved in the buying and selling of the "commodity" seem driven more by profit than altruism: the company Prolacta Bioscience, for one, is now selling its human milk–derived fortifier for extremely preterm infants to hospitals for around $10,000 a treatment. There is no doubt that others, including the big formula companies, are racing to distill human milk down to its essence so that they can profit, too. But do we really want what is free and available to nearly all mothers to one day be sold back to us, in a bottle? And would the environmental toll of that be sustainable, with seven billion people on the planet and counting?

This doesn't have to be our future. I see a world where . . .

The United States (along with Liberia, Sierra Leone, Suriname and Papua New Guinea) finally joins every other country on earth to provide paid maternity leave to mothers, so that every woman who wants to is given the means to rest and recuperate after birth and successfully establish breastfeeding. In this world, fathers and partners are given time off, too. Eventually, all the countries on the planet sign a treaty establishing six months as the global minimum, so that every human child has the best chance for life and health by receiving the six months of exclusive breastfeeding recommended by WHO.

In this enlightened new world, *all* hospitals are Baby-Friendly, allowing mothers to bond with their newborns from birth and giving them the best chance to succeed at breastfeeding without the interference of formula advertising and giveaways. The American Academy of Pediatrics extends its nursing recommendation to age two or beyond to meet WHO standards, and the AAP stops taking millions of dollars a year in donations from formula manufacturers. Mothers are given unlimited access to lactation consultants, both before and after leaving the hospital. All doctors and health care practitioners receive extensive education on human lactation in medical school, and each graduates fully understanding the risks to human health of *not* breastfeeding. Obstetricians and pediatricians also routinely add "lactation consultant" to their credentials and are able to assist mothers with any mechanical breastfeeding issues they encounter. If a mother does have trouble breastfeeding, diagnostic tests are available to test for function and normality. Ubiquitous, too, are breastfeeding medicine specialists. These doctors in the hottest new field in medicine (besides microbiome medicine) are able to provide treatment to any nursing mother who needs it, making insufficient milk supply no longer a common fear. Yes, formula is still available for mothers who want it or need it, but they, along with adoptive parents and same-sex male couples, also have access to fairly priced human milk via publicly managed banks.

And in the future I envision, the US government's WIC assistance program stops subsidizing free infant formula for half the country and offers formula (or banked milk) by prescription only, to those who truly need it. The government funnels the billions of dollars saved each year into breastfeeding support, opening WIC's twelve thousand clinics across the country to the public, so that anyone can have access to the program's top-notch breastfeeding educators. Insurance companies reimburse WIC directly, or mothers can pay on an affordable fee-for-service basis.

Governments worldwide also pass laws instituting hefty fines for anyone who kicks a breastfeeding mom and child out of a restaurant, out of a store, off an airplane, or out of *anywhere.* Breastfeeding in public becomes so routine that mothers feel comfortable nursing wherever, either with or without a cover, although super comfy lactation rooms are readily available in public places (especially airports!) for women who need a quiet place to nurse a distracted toddler or a shielded place to pump, or who just desire a little added privacy. And when women head back to work after six months of maternity leave, every work place, regardless of size, has a state-of-the-art room in which mothers can pump, although this is now the secondary choice to the new standard: on-site childcare, which medical centers, schools, tech companies, factories, and even employers like Target offer (after every forward-thinking CEO discovers that it greatly reduces worker turnover and increases productivity). There, in the childcare center, parents visit with their babies at junctures throughout the day, and moms are able to breastfeed as needed. And if mothers want to continue nursing for the recommended two years or more for optimum health and development, it's a no-brainer, since they never again have to choose between their work and their child.

In this informed world, we talk no longer about the "benefits" of breastfeeding but about the risks of *not* breastfeeding. Every child grows up thinking breastfeeding is the norm. Little boys and girls "feed" their dolls by pretending to nurse them, instead of giving them toy baby bottles. Children also grow up seeing supportive commercials about breastfeeding and breast milk on TV and online, but they and their parents do not see commercials for formula, since the advertising of formula for babies twenty-four months and under has been banned by governments around the world. Breastfeeding also becomes so normalized that new generations once again view breasts for their primary purpose. Plenty of men everywhere still adore breasts, of course, but breasts are no longer fetishized, and breast implants go completely out of style.

Attachment parenting is no longer controversial in this lovely world, since everybody recognizes that it's normal for babies to be close to their mothers and to be up a lot at night to breastfeed. Everyone knows, too, that frequent nursing during the day is normal and that putting a baby on a breastfeeding schedule can seriously derail milk production. New research continues to reveal amazing insights about how the emotional aspect of breastfeeding affects a child's intelligence and development, but research also reveals astounding things about the thousands of (now fully cataloged!) components of breast milk. Happily, we have more than the means to fund all this research, since governments have taken the billions of dollars being saved in health care costs (now that nearly everyone is exclusively breastfeeding) and put that money toward human-milk research. And now that we have unequivocally demonstrated the divine power of human milk and the microbiome and have used that knowledge to institute worldwide change to help every woman breastfeed, scientists are also using human milk to develop breakthrough treatments for cancer and autoimmune disease. In fact, lactation science, or human lactology as it's called, is now one of the most desirable fields for young scientists, and professorships in human lactology are some of the most coveted positions in academia.

IF EVERYTHING ABOVE SOUNDS IMPOSSIBLE OR, AT THE VERY least, like the crazy ramblings of a breastfeeding activist, it's not. Much of what I have detailed is already reality; I have described it, in this book. The laws I named are already in place somewhere in the world, and the initiatives I mentioned, such as the Baby-Friendly Hospital Initiative, are already in existence. Other ideas are in the works, as well, such as turning WIC's existing infrastructure into breastfeeding clinics for the public. The National WIC Association is now pursuing this concept, and its president and CEO, Rev. Douglas Greenaway, told me this was actually an idea that came from his daughter-in-law, who lives in Buffalo, New York. (She desperately needed a lactation consultant and couldn't find one, but wasn't income-qualified to visit the WIC clinic in her neighborhood.) The professorship in human lactology is a now-realized concept, too. The Family Larsson-Rosenquist Foundation (the nonprofit arm of pump-maker Medela) just donated nearly $27 million to establish the very first chairs of human lactology in the world, at the University of Zurich and the University of Western Australia. And the outdoor-apparel company, Patagonia, has had on-site childcare for its employees for *thirty years*. Child development–program staff are even trained to offer lactation assistance.

How simply can I say this? With more focused time to spend with our babies and our families, we will be happier. We will be healthier. Child malnutrition worldwide will plummet, as will deaths from infectious disease. The American obesity and diabetes epidemics will be no more, and each new generation will see lower rates of chronic illnesses such as asthma, crippling allergies, and autoimmune disease. Antibiotic resistance, too, will no longer be an urgent public health threat, since antibiotics will be prescribed far less frequently for once-routine baby illnesses like ear infections and even more serious ones like pneumonia. And in the face of an ever more complex and technologically advanced world—and even in the face of climate change—we will be more resilient and self-reliant. Never again will we have to look to industry rather than to the millions of years of biological wisdom embedded in our own bodies. Never again will we respond to industry instead of to our own children. And never, ever again will we take for granted connection, memory, love—the incredible gift of life and humanity that each of us has been given.

ACKNOWLEDGMENTS

The main thread of this story is my own, but all during the writing of this book I've felt more like a dot connector than anything else, stringing together the astounding work of scientists, historians, researchers, economists, educators, doctors, health workers, professors, policymakers, writers and, of course, mothers and fathers who have made the restoration of our unlatched world their life's work. I cannot begin this section without acknowledging these sources, and thanking them for so graciously sharing their knowledge and personal stories with me. Their names appear in the pages of this book.

I owe an extra note of appreciation to Lars Bode, Kathy Dettwyler, Betsy Frazão, Katie Hinde, Dr. Lawrence Gartner, Nemat Hajeebhoy, George Kent, Dr. Ruth Lawrence, Laurie Nommsen-Rivers, Dr. William Sears, as well as Baila and Rabbi Mendel Weiss. They went above and beyond the call of any interviewee—connecting me with sources, providing additional support, patiently responding to a seemingly never-ending chain of follow-up phone calls and e-mails and, in some cases, even cooking me dinner. A special thanks, too, to the mysterious Cedars-Sinai lactation consultant responsible for the epiphany that set me off on this incredible journey, as well as to all of my sources who remain unnamed for a variety of reasons. They know who they are.

I've been told that being a first-time author can be a harrowing ride, but I wouldn't know: Working with my entire team at HarperCollins has been the experience that writers at any stage in their careers only dream about. At every turn my editor, Amy Bendell, was a source of encouragement and wisdom, supplying the most spot-on suggestions imaginable and skillfully coaxing this book into the one I had always hoped it could be (all while providing inspiration as a working-and-pumping mom, to boot!). I only wish that I didn't live on the other side of the country so that I could spend more time with her. It was the incomparable Lisa Sharkey who initially saw the potential in this book; she has since been an enduring source of enthusiasm and brilliant ideas. I also deeply appreciate the efforts of Daniella Valladares, who kept me motivated and on track with her helpful notes last summer in the early stages of the writing process. I am additionally grateful to Amy Baker, Leslie Cohen, Mary Sasso, and Alieza Schvimer for their support and phenomenal behind-the-scenes efforts. And thank you to Joanne O'Neill for my breathtaking cover and to my wonderful copyeditor, Elise Morrongiello, who saved me from my relentless overuse of colons.

Of course, another profound thank you is owed to my original editor, my mom, Katherine Grayson, who first taught me to write and, more recently, delivered indispensable notes on every chapter of this book. Few writers are lucky enough to have a parent who is a professional editor, let alone a mother who remained enthusiastically open-minded while her daughter reexamined her childhood in print—and then was willing to be interviewed for the story! You are the most loving and devoted mom anyone could ever ask for. Thank you, too, to my stepfather (and writer), Ron Roman, who always seemed to have the perfect edit at the ready.

Have I already used the words incomparable and wise? I am wholly indebted to my agent, Mel Parker, who came into my life through a series of uncanny coincidences and connections, and who "got" this project from the beginning—expertly navigating the process of turning it into a reality, and providing support ever since. Mel is not only a fantastic agent; he's a wonderful person. Sometimes I wish I had extra issues to tackle just so I could listen to more of his sage advice. I am so grateful to Hilary Winston for the introduction.

This book would not have been the adventure it turned out to be without the generosity of Taiwan and its Ministry of Foreign Affairs, as well as Linda Hu and Kent Yang with the Taipei Economic and Cultural Office here in Los Angeles, who responded enthusiastically when I suggested turning my environmental press trip into an in-depth examination of the island's breastfeeding policy. (They then adeptly reshuffled all of my travel plans.) I am additionally obliged to my cheerful Taiwanese guide Diego Lin and my eager translator "Emily"; my gracious hosts at National Taiwan University Hospital; Dr. Shu-Ti Chiou and everyone at the Taiwan Health Promotion Administration; and all of the dedicated mothers (and fathers) at the Breastfeeding Association of Taiwan and Taiwan Academy of Breastfeeding. Journalist To-wen Tseng shared her stories with me both in Los Angeles and in Taipei, and kept me from getting too homesick in the bargain. I also owe a shout-out to the European journalists on my trip, who held on to their good sense of humor as I grilled them about the breastfeeding cultures in their respective countries. And of course, I am very thankful for my perpetually supportive in-laws Susan Handelman and Stuart Ralsky. "Nani Sooze" Handelman flew to Los Angeles from Chicago to keep Matthew and the girls well fed and laughing the entire week I was away.

There are so many who provided essential encouragement back when this book was still just an idea: Arianna Huffington, Ricki Lake and Abby Epstein, Christopher Gavigan, filmmaker Dana Ben-Ari, and Dr. Lauren Streicher, who offered words of support from the get-go, as did my cousins Annie and Adam Shulman. Lauren Cowen and Nancy L. Cohen were kind enough to read my original proposal and offer astute author-to-author feedback. Emily Parker provided valuable advice and editorial guidance. Matt Villano, Rachel Sarnoff, and Jenny Feldon extended writerly cheer. After he read my book proposal, my (soon-to-be married) brother-in-law Daniel Libman seemed so enthusiastic about the natural feeding of his future children, I knew I must have stumbled upon a good idea. I also owe special thanks to Cheryl Petran at The Pump Station in Los Angeles for helping me secure some crucial early endorsements. And I will be forever grateful to John Drimmer for helping me find my true path.

Later on, Paul Libman and Marcia Iacobucci provided the respite of a Wisconsin family vacation (and the inspiration of the aurora borealis), including grandparent care while I wrote. Angela Kung combed through her network to find me sources in China. Dr. Autumn Shurin dug through her residency notes. Lindsay Libman never failed to ask me how my writing was going. Jordan Cahan and Jane Steinberg were wonderful readers and cheerleaders, as was my friend Andrea Ruth, who has the added distinction of being my only extended-breastfeeding mom friend, and who unknowingly contributed so many ideas to this book. Jane, Andrea, and my ever-encouraging sister-in-law Sarah Grayson read the final draft of the manuscript with lightning speed and delivered a boost just when I needed it. I owe another big thank you to Sarah and to my other "seester" Samantha Rubin (and brother-in-law Brian Rubin) for allowing me to share their wonderful stories in these pages. And no one has been more steadfast in his belief in me than my brother, Noah Grayson; only he would turn around an entire manuscript in twenty-four hours. I credit his advice alone for the fact that everything magically fell into place just the way it did, and I will always be grateful for his unfaltering support.

To my adoring husband, Matthew, the love of my life, who to this day insists that he fell for me on our first date (when I was nineteen and he was twenty) because he knew that, one day, I would make an amazing mother. Thank you for knowing me, for loving me, for the countless years of being my sounding board as I tried to figure it all out, and for providing just enough resistance on the topic of breastfeeding to provide inspiration (but ultimately being open-minded enough to tramp down this road with me). Thank you, my TV-and-film-writer husband, for the comedy punch-ups on my (manu)script, the bourbon and chocolate as I burned the midnight oil, for helping me to carve out time everywhere possible this past year so that I could write, and for consistently being the voice of calm when I couldn't. More than anything, I'm just happy that we get to spend some "us" time together again.

And to the other two loves of my life—my *everythings*, Izzy and Mika—this book, of course, is my ode to you. At so many moments I wrote with you at my knee (and certainly at my breast), but any time with your mommy that may have been sacrificed in the process of authoring this book was, hopefully, for the greater good.

SOURCES

Included below are the primary works I've referred to in each chapter, as well as those that provided my facts and/or influenced my thinking over the course of my research. All essential interviews are noted directly in the text unless cited below. URLs are current as of January 2016.

INTRODUCTION

The Los Angeles Zoo's Curator of Mammals Jennie Becker was extremely helpful in filling me in on important details and facts I had missed with my observer's eye on my visit in January 2014.

Abello, M.T. and M. Colell. "Analysis of Factors That Affect Maternal Behaviour and Breeding Success in Great Apes in Captivity." *International Zoo Yearbook*, no. 40 (2006): 323–340. doi: 10.1111/j.1748--1090.2006.00323.x.

Choi, Charles Q. "Human and Chimp Genes May Have Split 13 Million Years Ago." LiveScience. June 12, 2014. http://www.livescience.com/46300-chimpanzee-evolution-dna-mutations.html.

Los Angeles Zoo & Botanical Gardens. "LA Zoo Welcomes Two Baby Chimpanzees." November 24, 2014. http://www.lazoo.org/2014/11/l-zoo-welcomes-two-baby-chimpanzees.

Mills, Elena. "Why Is Breastfeeding So Bloody Hard?" *Trust Your Baby* (blog). September 21, 2014. http://www.trustyourbaby.co.uk/?p=624.

National Park Service. "Griffith Park." http://www.nps.gov/samo/planyourvisit/griffithpark.htm.

Oftedal, Olav T. "The Mammary Gland and Its Origin During Synapsid Evolution." *Journal of Mammary Gland Biology and Neoplasia* 7, no. 3 (2002): 225-252. doi: 10.1023/A:1022896515287.

Smith, Harriet J. *Parenting for Primates*. Cambridge: Harvard University Press, 2006.

Volk, Anthony. "Human Breastfeeding Is Not Automatic: Why That's So and What It Means for Human Evolution." *Journal of Social, Evolutionary, and Cultural Psychology* 3, no. 4 (2009): 305-314. doi:10.1037/h0099314.

CHAPTER ONE: FORMULA-FED ME

A word about the breastfeeding statistics used in this chapter and throughout the book:

It's notable that up until very recently, the primary source for US breastfeeding statistics was formula manufacturer Ross Laboratories (later the Ross Products division of Abbott) via its national Ross Laboratories Mothers Survey, which the company began conducting in 1955. It wasn't until 2001 that the US government included questions in the CDC's National Immunization Survey (NIS) to assess the population's breastfeeding practices; the CDC's Breastfeeding Report Card was established in 2007. Unless otherwise noted, all twenty-first century US breastfeeding statistics in the book come from CDC (http://www.cdc.gov/breastfeeding/data/index.htm). Prior to that time, I've drawn from an array of sources, included below, as well as the Ross data—a nice snapshot of which can be viewed on the breastfeeding support site *KellyMom* (http://kellymom.com/fun/trivia/ross-data/).

American Academy of Pediatrics. "Breastfeeding and the Use of Human Milk." *Pediatrics* 129 no. 3 (2012): e827-e841. doi: http://dx.doi.org/10.1542/peds.2011-3552 .

American Pregnancy Association. "Breastfeeding vs. Bottle Feeding." http://americanpregnancy.org/breastfeeding/breastfeeding-and-bottle-feeding/.

Biagoli, Frances. "Returning to Work While Breastfeeding." *American Family Physician* 68, no. 11 (2003): 2199-2207. http://www.aafp.org/afp/2003/1201/p2201.html#afp20031201p2199-b3.

Bonyata, Kelly. "Breastfeeding Past Infancy: Fact Sheet." *KellyMom* (blog). http://kellymom.com/ages/older-infant/ebf-benefits/.

Collaborative Group on Hormonal Factors in Breast Cancer. "Breast Cancer and Breastfeeding: Collaborative Reanalysis of Individual Data From 47 Epidemiological Studies in 30 Countries, Including 50302 Women With Breast Cancer and 96973 Women Without the Disease." *The Lancet* 360, no. 9328 (2002): 187-95. doi: http://dx.doi.org/10.1016/S0140-6736(02)09454-0.

Eidelman, Arthur. "The Talmud and Human Lactation: The Cultural Basis for Increased Frequency and Duration of Breastfeeding Among Orthodox Jewish Women." *Breastfeeding Medicine* 1, no. 1 (2006): 36-40. doi:10.1089/bfm.2006.1.36.

Fomon, Samuel J. "Infant Feeding in the 20th Century: Formula and Beikost." *Journal of Nutrition* 131 no. 2 (2001): 409S-420S. http://jn.nutrition.org/content/131/2/409S.full.pdf+html.

International Labour Organization. "Maternity and Paternity at Work: Law and Practice Across the World." 2014. www.ilo.org/maternityprotection.

Muller, Mike. *The Baby Killer*. London: War on Want, 1974.

Palmer, Gabrielle. *The Politics of Breastfeeding: When Breasts Are Bad for Business*. London: Pinter & Martin, 2009.

Pickert, Kate. "The Man Who Remade Motherhood." *Time*, May 21, 2012.

Ryan, A.S., W.F. Pratt, J.L. Wysong, G. Lewandowski, J.W. McNally and F.W. Krieger. "A Comparison of Breast-Feeding Data from the National Surveys of Family Growth and the Ross Laboratories Mothers Surveys." *American Journal of Public Health* 81, no. 8 (1991): 1049-1052. doi: 10.2105/AJPH.81.8.1049.

Siegel Bernard, Tara. "In Paid Family Leave, US Trails Most of the Globe." *New York Times*. February 22, 2013.

Steube, Alison. "The Risks of Not Breastfeeding for Mothers and Infants." *Reviews in Obstetrics and Gynecology* 2, no. 4 (2009): 222-231. doi: 10.3909/riog0093.

Stuart-Macadam, Patricia. "Biocultural Perspectives on Breastfeeding." In *Breastfeeding: Biocultural Perspectives*, edited by Patricia Stuart-Macadam and Katherine A. Dettwyler, 1-38. New York: Aldine de Gruyter, 1995.

US Department of Agriculture Food and Nutrition Service. "About WIC: WIC at a Glance." http://www.fns.usda.gov/wic/about-wic-wic-glance.

US Department of Labor. "Break Time for Nursing Mothers." http://www.dol.gov/whd/nursingmothers/.

Van Esterik, Penny. "The Politics of Breastfeeding: An Advocacy Perspective." In *Breastfeeding: Biocultural Perspectives*, edited by Patricia Stuart-Macadam and Katherine A. Dettwyler, 145-166. New York: Aldine de Gruyter, 1995.

Victora, Cesar G, Bernardo Lessa Horta, Christian Loret de Mola, Luciana Quevedo, Ricardo Tavares Pinheiro, Denise P Gigante, Helen Gonçalves and Fernando C Barros. "Association Between Breastfeeding and Intelligence, Educational Attainment, and Income at 30 Years of Age: A Prospective Birth Cohort Study from Brazil. *The Lancet 3, no. 4 (2015): e199-e205.* http://dx.doi.org/10.1016/S2214-109X(15)70002-1.

WHO. "The World Health Organization's Infant Feeding Recommendation." http://www.who.int/nutrition/topics/infantfeeding_recommendation/en/.

Wright, Anne L. and Richard J. Schanler. "The Resurgence of Breastfeeding at the End of the Second Millenium." *Journal of Nutrition* 131 no. 2 (2001): 421S-5S.

CHAPTER TWO: WHAT WOULD BABY JESUS DRINK?

Dettwyler, Katherine A. "A Time to Wean: The Hominid Blueprint for the Natural Age of Weaning in Modern Human Populations." In *Breastfeeding: Biocultural Perspectives*, edited by Patricia Stuart-Macadam and Katherine A. Dettwyler, 39-74. New York: Aldine de Gruyter, 1995.

Ellicott, Charles John, editor. *A New Testament Commentary for English Readers*. New York: E.P. Dutton & Co., 1878.

Gibson, David. "Christmas' Missing Icon: Mary Breastfeeding Jesus." Religion News Service. December 10, 2012.

Gruber, Mayer I. "Breastfeeding Practices in Biblical Israel and in Old Babylonian Mesopotamia." *Journal of the Ancient Near Eastern Society* 19 (1989): 61-83.

Henn, Brenna M., Christopher R. Gignoux, Matthew Jobin, Julie M. Granka, J. M. Macpherson, Jeffrey M. Kidd, Laura Rodríguez-Botigué, Sohini Ramachandran, Lawrence Hon, Abra Brisbin, Alice A. Lin, Peter A. Underhill, David Comas, Kenneth K. Kidd, Paul J. Norman, Peter Parham, Carlos D. Bustamante, Joanna L. Mountain and Marcus W. Feldman. "Hunter-Gatherer Genomic Diversity Suggests a Southern African Origin for Modern Humans." *Proceedings of the National Academy of Sciences of the United States of America* 108 no. 13 (2011): 5154-5162. doi: 10.1073/pnas.1017511108.

Howell, Nancy. *Life Histories of the Dobe !Kung: Food, Fatness, and Well-Being Over the Life Span*. Berkeley and Los Angeles: University of California Press, 2010.

Jacobs, Jill. "Breastfeeding." *Kveller* (blog). September 16, 2010. http://www.kveller.com/article/breastfeeding/.

Kippley, Sheila M. *Breastfeeding and Catholic Motherhood: God's Plan for You & Your Baby*. Manchester: Sophia Institute Press, 2005.

Kippley, Sheila M. "Scriptural Mothering." *Natural Family Planning International* (blog). 2006. http://www.nfpandmore.org/bfscriptural.shtml.

Konner, Melvin and Carol Worthman. "Nursing Frequency, Gonadal Function, and Birth Spacing Among !Kung Hunter-Gatherers." *Science* 207 no. 4432 (1980): 788-91. doi: 10.1126/science.7352291.

Miles, Margaret R. *A Complex Delight: The Secularization of the Breast, 1350-1750*. Berkeley and Los Angeles: University of California Press, 2008.

Planned Parenthood. "A History of Birth Control Methods." https://www.plannedparenthood.org/files/2613/9611/6275/History_of_BC_Methods.pdf.

US Census Bureau. "Estimated Median Age at First Marriage, by Sex: 1890 to the Present." http://www.census.gov/hhes/families/data/marital.html.

Valenze, Deborah. *Milk: A Global and Local History*. New Haven: Yale University Press, 2012.

Yalom, Marilyn. *A History of the Breast*. New York: Ballantine, 1997.

CHAPTER THREE: MILK MYSTERIES AND MATERNAL DUTY

I could not have prepared for my conversations with Harvard's (now ASU's) Katie Hinde about the complexities of lactation biology and the uniqueness of mother's milk without the in-depth schooling I received via her blog *Mammals Suck . . . Milk!* (http://mammalssuck.blogspot.com). Hinde is not only a highly entertaining writer; she's a voice of scientific reason amidst the mommy wars. My conversation with Kathi Barber about African American breastfeeding heritage and the challenges that black mothers face proved particularly illuminating.

Barber, Katherine. *The Black Woman's Guide to Breastfeeding: The Definitive Guide to Nursing for African American Mothers.* Naperville: Sourcebooks, 2005.

Beck, Kristen, Darren Weber, Brett S. Phinney, Jennifer T. Smilowitz, Katie Hinde, Bo Lönnerdal, Ian Korf, and Danielle G. Lemay. "Comparative Proteomics of Human and Macaque Milk Reveals Species-Specific Nutrition during Postnatal Development." *Journal of Proteome Research* 14 no. 5 (2015): 2143-2157. doi: 10.1021/pr501243m.

Caulfield, Ernest. "Infant Feeding in Colonial America." *The Journal of Pediatrics* 41, no. 6 (1952): 673-687. doi: http://dx.doi.org/10.1016/S0022-3476(52)80288-4.

Chapkin, Robert S., Chen Zhao, Ivan Ivanov, Laurie A. Davidson, Jennifer S. Goldsby, Joanne R. Lupton, Rose Ann Mathai, Marcia H. Monaco, Deshanie Rai, W. Michael Russell, Sharon M. Donovan and Edward R. Dougherty. "Noninvasive Stool-Based Detection of Infant Gastrointestinal Development Using Gene Expression Profiles from Exfoliated Epithelial Cells." *American Journal of Physiology-Gastrointestinal and Liver Physiology* 298 no. 5 (2010): G582-9. doi: 10.1152/ajpgi.00004.2010.

Child Trends. "Child Care." http://www.childtrends.org/?indicators=childcare#sthash.5Uz3FMf9.dpuf.

Donovan, Sharon M., Mei Wang, Marcia H. Monaco, Camilia R. Martin, Laurie A. Davidson, Ivan Ivanov, and Robert S. Chapkin. "Noninvasive Molecular Fingerprinting of Host–Microbiome Interactions in Neonates." *FEBS Letters* 588 no. 22 (2014): 4112-9. doi 10.1016/j.febslet.2014.07.008.

Doyle, Nora. "'The Highest Pleasure of Which Woman's Nature Is Capable': Breastfeeding and the Sentimental Maternal Ideal in America 1750-1860" (Master's thesis). The University of North Carolina at Chapel Hill, 2009.

Fildes, Valerie. *Wet Nursing: A History from Antiquity to the Present.* New York: Basil Blackwell, 1988.

Franklin, Benjamin, William Temple Franklin, and William Duane. *Memoirs of Benjamin Franklin*. New York: Derby & Jackson, 1859.

Heslett, Cecily, Sherri Hedberg and Haley Rumble. "Did You Ever Wonder What's In . . . ?" Poster for the Douglas College Breastfeeding Course for Health Care Providers. 2007. http://3.bp.blogspot.com/-sGuXsLq_y3E/USGvvwrpGtI/AAAAAAAAAig/bI6Ur2X9Ack/s1600/whats-in-breastmilk-poster-canada.jpg.

Hinde, Katie, Amy L. Skibiel, Alison B. Foster Laura Del Rosso, Sally P. Mendoza, and John P. Capitanio. "Cortisol in Mother's Milk Across Lactation Reflects Maternal Life History and Predicts Infant Temperament." *Behavioral Ecology* 26 no. 1 (2014): 269-281. doi: 10.1093/beheco/aru186.

Hinde, Katie and Danielle Lemay. "Stop, Slow & Go: Hormonal Signals From Mother's Milk." *Splash! Milk Science Update*. International Milk Genomics Consortium. December 2014. http://milkgenomics.org/article/stop-slow-go-hormonal-signals-mothers-milk/.

Horta, Bernardo L., Bahl Rajiv, José C. Martines and Cesar G. Victora. "Evidence on the Long-Term Effects of Breastfeeding: Systematic Reviews and Meta-Analyses." Geneva: World Health Organization, 2007.

Hrdy, Sarah Blaffer. *Mother Nature: A History of Mothers, Infants, and Natural Selection*. New York: Pantheon Books, 1999.

Ip, S., M. Chung, G. Raman, P. Chew, N. Magula, D. DeVine, T. Trikalinos and J. Lau. "Breastfeeding and Maternal and Infant Health Outcomes in Developed Countries." *Evid Rep Tech Assess* 153 (2007): 1-186. doi: 10.1542/gr.18-2-15.

Koletzko, Berthold, Peter Cooper, Maria Makrides, Cutberto Garza, Ricardo Uauy and Weiping Wang, eds. "Table 1. Essential Composition of Infant Formula in Liquid or Powdered Form." In *Pediatric Nutrition in Practice*, 92. Basel: Karger, 2008.

Lepore, Jill. "Baby Food." *The New Yorker*, January 19, 2009.

Mays, Dorothy A. *Women in Early America: Struggle, Survival, and Freedom in a New World*. Santa Barbara: ABC-CLIO, 2004.

National Institutes of Health. "Human Microbiome Project." https://commonfund.nih.gov/hmp/index.

Porter, Roy and Mikulas Teich. *Sexual Knowledge, Sexual Science: The History of Attitudes to Sexuality*. Cambridge: Cambridge University Press, 1994.

Prentice, Ann. "Constituents of Human Milk." *Food and Nutrition Bulletin* 17, no. 4 (December 1996). http://archive.unu.edu/unupress/food/8F174e/8F174E04.htm.

Quinn, E.A. "Human Milk Has a Microbiome—and the Bacteria Are Protecting Mothers and Infants!" *Biomarkers & Milk* (blog). December 14, 2014. http://biomarkersandmilk.blogspot.com/2014/12/human-milk-has-microbiome-and-bacteria.html.

Quinn, E. A, F. Largado, J. B. Borja and C. W. Kuzawa. "Maternal Characteristics Associated with Milk Leptin Content in a Sample of Filipino Women and Associations with Infant Weight for Age." *Journal of Human Lactation* 31 no. 2 (2015): 273-81. doi:10.1177/0890334414553247.

Shy, John. *A People Numerous & Armed: Reflections on the American Military Struggle for Independence*. Ann Arbor: University of Michigan Press, 1990.

Sussman, George. *Selling Mother's Milk: The Wet-Nursing Business in France 1715-1914*. Urbana: University of Illinois Press, 1982.

US Census Bureau. "Who's Minding the Kids? Child Care Arrangements: Spring 2011." https://www.census.gov/prod/2013pubs/p70-135.pdf.

Williams, Florence. *Breasts: A Natural and Unnatural History*. New York: W. W. Norton & Company, 2012.

Wheaton, Robert and Tamara K. Hareven, editors. *Family and Sexuality in French History*. Philadelphia: University of Pennsylvania Press, 1998.

Yan W., A. A. Wiley, R. A. Bathgate, A. L. Frankshun, S. Lasano, B. D. Crean, B. G. Steinetz, C. A. Bagnell and F. F. Bartol. "Expression of LGR7 and LGR8 by Neonatal Porcine Uterine Tissues and Transmission of Milk-Borne Relaxin into the Neonatal Circulation by Suckling." *Endocrinology* 147 no. 9 (2006): 4303-4310. doi: 10.1210/en.2006-0397.

Zimmer, Carl. "In Mother's Milk, Nutrients, and a Message, Too." *New York Times*, November 6, 2014.

CHAPTER FOUR: INDUSTRIAL AGE VS. THE BREAST

Apple, Rima D. *Mothers & Medicine: A Social History of Infant Feeding 1890-1950*. Madison: The University of Wisconsin Press, 1987.

Babyhood: The Mother's Nursery Guide 14, no. 163. June 1898.

Brändström, Anders, Göran Broström and Lars Åke Persson. "The Impact of Feeding Patterns on Infant Mortality in a Nineteenth Century Swedish Parish." *Journal of Tropical Pediatrics* 30 no. 3 (1984) 154-159.

Dettwyler, Katherine. Phone interview by author. Los Angeles, March 5, 2015.

Eaton, P. J. "A Few of the Things a Pediatrician Should Teach," in *Transactions of the American Pediatric Society* 21, ed. Linnaeus Edford La Fétra, 40-47. New York: E. B. Treat & Co., 1910.

Fildes, *Wet Nursing*.

Fomon, "Infant Feeding in the 20th Century."

History.com. "Transcontinental Railroad." 2010. http://www.history.com/topics/inventions/transcontinental-railroad.

Jelliffe, Derrick B. "Culture, Social Change and Infant Feeding: Current Trends in Tropical Regions." *The American Journal of Clinical Nutrition* 10 no. 1 (1962): 19-45. http://ajcn.nutrition.org/content/10/1/19.long.

Levenstein, Harvey. "'Best for Babies' or 'Preventable Infanticide'? The Controversy over Artificial Feeding of Infants in America, 1880-1920." *The Journal of American History* 70 no. 1 (1983): 75-94. doi: 10.2307/1890522.

Li, Ruowei, Sara B. Fein, Jian Chen and Laurence M. Grummer-Strawn. "Why Mothers Stop Breastfeeding: Mothers' Self-Reported Reasons for Stopping During the First Year." *Pediatrics* 122 Supplement 2 (2008): S28-S35. doi:10.1542/peds.2008-1315i .

Library of Congress. "Pacific Railway Act." http://www.loc.gov/rr/program/bib/ourdocs/PacificRail.html.

Lower East Side Tenement Museum. "Marasmus and Scrofula." 2005. https://www.tenement.org/encyclopedia/diseases_marasmus.htm.

Lower East Side Tenement Museum. "Meehan-Moore Family." 2005. https://www.tenement.org/encyclopedia/97_moore.htm.

Morse, E. G. "Lactation." *Annals of Gynecology and Pediatry: A Monthly Review of Gynecology, Obstetrics, Abdominal Surgery and the Diseases of Children*, edited by Ernest W. Cushing, Charles G. Cumston and Robert W. Hastings, 597-605. Boston: Annals of Gynecology and Pediatry, 1897.

Mullaly, John. *The Milk Trade in New York and Vicinity*. New York: Fowlers and Wells, 1853.

New York City Department of Health and Mental Hygiene. "(Milk and Milk Products) and Article 117." 2010. http://www.nyc.gov/html/doh/downloads/pdf/notice/2010/notice-article-111-117-noa.pdf.

Palmer, *The Politics of Breastfeeding*.

Papademas, Photis, editor. *Dairy Microbiology: A Practical Approach*. Boca Raton: CRC Press, 2014.

Pollan, Michael. *In Defense of Food*. New York: Penguin, 2008.

Population Reference Bureau. "Human Population: Urbanization." http://www.prb.org/Publications/Lesson-Plans/HumanPopulation/Urbanization.aspx.

Scovil, Elisabeth Robinson. *The Care of Children*. Philadelphia: Henry Altemus, 1894.

"Shorter Factory Hours: Law Forbids Working Women and Boys More than 54 Hours a Week." *New York Times*. October 1, 1912.

Sussman, *Selling Mother's Milk*.

"Swill-Milk Investigation." *New York Times*. June 3, 1858.

WHO. "Session 2: The Physiological Basis of Breastfeeding." *Infant Young and Child Feeding: Model Chapter for Textbooks for Medical Students and Allied Health Professionals*. Geneva: World Health Organization, 2009.

The Week Staff. "How Marriage Has Changed Over Centuries." *The Week*. June 1, 2012. http://theweek.com/articles/475141/how-marriage-changed-over-centuries.

Wilson, Bee. *Swindled: The Dark History of Food Fraud, from Poisoned Candy to Counterfeit Coffee*. Princeton: Princeton University Press, 2008.

Wolf, *Don't Kill Your Baby*.

Yale, Leroy M., editor. *Nursery Problems*. New York: The Contemporary Publishing Company, 1897.

CHAPTER FIVE: DOCTOR KNOWS BEST

AAP. "Breastfeeding and the Use of Human Milk."

AAP. "Honor Roll of Giving." *AAP News*. August 25, 2014.

Apple, *Mothers and Medicine*.

Berg, Allan. *The Nutrition Factor: Its Role in National Development*. The Brookings Institution, 1973.

Bonyata, Kelly. "My Baby Is Sick—Should I Continue to Breastfeed?" *KellyMom* (blog). http://kellymom.com/bf/can-i-breastfeed/illness-surgery/baby-illness/.

Brosco, Jeffrey P. "Weight Charts and Well-Child Care: How the Pediatrician

Became the Expert in Child Health." *Archives of Pediatrics & Adolescent Medicine* 155 no. 12 (2001): 1385-1389.

Brush, Edward F. "How to Produce Milk for Infant Feeding." *JAMA: The Journal of the American Medical Association* 43 (1904): 1385-1387.

Caillé, Augustus. "The Need of Post-Graduate Instruction in Pediatrics." In *Contributions to the Science of Medicine and Surgery by the Faculty in Celebration Twenty-Fifth Anniversary—1882-1907—of the Founding of the New York Post-Graduate Medical School and Hospital*. New York: Directors of the New York Post-Graduate Medical School and Hospital, 1908.

CDC. National Center for Chronic Disease Prevention and Health Promotion. Division of Nutrition, Physical Activity, and Obesity. "Hospital Support for Breastfeeding: Preventing Obesity Begins in Hospitals." *CDC Vital Signs*. Atlanta: CDC, August 2011.

Davis, Lisa Selin. "Is the Medical Community Failing Breastfeeding Moms?" *Time.com*. January 2, 2013.

Dick-Read, Grantly. *Childbirth Without Fear*. 1942. Rev. ed. London: Pinter & Martin, 2004.

Feldman-Winter, Lori, Lauren Barone, Barry Milcarek, Krystal Hunter, Joan Meek, Jane Morton, Tara Williams, Audrey Naylor and Ruth A. Lawrence. "Residency Curriculum Improves Breastfeeding Care." *Pediatrics* 126 no. 2 (2010): 289-297. doi: http://dx.doi.org/10.1542/peds.2009-3250.

Feldman-Winter, Lori B., Richard J. Schanler, Karen G. O'Connor and Ruth A. Lawrence. "Pediatricians and the Promotion and Support of Breastfeeding." *Archives of Pediatric & Adolescent Medicine* 162 no. 12 (2008): 1142-1149. doi:10.1001/archpedi.162.12.1142.

Gaskin, Ina May. *Birth Matters: A Midwife's Manifesto*. New York: Seven Stories Press, 2011.

ILO, "Maternity and Paternity at Work."

Institute of Medicine. Food and Nutrition Board. Committee on the Evaluation of the Addition of Ingredients New to Infant Formula. "Comparing Infant Formulas with Human Milk." In *Infant Formula: Evaluating the Safety of New Ingredients*, 41-54. Washington, DC: The National Academies Press, 2004.

Lackey, W. Nicholas. "Pediatric Practice in the Small Towns and Country." *Pediatrics* 25 (1913): 366-374.

Lawrence, Ruth A. and Robert M. Lawrence. *Breastfeeding: A Guide for the Medical Professional, Eighth Edition*. Philadelphia: Elsevier, 2015.

MacDorman, Marian F., T.J. Mathews and Eugene Declercq. "Home Births in the United States, 1990-2009." *NCHS Data Brief* 84. Hyattsville: National Center for Health Statistics, 2012.

Margulis, Jennifer. *The Business of Baby: What Doctors Don't Tell You, What Corporations Try to Sell You, and How to Put Your Pregnancy, Childbirth, and Baby Before Their Bottom Line*. New York: Scribner, 2013.

Riddle, Sarah W. and Laurie A. Nommsen-Rivers. "A Case Control Study of Diabetes During Pregnancy and Low Milk Supply." *Breastfeeding Medicine* 11, no. 2 (2016). doi: 10.1089/bfm.2015.0120.

Seals Allers, Kimberly. "Does the AAP Logo Belong on Formula Gift Bags?" *Motherlode* (blog), *New York Times*. December 19, 2013. http://parenting.blogs.nytimes.com/2013/12/19/does-the-a-a-p-logo-belong-on-formula-gift-bags/.

Sehring, Dewey A. "Continuing Physician Education: the Ross Conference Approach." *American Journal of Clinical Nutrition* 46 no. 1 (1987): 192-197. http://ajcn.nutrition.org/content/46/1/192.

Sehring, Dewey A. Interview with Lawrence Gartner. *Oral History Project*. Blacklick: AAP Pediatric History Center, 2009.

US Department of Health, Education, and Welfare. *Vital Statistics of the United States 1950 Volume 1*. Washington, DC: United States Government Printing Office, 1954.

Wolf, Jacqueline H. *Deliver Me from Pain: Anesthesia & Birth in America*. Baltimore: The Johns Hopkins University Press, 2009.

Wolf, *Don't Kill Your Baby*.

WHO. *Country Implementation of the International Code of Marketing of Breast-milk Substitutes: Status Report 2011*. Geneva: World Health Organization, 2013 (revised).

WHO. "Diarrhoeal Disease." http://www.who.int/mediacentre/factsheets/fs330/en/.

WHO. "Exclusive Breastfeeding." http://www.who.int/nutrition/topics/exclusive_breastfeeding/en/.

WHO. *International Code of Marketing of Breast-milk Substitutes*. Geneva: World Health Organization, 1981.

CHAPTER SIX: EXTRAORDINARY ATTACHMENT

On the science of how early childhood experience profoundly impacts not only brain development but lifelong health, I gained a great deal of knowledge from the wonderfully accessible papers and multimedia resources on the website of the Center on the Developing Child at Harvard University (http://developingchild.harvard.edu).

Bartick, Melissa. "Pediatric Politics: How Dire Warnings Against Infant Bed Sharing 'Backfired.'" *CommonHealth* (blog), WBUR Boston. December 19, 2014. http://commonhealth.wbur.org/2014/12/dire-warnings-against-infant-bed-sharing-backfired.

Bhattacharjee, Yudhijit. "The First Year." *National Geographic Magazine*, January 2015.

Bowlby, John. *A Secure Base: Parent-Child Attachment and Healthy Human Development*. Reprint edition. New York: Basic Books, 1988.

Bruun, Ole and Ole Odgaard, eds. *Mongolia in Transition: Old Patterns, New Challenges*. Copenhagen: Nordic Institute of Asian Studies, 1996.

California Department of Public Health. "California Laws Related to Breastfeeding." http://cdph.ca.gov.

Dettwyler, "A Time to Wean."

Dick, Edwina. "What It's Like to Breastfeed in the Middle East." *News.com.au*, May 22, 2014. http://www.news.com.au/travel/travel-advice/what-its-like-to-breastfeed-in-the-middle-east/story-e6frfqfr-1226924832542.

Dickson, Isabel. "The Association Between Breastfeeding Practices in Mongolia and Geographical Location of the Mother and Child" (Master's thesis). University of Washington, 2012.

Dölen, G., A. Darvishzadeh, K. W. Huang and R. C. Malenka. "Social Reward Requires Coordinated Activity of Nucleus Accumbens Oxytocin and Serotonin." *Nature* 501 no. 7466 (2013): 179–184. doi: 10.1038/nature12518.

Fields, R. Douglas. "White Matter Matters." *Scientific American*, March 1, 2008.

Hinde, Katie. "When to Wean." *Mammals Suck . . . Milk!* (blog). January 17, 2015. http://mammalssuck.blogspot.com/2015/01/when-to-wean.html.

Hulbert, Ann. *Raising America: Experts, Parents and a Century of Advice about Children*. New York: Vintage Books, 2004.

International Labour Organization. *Maternity at Work: A Review of National Legislation*. 2nd ed. Geneva: International Labour Office, 2010.

Kamnitzer, Ruth. "Breastfeeding in the Land of Genghis Khan." *Mothering*, July/August 2009.

Katz, Brigit. "Breastfeeding a 6-Year-Old: Harmless, Helpful or Downright Crazy?" *Women in the World* (blog), *New York Times*. June 2, 2015. http://nytlive.nytimes.com/womenintheworld/2015/06/02/breastfeeding-a-6-year-old-harmless-helpful-or-downright-crazy/.

Legal Aid Society–Employment Law Center. "LAS–ELC Settles Breastfeeding Discrimination Claim against World Journal." August 25, 2014. https://las-elc.org/news/las-elc-settles-breastfeeding-discrimination-claim-against-world-journal.

Liedloff, Jean. *The Continuum Concept: In Search of Happiness Lost*. Rev. ed. Boston: Da Capo Press, 1977.

Matos, Kenneth and Ellen Galinsky. "2012 National Study of Employers." New York: Families and Work Institute, 2012.

"Mongolian Way of Life Threatened by Dramatic Climate Change." *The World*. Public Radio International. May 16, 2012. http://www.pri.org/stories/2012-05-16/mongolian-way-life-threatened-dramatic-climate-change.

Narvaez, Darcia. "Normal Infant Sleep: Night Nursing's Importance." *Moral Landscapes* (blog), *Psychology Today*. March 11, 2013. https://www.psychologytoday.com/blog/moral-landscapes/201303/normal-infant-sleep-night-nursings-importance.

National Scientific Council on the Developing Child. *Children's Emotional Development Is Built into the Architecture of Their Brains: Working Paper No. 2*. 2004. http://www.developingchild.net.

National Statistical Office, UNICEF. *Mongolia Child and Development 2005 Survey (MICS-3), Final Report.* Ulaanbaatar: National Statistical Office, 2007.

National Women's Health Resource Center and Medela. *The Survey of Working Moms.* May 2, 2007.

Pickert, "The Man Who Remade Motherhood."

Sears, Martha and William Sears. *The Breastfeeding Book: Everything You Need to Know About Nursing Your Child from Birth through Weaning.* New York: Little, Brown and Company, 2000.

Sears, William and Martha Sears. *The Attachment Parenting Book: A Commonsense Guide to Understanding and Nurturing Your Baby.* New York: Little, Brown and Company, 2001.

Sears, William, Martha Sears, Robert Sears and James Sears. *The Baby Book: Everything You Need to Know About Your Baby from Birth to Age Two.* 3rd ed. New York: Little, Brown and Company, 2013.

Stanford University Medical Center. " 'Love Hormone' May Play Wider Role in Social Interaction than Previously Thought." *ScienceDaily.* September 11, 2013. www.sciencedaily.com/releases/2013/09/130911131955.htm.

Stanford University Medical Center. "Stunning Details of Brain Connections Revealed." *ScienceDaily.* November 17, 2010. http://www.sciencedaily.com/releases/2010/11/101117121803.htm.

Tate, Julie F. "Feeding Practices of Mothers in the Gobi Desert of Mongolia" (Master's thesis). East Tennessee State University, 2011.

Tseng, To-wen. "Building a Breastfeeding Friendly Society." San Diego County Breastfeeding Coalition. January 2, 2015. https://www.breastfeeding.org/news_article.php?id=157.

Tseng, To-wen. *I'd Rather Be Breastfeeding* (blog). http://breastfeedingtowen.blogspot.com.

UNICEF. "At a Glance: Mongolia." http://www.unicef.org/infobycountry/mongolia_statistics.html.

US Department of Health and Human Services. Health Resources and Services Administration. Maternal and Child Health Bureau. "Maternity Leave." *Women's Health USA 2011.* Rockville: US Department of Health and Human Services, 2011.

US Department of Labor. "DOL Fact Sheet: Paid Family and Medical Leave." http://www.dol.gov/wb/PaidLeave/PaidLeave.htm.

US Department of Labor. Wage and Hour Division. "Fact Sheet #17A: Exemption for Executive, Administrative, Professional, Computer & Outside Sales Employees Under the Fair Labor Standards Act (FLSA)." http://www.dol.gov/whd/overtime/fs17a_overview.pdf.

United States Breastfeeding Committee. "Existing Legislation." http://www.usbreastfeeding.org/p/cm/ld/fid=25.

Vanderwert, Ross E., Charles H. Zeanah, Nathan A. Fox and Charles A. Nelson. "Normalization of EEG Activity among Previously Institutionalized Children Placed into Foster Care: A 12-Year Follow-Up of the Bucharest Early Intervention Project." *Developmental Cognitive Neuroscience* 17 (2016): 68-75. doi:10.1016/j.dcn.2015.12.004.

The World Bank. "World Development Indicators: Urbanization" (Mongolia). http://wdi.worldbank.org/table/3.12.

World Breastfeeding Trends Initiative. "Second Assessment of Status of Infant and Young Child Feeding (IYCF) in Mongolia: Practice, Policy and Program Achievements and Gaps." IBFAN, 2013.

CHAPTER SEVEN: LATCH OFF, LATCH ON

The poem at the opening of the chapter is *Written on the Wall at West Forest Temple*, by the famed Sung dynasty poet Su Shih (also known as Su Tung-p'o). The translation is by Burton Watson.

All Taiwan breastfeeding statistics not included below were supplied to me directly by the Health Promotion Administration, Ministry of Health and Welfare, Taiwan, R.O.C.

Anderson, G.C., D. Radjenovic, S. H. Chiu, M. Conlon and A. E. Lane. "Development of an Observational Instrument to Measure Mother-Infant Separation Post Birth." *Journal of Nursing Measurement* 12 no. 3 (2004): 215-234. doi: http://dx.doi.org/10.1891/jnum.12.3.215.

Bartick, M. and A. Reinhold. "The Burden of Suboptimal Breastfeeding in the United States: A Pediatric Cost Analysis." *Pediatrics* 125 no. 5 (2010): e1048-e1056. doi: 10.1542/peds.2009-1616.

Brazelton, T. Berry. "Psychophysiologic Reactions in the Neonate. II. Effect of Maternal Medication on the Neonate and His Behavior." *The Journal of Pediatrics* 58 no. 4 (1961): 513-518. doi: http://dx.doi.org/10.1016/S0022-3476(61)80185-6.

Central Intelligence Agency. "The World Factbook: Country Comparison: Birth Rate." https://www.cia.gov/library/publications/the-world-factbook/rankorder/2054rank.html.

Chiou, Shu-Ti, Li-Chuan Chen, Hsing Yeh, Shu-Ru Wu and Li-Yin Chien. "Early Skin-to-Skin Contact, Rooming-in, and Breastfeeding: A Comparison of the 2004 and 2011 National Surveys in Taiwan." *Birth* 41, no. 1 (2014): 33-38. doi: 10.1111/birt.12090.

Dunn, Lindsey and Scott Becker. "50 Things to Know About the Hospital Industry." Becker's Hospital Review. 2013. http://www.beckershospitalreview.com/hospital-management-administration/50-things-to-know-about-the-hospital-industry.html.

Harney, Alexandra. "Special Report: How Big Formula Bought China." *Reuters*, November 7, 2013.

Hellerstein, S., S. Feldman and T. Duan. "China's 50% Caesarean Delivery Rate: Is It Too High?" *BJOG: An International Journal of Obstetrics & Gynaecology* 122 no. 2 (2014): 160-164. doi: 10.1111/1471-0528.12971.

Hou, Arnold. "Rate of Exclusive Breastfeeding Declining in China." All-

China Women's Federation. May 21, 2014. http://www.womenofchina.cn/womenofchina/html1/17/3045-1.htm.

Lee, Chia-Chian, Shu-Ti Chiou, Li-Chuan Chen and Li-Yin Chien. "Breastfeeding-Friendly Environmental Factors and Continuing Breastfeeding Until 6 Months Postpartum: 2008-2011 National Surveys in Taiwan." *Birth* 42, no. 3 (2015): 242-248. doi: 10.1111/birt.12170.

Manthorpe, Jonathan. *Forbidden Nation: A History of Taiwan*. New York: St. Martin's Griffin, 2008.

Meyer, Eric. "China and Its Coming Great Milk Battle." *Forbes*, October 30, 2014.

Minter, Adam. "China's Growing Breastfeeding Problem." *BloombergView*. April 22, 2015.

Moore, E. R., G. C. Anderson, N. Bergman and T. Dowswell. "Early Skin-to-Skin Contact for Mothers and Their Newborn Healthy Infants." *Cochrane Database of Systematic Reviews* 5 no. CD003519 (2012). doi 10.1002/14651858.CD003519.pub3.

Taiwan Government Information Office. "The Republic of China at a Glance (2011)." http://www.roc-taiwan.org/glance/en/ch3.htm.

Taiwan Today. "Taiwan Birthrate Falls in 2013 After Dragon Year." June 20, 2014. http://www.taiwantoday.tw/ct.asp?xItem=218788&ctNode=445.

Temkin, Elizabeth. "Rooming-In: Redesigning Hospitals and Motherhood in Cold War America." *Bulletin of the History of Medicine* 76, no. 2 (2002): 271-298. doi: 10.1353/bhm.2002.0101.

Tseng, *I'd Rather Be Breastfeeding*.

USDA. Foreign Agricultural Service. Global Agricultural Information Network. *GAIN Report: China's Baby Formula Market*. By Sasha Small. Washington, DC: GAIN, 2013.

WHO. *Information Concerning the Use and Marketing of Follow-up Formula*. July 17, 2013. http://www.who.int/nutrition/topics/WHO_brief_fufandcode_post_17July.pdf.

WHO, UNICEF. *Baby-Friendly Hospital Initiative: Revised, Updated and Expanded for Integrated Care*. Geneva: WHO Press, 2009.

CHAPTER EIGHT: BREASTS ARE FOR MEN

I searched for a long time for a fitting epigraph for this chapter, but nothing more perfectly encapsulated (no pun intended) the singular situation of breasts in modern-day America than the one I had already found at the beginning of Katherine Dettwyler's chapter, "Beauty and the Breast: The Cultural Context of Breastfeeding in the United States," in *Biocultural Perspectives*. (The entire chapter, too, proved essential reading as I researched this chapter.) Thank you, Kathy, for letting me "borrow" the quote here and of course to the inimitable writer Glenn O'Brien, who penned those words back in 1995 in—where else?—*Playboy*.

The American Society for Aesthetic Plastic Surgery. *Cosmetic Surgery National Data Bank Statistics*, 2014. http://www.surgery.org/sites/default/files/2014-Stats.pdf.

American Society of Plastic Surgeons. *2013 Plastic Surgery Statistics Report*. http://www.plasticsurgery.org/Documents/news-resources/statistics/2013-statistics/plastic-surgery-statistics-full-report-2013.pdf.

Badinter, Elisabeth. *The Conflict: How Overzealous Motherhood Undermines the Status of Women*. Translated by Adriana Hunter. New York: Picador, 2013.

Baldwin, Elizabeth N. "Extended Breastfeeding and the Law." 1993. La Leche League International. http://www.llli.org/law/lawextended.html.

Blum, Linda M. *At the Breast: Ideologies of Breastfeeding and Motherhood in the Contemporary United States.* Boston: Beacon Press, 1999.

Clark, Robert K. *Anatomy and Physiology: Understanding the Human Body*. Sudbury: Jones and Bartlett Publishers, 2005.

Dölen et al., *Nature*.

Duncan, Evelyn Kennedy. "The Naughty Side of 18th Century French Fashions." *My Fanciful Muse* (blog). March 5, 2012. http://www.ekduncan.com/2012/03/naughty-side-of-18th-century-french.html.

Elabd, Christian, Wendy Cousin, Pavan Upadhyayula, Robert Y. Chen, Marc S. Chooljian, Ju Li, Sunny Kung, Kevin P. Jiang and Irina M. Conboy. "Oxytocin Is an Age-Specific Circulating Hormone that Is Necessary for Muscle Maintenance and Regeneration." *Nature Communications* 5, no. 4082 (2014). doi:10.1038/ncomms5082.

Ford, Clellan S. and Frank A. Beach. *Patterns of Sexual Behavior*. New York: Harper & Brothers, 1951.

Foreman, Amanda. "Why Footbinding Persisted in China for a Millenium." *Smithsonian Magazine*, February 2015.

International Society of Aesthetic Plastic Surgery. *ISAPS International Survey on Aesthetic/Cosmetic Procedures Performed in 2014*. http://www.isaps.org/Media/Default/global-statistics/2015%20ISAPS%20Results.pdf.

"Justice Department Covers Partially Nude Statues." *Associated Press*, January 29, 2002.

Komisaruk, B. R., N. Wise, E. Frangos, W. C. Liu, K. Allen and S. Brody. "Women's Clitoris, Vagina and Cervix Mapped on the Sensory Cortex: fMRI Evidence." *Journal of Sexual Medicine* 8, no. 10 (2011): 2822-2830. doi: 10.1111/j.1743-6109.2011.02388.x.

Lansinoh. *2014 Lansinoh Global Breastfeeding Survey*. https://www.lansinoh.com/globalsurvey.

Latteier, Carolyn. *Breasts: The Women's Perspective on an American Obsession*. Binghamton: The Haworth Press, 1998.

Lundberg, Claire. "The French Government Wants to Tone My Vagina." *Slate*, February 15, 2012.

Montagna, William and Elizabeth E. Macpherson. "Some Neglected Aspects of the Anatomy of Human Breasts." *Journal of Investigative Dermatology* 63, no. 1 (1974): 10-16.

National Conference of State Legislatures. "Breastfeeding State Laws." http://www.ncsl.org/research/health/breastfeeding-state-laws.aspx.

Neifert, M., S. DeMarzo, J. Seacat, D. Young, M. Leff and M. Orleans. "The Influence of Breast Surgery, Breast Appearance, and Pregnancy-Induced Breast Changes on Lactation Sufficiency as Measured by Infant Weight Gain." *Birth* 17, no. 1 (1990): 31–38. doi: 10.1111/j.1523-536X.1990.tb00007.x.

New York City Department of Health and Mental Hygiene. "Breastfeeding Disparities in New York City." *Epi Data Brief* no. 57, August 2015.

Roberts, Christine L., Amanda J. Ampt, Charles S. Algert, Mark S. Sywak and Jian Sheng C. Chen. "Reduced Breast Milk Feeding Subsequent to Cosmetic Breast Augmentation Surgery." *The Medical Journal of Australia* 202, no. 6 (2015): 324-328.

doi: 10.5694/mja14.01386.

Rosenberg, Kenneth D., Claire McMurtrie, Bonnie D. Kerker, Yingjian Na and Elizabeth H. Graham. "Breast-feeding Initiation in New York City, 1979 to 1996." *American Journal of Public Health* 88, no. 12 (1998): 1850-1852. doi: 10.2105/AJPH.88.12.1850.

Schiff, Michael, Charles S. Algert, Amanda Ampt, Mark S. Sywak and Christine L. Roberts. "The Impact of Cosmetic Breast Implants on Breastfeeding: A Systematic Review and Meta-Analysis." *International Breastfeeding Journal* 9 (2014): 17. doi: 10.1186/1746-4358-9-17.

Schlussel, Debbie. "Breastfeeding & Attachment Parenting Militants: Theirs—Jamie Lynn Grumet & 'Ours'—Michelle Fraudkin." *Debbie Schlussel* (blog). May 15, 2012. http://www.debbieschlussel.com/49620/breastfeeding-attachment-parenting-militants-theirs-jamie-lynne-grumet-ours-michelle-fraudkin-video/.

Smith, Merril D., editor. *Cultural Encylopedia of the Breast*. Lanham: Rowman & Littlefield, 2014.

"Titillate, teat, tit." Online Etymology Dictionary. http://www.etymonline.com/.

Wagner, Erin A., Caroline J. Chantry, Kathryn G. Dewey and Laurie A. Nommsen-Rivers. "Breastfeeding Concerns at 3 and 7 Days Postpartum and Feeding Status at 2 Months." *Pediatrics* 132, no. 4 (2013): e865-e875. doi: 10.1542/peds.2013-0724.

Wagner S., C. Kersuzan, S. Gojard, C. Tichit, S. Nicklaus, B. Geay, P. Humeau, X. Thierry, M.A. Charles, S. Lioret and B. de Lauzon-Guillain. "Breastfeeding Duration in France According to Parents and Birth Characteristics: Results from the ELFE Longitudinal French Study 2011." Bulletin Épidémiolgique Hebdomadaire 29 (2015): 522-32. http://www.invs.sante.fr/beh/2015/29/2015_29_1.html.

Williams v. Saxbe, 413 F. Supp. 654 (D.D.C. 1976).

Yalom, *A History of the Breast*.

CHAPTER NINE: BIG BROTHER AND THE BREAST

There is no source better able to navigate the complexities of the federal government's WIC program than the federal government itself, via scores of exhaustively thorough reports prepared by USDA's Economic Research Service economists (all reports publicly available online at http://www.ers.usda.gov/). There are far too many to list them all here, but I've included the reports that provided the bulk of my information and insight. Dairy supply and consumption data also come from ERS (http://www.ers.usda.gov/data-products/dairy-data.aspx). Additional facts and figures were accessed through the WIC portal on the USDA Food and Nutrition Service website (http://www.fns.usda.gov/wic/women-infants-and-children-wic).

Baumgartel, Kelley L. and Diane L. Spatz. "WIC (The Special Supplemental Nutrition Program for Women, Infants and Children): Policy versus Practice Regarding Breastfeeding." *Nursing Outlook* 61, no. 6 (2013): 466-470. doi: 10.1016/j.outlook.2013.05.010.

Baumslag, Naomi and Dia L. Michels. *Milk, Money, and Madness: The Culture and Politics of Breastfeeding.* Westport: Bergin & Garvey, 1995.

Betson, David. *Impact of the WIC Program on the Infant Formula Market*. CCR-51. USDA. Economic Research Service. January 2009.

Burrington, Kimberlee. "Milk Fractionation Technology and Emerging Milk Protein Opportunities." Dairy Research Institute and US Dairy Export Council. http://www.usdairy.com/~/media/usd/public/technicalreport milkfractionationtechnology.pdf.pdf.

Carroll M.D., T. Navaneelan, S. Bryan and C. L. Ogden. "Prevalence of Obesity among Children and Adolescents in Canada and the United States." *NCHS Data Brief*, no 211. Hyattsville, MD: National Center for Health Statistics. 2015.

Carlson, Steven, Robert Greenstein and Zoë Neuberger. *WIC's Competitive Bidding Process for Infant Formula Is Highly Cost-Effective.* Center on Budget and Policy Priorities. September 14, 2015.

Carlson, Steven and Zoë Neuberger. *WIC Works: Addressing the Nutrition and Health Needs of Low-Income Families for 40 Years.* Center on Budget and Policy Priorities. May 4, 2015.

CDC. National Center for Health Statistics. "WHO Growth Standards Are Recommended for Use in the U.S. for Infants and Children 0 to 2 Years of Age." http://www.cdc.gov/growthcharts/who_charts.htm#The%20WHO%20Growth%20Charts.

Edwards, Chris. "Food Subsidies." *Downsizing the Federal Government* (blog). CATO Institute. July 2009. http://www.downsizinggovernment.org/agriculture/food-subsidies#WIC.

Jensen, Elizabeth and Miriam Labbok. "Unintended Consequences of the WIC Formula Rebate Program on Infant Feeding Outcomes: Will the New Food Packages Be Enough?" *Breastfeeding Medicine* 6, no. 3 (2011): 145-149. doi: 10.1089/bfm.2010.0022.

Kent, George. *Regulating Infant Formula*. Amarillo: Hale Publishing, 2011.

Kent, George. "US Government Violates International Code of Marketing of Breast-milk Substitutes." Draft of October 1, 2015. http://www2.hawaii.edu/~kent/usgovernmentviolatescode.docx.

Kent, George. "WIC's Promotion of Infant Formula in the United States." *International Breastfeeding Journal* 1, no. 8 (2006). doi: 10.1186/1746-4358-1-8.

Kennedy, Eileen and Edward Cooney. "Development of the Child Nutrition Programs in the United States." *The Journal of Nutrition* 131, no. 2 (2001): 431S-436S. http://jn.nutrition.org/content/131/2/431S.full.

Levine, James A. "Poverty and Obesity in the US." *Diabetes* 60, no. 11 (2011): 2667-2668. doi: 10.2337/db11-1118.

Maryland WIC. "Story of WIC – Part 1." YouTube video, 10:12. Posted September 22, 2011. https://www.youtube.com/watch?v=r3RtBW-J5Z4.

Maryland WIC. "Story of WIC – Part 2." YouTube video, 13:40. Posted September 20, 2011. https://www.youtube.com/watch?v=fBnmXEogo2M.

Moss, Michael. *Salt, Sugar, Fat: How the Food Giants Hooked Us*. New York: Random House, 2013.

Office of Management and Budget. *Budget of the US Government, Fiscal Year 2015*. Washington, DC: US Government Printing Office, 2014.

Office of Management and Budget. "Public Budget Database." 2015. https://www.whitehouse.gov/omb/budget/Supplemental.

Nestle, Marion. *Food Politics: How the Food Industry Influences Nutrition and Health*. Rev. ed. Berkeley: University of California Press, 2007.

Oliveira, Victor and Elizabeth Frazão. "Legislative and Regulatory History of the WIC Program" in *The WIC Program: Background, Trends, and Economic Issues, 2009 Edition*. ERR-73. US Department of Agriculture. Economic Research Service. April 2009.

Oliveira, Victor and Elizabeth Frazão. *The WIC Program: Background, Trends, and Economic Issues, 2015 Edition*. EIB-134. US Department of Agriculture. Economic Research Service. January 2015.

Oliveira, Victor, Elizabeth Frazão and David Smallwood. *The Infant Formula Market: Consequences of a Change in the WIC Contract Brand*. ERR-124. US Department of Agriculture. Economic Research Service. August 2011.

Oliveira, Victor, Elizabeth Frazão and David Smallwood. *Rising Infant Formula Costs to the WIC Program: Recent Trends in Rebates and Wholesale Prices*. ERR-93. US Department of Agriculture. Economic Research Service. February 2010.

Oliveira, Victor, Mark Prell, David Smallwood and Elizabeth Frazão. *Infant Formula Prices and Availability: Final Report to Congress*. E-FAN-02-001. US Department of Agriculture. Economic Research Service. 2001.

Oliveira, Victor, Mark Prell, David Smallwood and Elizabeth Frazão. *WIC and the Retail Price of Infant Formula*. FANRR-39. US Department of Agriculture. Economic Research Service. 2004.

The Physicians Committee for Responsible Medicine. "Agriculture and

Health Policies in Conflict: How Food Subsidies Tax Our Health." http://www.pcrm.org/health/reports/agriculture-and-health-policies-unhealthful-foods.

Sharma, A., A. H. Jana and R. S. Chavan. "Functionality of Milk Powders and Milk-Based Powders for End Use Applications—A Review." *Comprehensive Reviews in Food Science and Food Safety* 11 (2012): 518–528. doi: 10.1111/j.1541-4337.2012.00199.x.

Sinclair, Ward. "Under Missouri: A Monument to the Output of the American Cow." *The Washington Post*, December 21, 1981.

Thorn, B., C. Tadler, N. Huret, C. Trippe, E. Ayo, M. Mendelson, K. L. Patlan, G. Schwartz and V. Tran. *WIC Participant and Program Characteristics 2014*. Prepared by Insight Policy Research. Alexandria, VA: U.S. Department of Agriculture, Food and Nutrition Service. 2015.

Thomas, Karen Kruse. Interview with David Paige. "Rx for the Future." *Johns Hopkins Public Health,* Special Issue 2014.

Tracy, Tennille. "Makers of Baby Formula Press Their Case on WIC Program." *The Wall Street Journal*, April 27, 2015.

USDA. Food and Nutrition Service. "Special Supplemental Nutrition Program for Women, Infants and Children (WIC): Revisions in the WIC Food Packages, Final Rule." *Federal Register* 79, no. 42 (March 4, 2014): 12274. http://www.fns.usda.gov/sites/default/files/03-04-14_WIC-Food-Packages-Final-Rule.pdf.

US Dairy Export Council. *US Milk Powder: Enhancing Our Product Offerings*. 2015. http://www.thinkusadairy.org/assets/Documents/Supplier%20Site/Global%20Marketing/U.S.%20Milk%20Powder%20Overview.pdf.

USDA. Food and Nutrition Service. Supplemental Food Programs Division. *WIC Breastfeeding Data: Local Agency Report.* FY 2012.

USDA. Food and Nutrition Service. Supplemental Food Programs Division. *WIC Funding Update.* National Advisory Council on Maternal, Infant and Fetal Nutrition. July 2013.

Wang, Dong. D., Cindy W. Leung, Yanping Li, Eric L. Ding, Stephanie E. Chiuve, Frank B. Hu and Walter C. Willett. "Trends in Dietary Quality Among Adults in the United States, 1999 Through 2010." *JAMA Internal Medicine* 174, no. 10 (2014): 1587-1595. doi:10.1001/jamainternmed.2014.3422.

Ward, Ronald W. and Bruce L. Dixon. "Effectiveness of Fluid Milk Advertising Since the Dairy and Tobacco Adjustment Act of 1983." *American Journal of Agricultural Economics* 71, no. 3 (1989): 730–740. http://www.jstor.org/stable/1242029.

Wilde, Park, Anne Wolf, Meena Fernandes and Ann Collins. "Food-Package Assignments and Breastfeeding Initiation before and after a Change in the Special Supplemental Nutrition Program for Women, Infants, and Children." *The American Journal of Clinical Nutrition* 96, no. 3 (2012): 560-566. doi: 10.3945/ajcn.112.037622.

CHAPTER TEN: "WE COMPLETE, NOT COMPETE"

All information and data regarding Alive & Thrive's programs not supplied during my conversations with Nemat Hajeebhoy and Jean Baker come from the briefs, reports, manuals, and other resources available on the Alive & Thrive website (http://aliveandthrive.org/resources-main-page/).

Black, Robert E., Cesar G. Victora, Susan P. Walker and the Maternal and Child Nutrition Study Group. "Maternal and Child Undernutrition and Overweight in Low-Income and Middle-Income Countries." *The Lancet* 382, no. 9890 (2013): 427-451. doi: http://dx.doi.org/10.1016/S0140-6736(13)60937-X.

Burke-Kennedy, Eoin. "Ireland Now Second Biggest Exporter of Infant Formula to China." *The Irish Times*, September 22, 2015.

Cannon, Anna M., Foteini Kakulas, Anna R. Hepworth, Ching Tat Lai, Peter E. Hartmann and Donna T. Geddes. "The Effects of Leptin on Breastfeeding Behaviour."

International Journal of Environmental Research and Public Health. 12, no. 10 (2015): 12340-12355. doi: 10.3390/ijerph121012340.

Daly, S. E. J. and P. E. Hartmann. "Infant Demand and Milk Supply. Part 1: Infant Demand and Milk Supply in Lactating Women." *Journal of Human Lactation* 11, no. 1 (1995): 21-26. doi: 10.1177/089033449501100119.

Daly, S. E. J. and P. E. Hartmann. "Infant Demand and Milk Supply. Part 2: The Short-Term Control of Milk Synthesis in Lactating Women." *Journal of Human Lactation* 11, no. 1 (1995): 27-31. doi: 10.1177/089033449501100120.

Daly, S. E. J., J. C. Kent, R. A. Owens and P. E. Hartmann. "Frequency and Degree of Milk Removal and the Short-term Control of Human Milk Synthesis." *Experimental Physiology* 81, no. 5 (1996) 861-875. doi: 10.1113/expphysiol.1996.sp003982.

Dewey, K. G. and K. Begum. "Long-term Consequences of Stunting in Early Life." *Maternal & Child Nutrition* 7, Supplement 3 (2011): 5-18. doi: 10.1111/j.1740-8709.2011.00349.x.

Food and Agriculture Organization of the United Nations. "Milk Production Facts." http://www.fao.org/agriculture/dairy-gateway/milk-production/en/#.Vqa7aBEks8R.

Kakulas, Foteini. "How Breastfed Babies Control Their Own Appetite." *Splash! Milk Science Update*. International Milk Genomics Consortium, June 2013. http://milkgenomics.org/article/how-breastfed-babies-control-their-own-appetite/.

Kent, Jacqueline C., Elizabeth Ashton, Catherine M. Hardwick, Marnie K. Rowan, Elisa S. Chia, Kyle A. Fairclough, Lalitha L. Menon, Courtney Scott, Georgia Mather-McCaw, Katherine Navarro and Donna T. Geddes. "Nipple Pain in Breastfeeding Mothers: Incidence, Causes and Treatments." *International Journal of Environmental Research and Public Health* 12, no. 10 (2015): 12247-12263. doi: 0.3390/ijerph121012247.

Mason, Frances, Kathryn Rawe and Simon Wright. *Superfood for Babies: How Overcoming Barriers to Breastfeeding Will Save Children's Lives*. London: Save the Children, 2013.

Nguyen, Phuong H., Sarah C. Keithly, Nam T. Nguyen, Tuan T. Nguyen, Lan M. Tran and Nemat Hajeebhoy. "Prelacteal Feeding Practices in Vietnam: Challenges and Associated Factors." *BMC Public Health* 13 (2013): 932. doi:10.1186/1471-2458-13-932.

The Nielsen Company. *Nielsen Global Baby Care Report*. August 2015.

Ramsay, D. T., J. C. Kent, R. A. Hartmann and P. E. Hartmann. "Anatomy of the Lactating Human Breast Redefined with Ultrasound Imaging." *Journal of Anatomy* 206 no. 6 (2005): 525-534. doi: 10.1111/j.1469--7580.2005.00417.x.

Ruowei et al. "Why Mothers Stop Breastfeeding," *Pediatrics*.

US Office of the Surgeon General, CDC and US Office on Women's Health. "Barriers to Breastfeeding in the United States." In *The Surgeon General's Call to Action to Support Breastfeeding*. Rockville: US Office of the Surgeon General, 2011.

Victora, Cesar G. "Nutrition in Early Life: A Global Priority." *The Lancet* 374, no. 9696 (2009): 1123-1125. doi: http://dx.doi.org/10.1016/S0140-6736(09)61725-6.

Wagner et al. "Breastfeeding Concerns," *Pediatrics*.

CHAPTER ELEVEN: THE HUMAN EXPERIMENT

All information regarding the US regulation of commercial infant formulas, as well as GRAS ingredients (which includes the GRAS Substances Database, searchable by ingredient) comes directly from the US Food and Drug Administration website (http://www.fda.gov).

Aragon, George, Deborah B. Graham, Marie Borum and David B. Doman. "Probiotic Therapy for Irritable Bowel Syndrome." *Journal of Gastroenterology and Hepatology* 6, no. 1 (2010): 39-44. http://www.ncbi.nlm.nih.gov/pmc/articles/PMC2886445.

"The Archean Eon." Smithsonian National Museum of Natural History. http://forces.si.edu/atmosphere/02_02_02.html.

Bar-El, D. S. and R. Reifen. "Soy as an Endocrine Disruptor: Cause for Caution?" *Journal of Pediatric Endocrinology and Metabolism* 23, no. 9 (2010): 855-861. doi: 10.1515/jpem.2010.138.

Biello, David. "Primeval Precipitation: What Fossil Imprints of Rain Reveal about Early Earth." *Scientific American*, March 28, 2012.

Bode, Lars. "Human Milk Oligosaccharides: Every Baby Needs a Sugar Mama." *Glycobiology* 22, no. 9 (2012): 1147-1162. doi: 10.1093/glycob/cws074.

Bode, Lars. *The Role of Oligosaccharides in Infant Nutrition*. Podcast audio. Pediatrix University Grand Rounds. October 6, 2014. https://itunes.apple.com/us/podcast/pediatrix-university-grand/id429676160?mt=2.

Bode, Lars, Mark McGuire, Juan M. Rodriguez, Donna T. Geddes, Foteini Hassiotou, Peter E. Hartmann and Michelle K. McGuire. "It's Alive: Microbes and Cells in Human Milk and Their Potential Benefits to Mother and Infant." *Advances in Nutrition* 5 (2014): 571-573. doi: 10.3945/an.114.006643.

"Breast Cancer and Breastfeeding: Collaborative Reanalysis," *The Lancet*.

California WIC Association and the UC Davis Human Lactation Center. "San Diego County: 2013 Data." *Bringing Breastfeeding Home: Building Communities of Care*. August 2014. http://calwic.org/storage/documents/FactSheets2014/SanDiego.pdf.

Chiang, W. C., C. H. Huang, G. V. Llanora, I. Gerez, S. H. Goh, L. P. Shek, A. J. Nauta, W. A. Van Doorn, J. Bindels, L. H. Ulfman, K. Knipping, D. J. Delsing, E. F. Knol and B. W. Lee. "Anaphylaxis to Cow's Milk Formula Containing Short-chain Galacto-oligosaccharide." *Journal of Allergy and Clinical Immunology* 130, no. 6 (2012): 1361-1367. doi: 10.1016/j.jaci.2012.08.048.

Clemente, Jose C., Erica C. Pehrsson, Martin J. Blaser, Kuldip Sandhu, Zhan Gao, Bin Wang, Magda Magris, Glida Hidalgo, Monica Contreras, Óscar Noya-Alarcón, Orlana Lander, Jeremy McDonald, Mike Cox, Jens Walter, Phaik Lyn Oh, Jean F. Ruiz, Selena Rodriguez, Nan Shen, Se Jin Song, Jessica Metcalf, Rob Knight, Gautam Dantas and M. Gloria Dominguez-Bello. "The Microbiome of Uncontacted Amerindians." *Science Advances* 1, no. 3 (2015). doi: 10.1126/sciadv.1500183.

Committee on the Evaluation of the Addition of Ingredients New to Infant Formula. Food and Nutrition Board. Institute of Medicine. *Infant Formula: Evaluating the Safety of New Ingredients*, 41-54. Washington, DC: The National Academies Press, 2004.

Dabelea, Dana, Elizabeth J. Mayer-Davis, Sharon Saydah, Giuseppina Imperatore, Barbara Linder, Jasmin Divers, Ronny Bell, Angela Badaru, Jennifer W. Talton, Tessa Crume, Angela D. Liese, Anwar T. Merchant, Jean M. Lawrence, Kristi Reynolds, Lawrence Dolan, Lenna L. Liu and Richard F. Hamman. "Prevalence of Type 1 and Type 2 Diabetes Among Children and Adolescents from 2001 to 2009." *JAMA: The Journal of the American Medical Association* 311, no. 17 (2014): 1778-1786. doi: 10.1001/jama.2014.3201.

Faupel-Badger, Jessica M., Kathleen F. Arcaro, Jane J. Balkam, A. Heather Eliassen, Foteini Hassiotou, Carlito B. Lebrilla, Karin B. Michels, Julie R. Palmer, Pepper Schedin, Alison M. Stuebe, Christine J. Watson and Mark E. Sherman. "Postpartum Remodeling, Lactation, and Breast Cancer Risk: Summary of a National Cancer Institute–Sponsored Workshop." *Journal of the National Cancer Institute* 105, no. 3 (2013): 166-174. doi: 10.1093/jnci/djs505.

Holmes, Jamie. "The Case for Teaching Ignorance." *New York Times*, August 24, 2015.

Knight, Rob. "How Our Microbes Make Us Who We Are." *TED* talk, February 2014. https://www.ted.com/talks/rob_knight_how_our_microbes_make_us_who_we_are.

Koletzko et al., "Essential Composition of Infant Formula."

Maixner, Frank, Anton Thomma, Giovanna Cipollini, Stefanie Widder, Thomas Rattei and Albert Zink. "Metagenomic Analysis Reveals Presence of Treponema Denticola in a Tissue Biopsy of the Iceman." *PLOS ONE* 9, no. 6 (2014): e99994. doi: 10.1371/journal.pone.0099994.

National Institutes of Health. National Cancer Institute. "Cancer Statistics." http://www.cancer.gov/about-cancer/what-is-cancer/statistics.

Neville, M. C., S. M. Anderson, J. L. McManaman, T. M. Badger, M. Bunik, N. Contractor, T. Crume, D. Dabelea, S. M. Donovan, N. Forman, D. N. Frank, J. E. Friedman, J. B. German, A. Goldman, D. Hadsell, M. Hambidge, K. Hinde, N. D. Horseman, R. V. Hovey, E. Janoff, N. F. Krebs, C. B. Lebrilla, D. G. Lemay, P. S. MacLean, P. Meier, A. L. Morrow, J. Neu, L. A. Nommsen-Rivers, D. J. Raiten, M. Rijnkels, V. Seewaldt, B. D. Shur, J. VanHouten and P. Williamson. "Lactation and Neonatal Nutrition: Defining and Refining the Critical Questions." *Journal of Mammary Gland Biology and Neoplasia* 17, no. 2 (2012): 167-188. doi: 10.1007/s10911-012-9261-5.

Prentice, "Constituents of Human Milk."

Proctor, Robert N. and Londa Schiebinger, eds. *Agnotology: The Making & Unmaking of Ignorance*. Stanford: Stanford University Press, 2008.

Ravel, Jacques, Martin J. Blaser, Jonathan Braun, Eric Brown, Frederic D. Bushman, Eugene B. Chang, Julian Davies, Kathryn G. Dewey, Timothy Dinan, Maria Dominguez-Bello, Susan Erdman, B. Brett Finlay, Wendy Garrett, Gary B. Huffnagle, Curtis Huttenhower, Janet Jansson, Ian B. Jeffery, Christian Jobin, Alexander Khoruts, Heidi H. Kong, Johanna W. Lampe, Ruth E. Ley, Dan R. Littman, Sarkis K. Mazmanian, David A. Mills, Andrew S. Neish, Elaine Petrof, David A. Relman, Rosamond Rhodes, Peter J. Turnbaugh, Vincent B. Young, Rob Knight and Owen White. "Human Microbiome Science: Vision for the Future, Bethesda, MD, July 24 to 26, 2013." *Microbiome* 2, no. 1 (2014): 16. doi:10.1186/2049-2618-2-16.

Steube, "The Risks of Not Breastfeeding."

UBIC Consulting. *Ingredients for the World Infant Formula Market*. 2014.

WHO. *How to Prepare Powdered Infant Formula in Care Settings*. Food Safety Authority of Ireland and World Health Organization, 2007.

CHAPTER TWELVE: THE WEANING

Assadourian, Erik. "Baby Formula Has No Place in a Sustainable Future." *The Guardian*, February 3, 2014.

Catalini, Michael. "The Battle for Control of the Growing Breast Milk Industry." *Associated Press*, July 7, 2015.

Family Larsson-Rosenquist Foundation. "World's First Medical Chair in Human Lactology." http://www.larsson-rosenquist.org/en/news/worlds-first-chair-in-human-lactology-in-medicine.html.

Griffin, Dan and Katherine Russell. "Parents Can Track Whether Their College-Aged Kids Are Going to Classes. They Shouldn't." *PostEverything, The Washington Post*, August 28, 2015. https://www.washingtonpost.com/posteverything/wp/2015/08/28/parents-can-track-whether-their-college-aged-kids-are-going-to-classes-but-they-shouldnt/.

ILO Working Conditions Laws Database. http://www.ilo.org/dyn/travail.

Pollack, Andrew. "Breast Milk Becomes a Commodity, With Mothers Caught up in Debate." *New York Times*, March 20, 2015.

Stuart-Macadam and Dettwyler, *Biocultural Perspectives*.

US Department of Health and Human Services. Health Resources and Services Administration. Maternal and Child Health Bureau. *The Business Case for Breastfeeding: Steps for Creating a Breastfeeding Friendly Worksite*. 2008.

US Office of the Surgeon General, CDC and US Office on Women's Health. "The Importance of Breastfeeding." In *The Surgeon General's Call to Action to Support Breastfeeding*. Rockville: US Office of the Surgeon General, 2011.

ABOUT THE AUTHOR

JENNIFER GRAYSON is an environmental journalist and *Huffington Post* columnist whose work has appeared in publications including *USA Today*, the *Washington Post*, and *American Baby*. She lives in Los Angeles with her husband and two young daughters.